THE WAR DIARIES OF NEVILLE DUKE

The
War Diaries of
Neville Duke

The Journals of Squadron Leader N F Duke
DSO, OBE, DFC & 2 Bars, AFC, MC (Cz)
1941–44

Edited by

Norman Franks

GRUB STREET · LONDON

Published by
Grub Street
4 Rainham Close
London SW11 6SS

Reprinted 2006

A catalogue record for this book is available from the British Library

ISBN 1-898697-16-7

Typeset by Pearl Graphics, Hemel Hempstead

Printed and bound in Great Britain by
Biddles Ltd, King's Lynn, Norfolk

CONTENTS

INTRODUCTION

There can be few people in the world of aviation who have not heard the name Neville Duke. From successful World War Two fighter pilot to equally successful test pilot, Neville Duke has been flying for well over fifty years.

A fact virtually unknown except among his very close friends, because of his modest outlook on his flying life, is that during the crucial four years of his combat flying, starting from RAF Biggin Hill in 1941 and continuing throughout the battles in North Africa and Tunisia between 1942-1943, and finally over Italy in 1944, he kept an almost daily diary of those years.

The first one was begun in the privacy of his room in the Mess while training at RAF Ternhill and later at Biggin Hill. He could not know if this diary would be short or long term, for life expectancy for any fighter pilot was an unknown factor. If anything, the odds were against him and his diary having a long life. However, having survived the summer of 1941 flying offensive operations over the Channel and Northern France, with Fighter Command beginning to take the war to the enemy, Neville Duke was then posted to North Africa. Here he continued with his daily diary entries, now written not in the comparative comfort of a stone-built mess bedroom but in a sand-swept, fly-infested, hot, dusty tent.

The North African campaign covered hundreds of miles, fought first westwards, then retreating eastwards, then back again in those 'see-saw' desert battles between the British 1st and 8th Armies and the German Afrika Korps, the Allied forces finally beating back Rommel's Axis forces into Tunisia. Despite the intense operations, the diary entries continue, sometimes in ink, more often in pencil, jotted down as the events occurred. In between times, he was rested from operations, and flew as an instructor back in the Canal Zone. Oddly enough, Neville had believed his superiors when they said he would only be in the Middle East for a few weeks, but these turned into three years. Nevertheless for him they were very success-ful: they brought him high awards and set him on his way into a life of flying.

With the fight for North Africa won, Neville Duke, now a squadron commander, went to Italy to lead a fighter squadron in air and ground actions as the Allied armies pushed their way up the Italian 'boot'. Volume four of the diaries, covering this period in 1944, ends with his final wartime sorties.

In addition to these very personal observations on his air war, the men he flew with, and those who commanded him and whom he in turn com-manded, are his combat reports. He retained virtually all his reports and these too are recorded in the appropriate places, giving the overall up-to-the-minute feel of a fighter pilot's war.   *N.F. 1995*

CHAPTER I

STARTING ALONG THE ROAD

Neville Duke today is tall and lean. His hair is grey and there is less of it than in his youth, but in many ways his angular frame and boyish features remain unchanged. His eyes are just as alert as they were when he saw his first Messerschmitt 109 fighter over the English Channel in 1941. They have to be and so does his brain, for regardless of his 70-plus years he still flies, still tests aeroplanes, despite the almost obligatory occupational hazard of deafness from years listening to the noise of aero engines, and still knows all there is to know about aviating.

He was born on 11 January 1922, in Tonbridge, Kent, and was a keen aero-modeller from an early age. This interest in flight and flying began due to the close proximity to his home of two airfields that would gain undying fame in WW2, Kenley and Biggin Hill. He started collecting aeroplane photographs and as a youngster had quite a collection of model aircraft. His first joy-ride flight at the age of ten made the young Duke determined to fly himself.

Leaving Judd's School, Tonbridge, he had to wait six months to be old enough to apply to join the Royal Air Force, by which time Britain and her empire was at war with Germany for the second time this century' W"""""ting he worked in an auctioneer's office. Initially he tried to join the Fleet Air Arm but was turned down—bad luck for the Navy!

Finally, in June 1940, just as the Battle of Britain was about to start which put both Kenley and Biggin Hill in the forefront of the daily air actions, the would-be pilot passed his initial examinations and was soon on his way to No.4 Initial Training Wing (ITW), first at Bexhill on the Sussex coast, then at Paignton, Devon. By mid-August he was starting his flying training at No.13 Elementary Flying Training School (EFTS), at RAF White Waltham, Berkshire, Pilot Officer Thompson taking him aloft for the first time in Tiger Moth N6790 on 20 August 1940. After

1

this his flying instructor became Flying Officer Rea. Neville's first solo flight was made on 6 September, in a civil Moth—G-ADHR. By this time he had a total of 8 hours 25 minutes in his log book.

September 8 was a busy day with no fewer than four solo flights plus three more with Rea. Rea now took him through all the usual training exercises; then came the first tentative cross-country flights, aerobatics, spins and mock forced-landings. On 22 September he was off to No.1 EFTS at Hatfield, having been assessed 'Above Average' by his former Chief Flying Instructor at White Waltham.

In October he moved to No.5 FTS at RAF Sealand, going on to the Miles Master two-seat trainer. His training continued into the winter months, including a move to Ternhill, his flying hours reaching exactly 100 by the close of the year.

It was on the first day of the new year that Neville decided to keep a diary. He purchased a T J & J Smith Ltd, 8″ × 10″ diary, at the princely sum of 3/- (when three shillings was three shillings, and nowhere near the present day 15p!), making the following entry:

> Decided to try and keep a diary this year. I wish I had started before as the past year has been the best and most successful of my life. I started flying last August. Some of my friends are dead but many of my other brother pupils will last this war out; perhaps, if I should one day fall, this diary will be of some slight interest to those who will in the future become pilots, and many will do so. Or it perhaps will stir a chord in the minds of those I once knew as keen and eager to fly and who were fearful lest they fall down under the CFI's test or some other nightmare test of their flying ability.
>
> Snowing today, but got in some formation this morning with McArthur and Gordon Brettell.

True to his New Year's resolution, his diary entries came thick and fast—for the first four days!

Thursday, 2 January 1941

Very much a 'clamp' this morning; more snow on the way I'm afraid. Not a hope of flying this morning. However, the weather lifted in the afternoon and I got up with F/O Chappell for a height test. Climbed to 15,000, did a few spins and aerobatted down to ground level. Half rolls, barrel rolls, also rolls, aileron turns, stall turns, upward rolls—some fun indeed. Did a forced landing and a precautionary. Yelled until I was put down for some solo in the same machine but found it was u/s. It was simply glorious up this afternoon—the sun shining on the snow-covered ground and not a bump in the air. It's good to be alive and flying.

Friday, 3 January 1941

No flying again this morning. These clamps are the usual thing around here this time of year. We've had no more snow but it's terrifically cold. We were taken on a route march this afternoon by the Adjutant, if you please. I suppose he considers we need exercise. No.53 Course is just about finished. All those getting commissions are, it is said, going onto Army Co-Op—8 are going to CFS [Central Flying School] and the NCOs are going on Spitfires at Harwarden. Sincerely hope I don't go on Army Co-Op or CFS.

Neville, like most new pilots, hated the idea of Army Co-Operation Command, where he could see himself flying Westland Lysanders for ever. Much of Army Co-Op's work, now that the British army had been kicked out of France, was practising for land battles of the future, whenever they might occur. While going to the Central Flying School would be an achievement, the danger then would be the strong possibility of becoming an instructor.

Saturday, 4 January 1941

A good day for flying. Got a plane this afternoon and did some IF [instrument flying] with Johnny Booth. Got my IF cross-country done—Ternhill-Welshpool-Wrexham-Ternhill. We landed and changed over after a time. It seems very strange flying from the rear cockpit of the Master. Saw McArthur on his cross-country, steaming along with hydraulic fluid leaking out.

Thursday, 9 January 1941

Have neglected my diary somewhat. I went up this morning with F/O Chappell for some formation—vic, echelon, line astern. P/Os Broad and Lockyer in one machine and Munro and Hendry in the other. Most of our chaps are off on their long cross-countries today to South Cerney. Some of them never got there and the others went in formation and were lost half the time. I think it is far better and much more fun if you do cross-countries without another plane or person about and rely completely upon yourself. Went up in the afternoon with Lockyer. He likes to show off too much—was not impressed.

Monday, 13 January 1941

Flew in the afternoon with Booth as Safety Pilot for some IF Had some fun and games. One of the nearest shaves so far I think. We decided that I should IF to Leicester (where JB lives) and shoot the place up. Got there OK in pretty thick weather and did our stuff. Started following a railway [line] back but it was the wrong one—couldn't see a thing by this time. Suddenly surrounded by barrage balloons! Climbed frantically right through them. Completely lost and above 10/10ths cloud. Eventually found a gap and came down over Worcester. Arrived home just as they were laying the flare path out! Indeed the gods were with us this afternoon.

Wednesday, 15 January 1941

Night flying! Was raked out of bed at 2 am and tottered down in bright moonlight, but very cold. Instructors were not keen on flying as ice was forming on the wings. Eventually P/O Munro took off with McArthur, and I went off with F/O Dean. Jerry came over, they put out the flare path, which didn't help any, and stopped our fun for the night.

By early 1941, he still carried the 'Above Average' assessment, prior to leaving Sealand to go to No.58 OTU (Operational Training Unit), Grangemouth, in February. A couple more trips on the Master, one under the direction of Squadron Leader West, the CFI (Chief Flying Instructor), and he was finally allowed to get into Britain's premier day fighter—the Spitfire (K1071). On 2 March he flew this machine for 25 minutes, followed immediately by a further 45 minutes in K9924.

Of interest here might be the list of young hopefuls that attended No.58 OTU Number 2 Course, which began in February 1941. The 29 pilots in the Course photo had a long way to go—some, unhappily, only a short way to go. In charge was Flight Lieutenant A G Douglas, but of the others, approximately 50% did not survive the war:

F/Lt G E Brettell DFC 133 Sqdn PoW/killed 29 March 1944
Sgt R L Brewer 616 Sqdn KIA 25 June 1941
Sgt R R Carson (46,126 Sqdns Malta 1941)
Sgt K D Cox 485 Sqdn KIA 18 June 1941
Sgt D Fair

Sgt B W Feely 611 Sqdn KIA 8 July 1941
Sgt G S Fraser (609 Sqdn 1941)
Sgt L J Frecklington
P/O J C Gilbert 249 Sqdn KIA (Malta) 8 July 1942
F/Sgt M B Green 118 Sqdn KIA 9 May 1942
Sgt A C Hendry No.1 ADF Killed 21 Oct 1941
Sgt W N Hendry 485 Sqdn KIA 8 July 1941
P/O G T Hugill (Hawkinge 1941)
Sgt C H Jacka 234 Sqdn KIA 26 Aug 1941
F/Sgt T W Jupp No.2 (O)AFU Killed 20 Sept 1942
F/Lt J M P Lintott DFC 85 Sqdn KIA 9 July 1943
P/O A S C Lumsden (229 Sqdn Malta 1942)
Sgt C J Mason
Sgt D S McGregor
Sgt M K McHugh 611 Sqdn KIA 3 July 1941
P/O K J McKelvie 603 Sqdn KIA 24 June 1941
Sgt P J McMullen
Sgt H A Newman 234 Sqdn KIA 15 Nov 1941
P/O E D M Rippon (92 Sqdn 1941)
Sgt L M Scott
P/O J R Stoop (F/O 185 Sqdn Malta 1942)
Sgt J H Walker 234 Sqdn KIA 5 Dec 1941
Sgt J G West (616 Sqdn DFM—Malta—ret'd Sqn Ldr)

Neville's assessment dropped to just average at Grangemouth, but with this and a mighty 145.50 flying hours (!) in his log, his road to the war truly started with a posting to one of the RAF's top fighter units. On 2 April 1941 he was sent to 92 Squadron at Biggin Hill—the same airfield from which, as a boy, he had watched the silver biplanes of a by-gone age climb into a pristine blue sky. Also posted to 92 was Gordon Brettell whom Neville had come to know at FTS. No.92 Squadron had seen action over Dunkirk, and throughout the Battle of Britain. Its Commanding Officer now, and the one who welcomed him to the Squadron, was Squadron Leader Jamie Rankin DFC, who was soon to become one of the RAF's top-scoring fighter pilots. Neville had his first flight in an operational Spitfire on the 7th (X4484), for 75 minutes of local flying.

Being on an operational squadron did not mean an immediate dash into combat. Even the best of pilots were not allowed such freedom, for there was still much to learn and much to understand from the seasoned veterans about him. Such men as Allan Wright, Brian Kingcome, Tony Bartley, Dutch Holland and Tommy Lund could give him this understanding. Surviving in a hostile sky, where eagle-eyed Messerschmitt pilots quickly picked off the unwary, had to be learnt just as religiously as one learned how to handle an aeroplane.

Despite his resolution to maintain a diary, entries were few and far between during the early weeks of 1941, but upon being posted to 92 Squadron, he galvanised himself once more, and this time he rarely neglected to write something each day, even though it began with jottings on headed paper from RAF Uxbridge.

Wednesday, 2 April 1941

Drove to Biggin Hill in one of Charlton's Fords—quite a decent car. I really need a car here, then I could get home almost any time. The first thing I was greeted with when I saw the Station Adj, was that I was leaving Biggin on Friday and going to Uxbridge for a 3-day Fighter R/T course. Ah well, there is not much I can do about it except moan a bit.

Poor old Biggin is in a pitiful state—not a hangar standing, nearly all windows smashed, walls spattered and oceans of mud. But under all the stinking mire of war is the old Biggin I knew on Empire Air Days.

The aircraft are Spitfire Vs; wizard machines, equipped with two cannon and four machine-guns, the new Merlin 45 engine, giving +12 boost on the take-off and, although I haven't got my hands on one yet, they climb like monkeys. The chaps are having a little teething trouble with the engine and oil cooling is a little difficult—and they are known to cut. However, they have a new hood release—you just pull a sort of plug on the perspex and bang the sides of the hood and it comes apart, thus facilitating hasty exit. We're also fitted with VHF which I haven't used before but I understand it's more efficient than HF. The ceiling is much better in these Spits— 38,000 ft is a cinch.

This fight for height is, I think, the answer to the mastery of the air. The Hun is still above us in this but I believe we are on the right track. The cannons are another good thing; one is thus enabled to sit astern of a Hun and pump shells into it until pieces start to fall off. I suppose the Jerries will soon get some new armour plating that will stop the shells then we shall have to think of the answer to that. So it goes on.

This Squadron, No.92 (East India) is financed by the East India Company and has the top score of confirmed Huns in the Air Force—135. It has been at Biggin since about last September-October and was a while at Pembroke. The

Biggin Wing, consisting of 92, 609 and 74 Squadrons (*The three Squadrons*) has over 600 [enemy aircraft] to its bag. Tops the lot.

We have a Defiant night-fighting squadron here (264) at the moment but they are leaving and 74 is coming back from Manston. The chaps on 92 are really wizard and I don't think anybody could want a better lot of blokes around in a fight. I can never remember names and although I've met nearly all of them I can only recall a few of them. Squadron Leader Rankin is our CO, and he has not been with the Squadron long, having come from Training Command, but he is a good type.

F/O 'Tommy' Lund[1] is another I can remember and a useful bloke who has been here a long time but is at present off operations as he is under the Doc. Then there is F/L Brian Kingcome DFC of 'A' Flight—an amazing chap, completely unmoved by anything. P/O Mottram is our deputy flight commander and seems to have taken it upon himself to look over Gordon and myself. Also 'Sam' Saunders, who I think never turns a hair at the gaze of a woman.

A word for Gordon Brettell—the quiet, the incredible, the likeable Gordon. A person as deep as the very ocean itself, who I am sure I shall never quite understand. I'm very glad to have him here with me. We were together in my week at Hatfield, (although I did not come into contact with him till later at Ternhill) at Sealand and Ternhill and very much together at Grangemouth.

He arrived at Biggin just after dinner, much to my relief as he had all my flying kit with him, and we were taken by the chaps down to the White Hart [Brasted], a good spot, the other side of Westerham. We suitably consumed a quantity of liquor and in due course removed ourselves to bed.

My room-mate is one Thompson, ex-public school heavy-weight champ who goes around in a much tattered uniform. Another 92 chap is a Frenchman, 'Monty' Montbron, while the adjutant is a useful man, MacGowan, and our Intelligence

---

[1] Flying Officer John W Lund, posted to 92 from 611 Squadron on 2 October 1940. Killed in action one year later, 2 October 1941, aged 22. Flying Officer Roy Mottram joined 92 in June 1940. Killed in action 31 August 1941 as a flight commander with 54 Squadron. Flying Officer C H Saunders joined 92 in April 1940, and went to 74 Squadron as a flight commander in May 1941. Later a flight commander with 145 Squadron in the Middle East—awarded DFC in December 1942. Retired from the RAF as a Wing Commander in 1958.

Officer is a Norwegian by the name of Weise.[1]

Thursday 3 April 1941

Intend getting things a bit more organised today. After breakfast Gordon and myself were button-holed by the IO [Intelli-
gence Officer] and taken along to his sanctum-sanctorum and
peered over maps and photographs of Hun aerodromes one
might sometime shoot-up. Next we sped down to 'B' Flight
dispersal point and met some more of the chaps and some
NCOs of the ground crews.

The crew room is a holy of holies—a complete shambles,
with the inevitable gramophone, the smoky old stove in the
middle of the room, parachutes and flying kit adorning the
walls. The untidy desk covered in Flying Orders, gramophone records, numerous technical books on the Spitfire
engine and airframe and unmentionable other odds and ends.

The absolutely smothered notice board draped with hand-
ling notes on the Spit V and other papers full of gen. There is
a board showing the state of the Squadron, ie: Released,
Readiness, 15 mins available, 30 mins available etc, and the
pilot's board with the names of the pilots and the machines
they are to fly and their position in the section.

The two Squadrons—92 and 609—went along to a chat by
one of the Rolls-Royce blokes on the best boost and revs to
get maximum range. Most interesting but highly technical.

Just after that the 'WingCo', Wing Commander Malan
DSO DFC and bar, brought up these new formations we are
supposed to be going to use. So far there are two types to be
tried out. Two sections in echelon, one stepped up and the
other stepped down—not so hot for turns they say. The other
is known as American pairs and seems feasible, consisting of
six pairs in formation while two or more weave.

Squadron Leader Rankin went into the subject with the
gang after lunch in the crew-room and they intend trying them
out soon. The CO prefers the vic type with two weavers.

We were fixed up with a 'chute and then Mottram suggested he should take Gordon and myself, with Rippon,
along to the Ops Room. It's quite a way from the 'drome—the
last one had a bomb come to rest in the middle of same, thus
causing some confusion. This Ops Room is a great deal better
than the Turnhouse one and the controllers at Biggin are keen
to help you if you are interested.

---

[1] Flying Officer Tom Weise.

I decided to leave tonight for Uxbridge and stop the night in London. Persuaded Gordon to come with me and have a night among the bright lights. It was a great success. We got a room at the Strand Palace and then sallied forth to the Windmill Theatre to see the show. Later we snooped around the Café Royal and had dinner in true fashion. Eventually struggled back to the Strand and having downed a suitable nightcap, retired to bed.

Neville completed his R/T course at Uxbridge and he and Gordon were back at Biggin on the 7th. Over the next couple of days he began to fly the Spitfire V, the first bit of excitement coming on the Thursday, but before then he flew a Spitfire Mark V for the first time and had another problem following railway lines:

Monday, 7 April 1941
I went up after lunch with Tommy Lund to do some formation. Had a bit of a dogfight and he was apparently satisfied with my stuff. Went off after this in a Spit V. Wizard machine and seems to handle smoother than the Is—bags of power. Did a few landings to get things taped a bit.

Tuesday, 8 April 1941
Gordon and self started out for Farnborough in two Spits but weather duff so came back. Followed some railway lines and got somewhat confused. Did a spot of formation with him but his windscreen was covered in oil so he broke away and beetled off home.

I broke away with no idea where I was but eventually pinpointed West Malling. Beat up Tonbridge in a mild manner. Went up late with Sgt Rippon and Gordon to do some dogfighting at 10,000. Wizard fun—got on quite well, shook Gordon off my tail and managed to keep on his. Led them back to base and then indulged in some low aerobatics over Tonbridge as weather was so glorious—great fun.

Thursday, 10 April 1941
(Maundy Thursday)
Up with P/O Fokes, Sgt Kingaby and Gordon to 35,000 ft this morning. They tested their cannons at that height. Ops then vectored us on to a Hun at 10,000 ft. We came down like bombs; 340 mph indicated at 30,000 is 518 mph true.

Circled above cloud where Ops said Jerry was, but saw

nothing. Damned cold at 35,000 and my right hand was frozen. We were leaving terrific smoke trails and ice was formed on my hood but it cleared after a while. We were very short of petrol after chasing the Hun nearly to France; thought perhaps I'd have to force-land but was OK. Fired cannons into sea off Beachy Head—very satisfying. Considerable Hun activity—things will pop soon.

Over the next few days Neville continued with practice flights, several being with experienced pilots such as 'Titch' Havercroft, Roy Mottram and Geoff Wellum. Very gradually he was eased into some early operational sorties—standing patrols. He was also getting into the habit of flying over Tonbridge where his family would guess who was in the aeroplane above the town.

Thursday, 24 April 1941

Up at 4.15 for dawn readiness this morning! Nothing doing until about 8.30 when heard CO and one of our Netherlands East Indies boys, F/L Bruinier, had shot down a 109 over Dungeness. It came down in flames, the pilot baled out and was taken prisoner. He evidently mistook our chaps for his friends as he made no attempt to duck into cloud and even waggled his wings to them! He was machine-gunning some town—Rye I think. Some people have all the luck. Went up at about 12.30 on a standing patrol over Maidstone. Took F/L Wright on leave in the Maggie and landed him in a field near Maidenhead. One hell of a party to celebrate the Hun!

This was Rankin's first solo success. He had shared in a Heinkel 59 floatplane earlier in April and had damaged a 109, so no wonder there was a celebration.

At this period Luftwaffe fighters were very active over the south east of England, shooting up airfields such as Manston or Lympne, as well as dropping bombs on Dover or Ramsgate harbours, so Fighter Command were kept pretty busy in an area that was being dubbed 'Hell-fire Corner'.

Friday, 25 April 1941

Struggled out of bed about 11.30 this morning after a stupendous party last night. We got some girls from Orpington Hospital to provide the company. Started off in the White Hart then proceeded to Knockholt and really got down to the consumption of liquor. I am getting quite good at this dancing business but only when pleasantly oiled. Took the girls back to Orpington and crawled into bed about 4 am.

Saturday, 26 April 1941

Dawn readiness sweep at 7.30, Dunkirk to Calais 32,000 ft. Pretty cold and nothing seen. R/T was very bad and Mottram, our leader, was out of touch for some time with base. Took off at 12.30 to do another sweep up the Channel at maximum altitude.

After taking off, control vectored us on to some Huns that were about. Intercepted a flight of Hurricanes at 32,000. Saw five Me109s and tackled them. Got a shot at one from astern as he dived for the sea—flaming from his exhaust. Another Spitfire cut between us and I had to break away without seeing whether I got it or not. Ronnie Fokes got one down in the sea. Same one as I shot at?

Apart from feeling strongly that this Me109 was really his—and he still does—Neville had to be content with surviving his first air battle. At least he had seen the enemy close-to, and was credited with a 109 'damaged'.

There was a bit of excitement on 3 May not recorded in his diary, but noted in his log book on this date: 'Intercepted two 109s at 34,000 ft. Roy and self chased but they flew circles round us. Roy gave a burst from 1,400 yds. Fuel gauge registered "O" at 34,000 ft so hastily proceeded earthwards towards Manston. Gauge was frozen up as there was still gas left when landed at Biggin.'

Little of interest followed for several days, and he made few notes in his diary. He now had his own Spitfire—R6906 QJ-Y—which was nice although he experienced some cannon problems at first.

Mid-May was fairly dull, but on the 21st the Squadron provided top cover for 18 Blenheims bombing Bethune. Then on the 25th Monty Montbron and Neville flew a 'Rhubarb' sortie. Unfortunately he makes no mention of this in his diary, but he noted in his log book: 'Monty and self left CO and Kingaby off Boulogne. Crossed coast in cloud; Monty dived onto a hangar and I lost him. Prowled off on my own inland, in and out of cloud at 4,000 ft. Nothing flying. Came out at Dunkirk— accurate AA fire. Not a shot at anything; "O" feet next time. Anxious moments coming back, miles of sea, low petrol. Hit coast south of Harwich! Force-landed at Gravesend.'

Tuesday, 27 May 1941

Took 'Y' up in the afternoon. She is just back from Hucknall and as good as ever. Considerable vigorous low flying and made attacks on a Lysander, stalking it in and out of cloud. Shot-up a Havoc, from Malling I think. A really good evening —some scattered cloud. Took 'Y' up to 10,000 ft over Tonbridge and aerobatted down to ground level for 40 minutes. Best show yet. Cloud-hopped back, great fun with the sun on the clouds; really beautiful evening for flying.

Wednesday, 28 May 1941
609, 74 and us plus Hornchurch Wing off on a Sweep over France. I had to return as I could not turn the oxygen on. Damn and blast! Wimpey Wade was shot-up a bit by a 109. Got cannon shell and m.g. in the wings. Went down out of control in weird spin. Spun for 15,000 ft but landed OK at Manston. Roy [Mottram] and Sam [Saunders] landed at Gravesend and Manston out of petrol. Not a very successful trip.

Trevor 'Wimpey' Wade was a couple of years older than Neville and had been in the RAFVR pre-war. He had flown with 92 during the Battle of Britain and had a number of victories already. After the war he too became a test pilot with Hawkers, Neville being his No.2 for a while, but he was killed flying the P1081 prototype in April 1951.

Tuesday, 3 June 1941
Convoy patrol this morning over 16 ships off the Thames Estuary—cloud about 800 ft. Ships flying balloons in cloud! Went with Sgt Kingaby, Allan Wright and Gordon. Some of 74 Squadron joined in and eight of us were milling around this convoy in all directions and heights from '0' to 700 ft!!

Nothing about and rather dull although some relief was gained by low flying over the water. Huge clamp on when we got back to Biggin, and Squadron was put to bad weather state—one Flight on and rest of us at 15 minutes available.

Saturday, 7 June 1941
Some aviation today. Went down to dispersal after brekkers and took 'Y' up for a flip to Kenley, Hawkinge, Manston, Canterbury and Tonbridge. Squadron called to Readiness just as I was landing. Sent off on a Sweep with W/C Malan leading 74 Squadron. Nothing came up at all.

Convoy patrol in afternoon with Monty. Never have I had such an uncomfortable trip. Trying to format on Monty is like being in a dog-fight. It was baking hot, helmet and mask were uncomfortable, CO_2 bottle in the dinghy pack was sticking into me!! Then it started to rain with thunder and lightning on the way back. What a trip.

Thursday, 12 June 1941

From West Malling to Biggin. Beat-up Tonbridge on way back and shot-up some blokes drilling on Penshurst aerodrome; shall get most unpopular with them. Flew 'Y' on this trip, first time since metal ailerons fitted. Superb machine.

Escort at sea level for three Blenheims bombing a couple of ships off the coast east of Calais. Some AA fire near us. Patrolled between Dover and Calais at about 1,000-4,000 ft. Two Me109s engaged over Dover harbour. CO did head-on attack and later EA reported down in the sea.

Saturday, 14 June 1941

Operation by 200 fighters from Biggin, Kenley, Hornchurch and North Weald Wings over Northern France with 24 Blenheims bombing St. Omer. 92 and 74 Squadrons covered Calais-Boulogne area at 7-10,000 ft. I was with Allan Wright but got separated and attacked a 109 and went into small circles. Gave long bursts but no visible damage done.

Came up behind a 109 flying straight and level, throttled right back. Almost overshot him at about 10-20 yards by 'swish-tailing'. Frantically pressing the gun-button but all ammunition was gone. Daren't break away or he would have got on my tail so followed him about for some time. A horrible state of affairs—doubt if I shall ever get such a chance again.

Eventually the 109 started turning and I broke away, screamed down out over Boulogne at 1,500 ft at +12 boost, about 320 mph. Some AA fire but not too close. Crossed the Channel at sea level and crossed the coast at Dungeness.

Wednesday, 18 June 1941

Show in the afternoon, 6 o'clock. Top cover for Blenheims bombing troops in a wood near Calais. Two 109s dived on Allan and self but did not engage us. Got a good view of one's silver wings and belly and enormous black crosses, as he whizzed past and then one went above and shot behind me. Gordon took a pass at a 109 with the CO. It crashed in France.

Saturday, 21 June 1941

Another show this morning at 12 o'clock. Cover patrol off the

Goodwins for Blenheims bombing a German HQ. Nothing seen. CO got a 109, pilot baled out. I was off this afternoon but Squadron did another show and Aston shot down into the sea after getting a 109. He was picked up OK. Titch Havercroft got a probable, CO got another. Squadron total now 148.

Monday, 23 June 1941

Circus: Blenheims bombing Bethune. We were cover over Bethune and were engaged by 109s. CO got one in flames—wizard sight. He got another later, so did Archer and Kingaby. I was separated from the rest in the general mix-up and was attacked by five Me109Fs near Le Touquet. One did a head-on attack; saw flashes from his guns and tracer whistling past. Gave him a burst and he skimmed just over me with white and black smoke coming from his engine. Claimed as a probable. Dog-fought with other four down to sea level. Hit by machine-gun bullets twice in wing. Pretty warm time.

Another Circus later in the evening. Engaged 109s near Boulogne and Squadron split up. Archer and Brettell joined up with me and I led them across to Dunkirk, all three weaving madly. A 109 took a look at us but was away before we could get near him. Snooped to and fro between Dover and Dunkirk with Archer, then landed at Hawkinge to refuel.

Combat Report for 23 June
Time: 1415 hrs, south-east of Boulogne

As Blue 2 I broke away to the left and dived after five Me109Fs. They broke up into pairs, one to the left and one to the right while the fifth enemy aircraft climbed right above me in front and came back head-on to me. He opened fire from very long range (700 yards). I got him in my sights and opened fire with cannons and machine-guns for a few seconds.

Enemy aircraft passed a few yards over my head and I saw a lot of black and white smoke come out from his engine. I then had a regular dog-fight with the other four right down to sea level where they left me.

I experienced some difficulty in turning inside the enemy aircraft and received two bullet holes in starboard wing. On my way back I saw a yellow parachute in the sea half-way between Dungeness and Le Touquet. I landed at Lympne and reported the parachute.

Claim: 1 Me109 Damaged.

Philip Leslie Irving Archer came from the British West Indies, via the RCAF. He flew with 92 Squadron in 1941 and later with 416 RCAF Squadron, winning the DFC. As a squadron leader flying with 421 RCAF Squadron in 1943, he was lost over Belgium in June.

Tuesday, 24 June 1941

Circus at 8 pm. Blenheims bombing north-west of Lille ; about 170 fighters altogether. I was No.2 to Allan Wright; we broke away and went down after five or six Huns near Dunkirk but couldn't catch them. Nearly jumped by 109s diving down behind us. Sgt Payne got two.

Wednesday, 25 June 1941

Circus about mid-day, Blenheims bombing St Omer. 92, 609 and 74 Squadrons top cover over target at 30,000 ft. Allan and self dived down on two 109s over St Omer—couldn't catch them—going at a phenomenal airspeed. 109s pulled up vertically—blacked out and broke away just avoiding stalling. Saw Allan and 109 diving with glycol coming from the 109.

I was attacked by two 109s from astern but saw them just in time and did a terrific turn, seeing tracer whistle past behind. Came out over Dunkirk and passed two 109s on way. Turned and saw dog-fight going on near Dunkirk so went back and joined in. Sat on the tail of a 109 which was shooting at another Spit. Fired several bursts of cannon and machine-gun into him from about 50 yards range. Glycol streamed out and he started going down. Got just above him and looked down into his cockpit. Pilot was crouched over stick and did not look up. Think perhaps I hit him.

The 109 went down and crashed a few miles inland. Sped home at sea level at terrific bat. Bad AA fire from a convoy which I came out over at 1,000 feet and also from Dunkirk. Engine stopped just as I touched down on 'drome for lack of petrol!

Combat Report for 25 June
Time: 1245 hrs off Dunkirk

When at sea level flying west of Dunkirk, I looked back and saw six Me109s having a dog-fight with two Spitfires. I turned and joined in and managed to get on the tail of one 109F which was on the tail of a Spitfire. I opened fire with cannons and machine-guns and gave him two bursts and closed to 50 yards, when I had to pull away as I got into his slipstream.

I came back on top of him and saw the pilot sitting quite quietly without looking around or up and proceeded to go down in a gentle dive from 2,000 feet, and hit the ground just east of Dunkirk and blow up.

On my way back I saw two orange-coloured parachutes going down, but no persons attached. I also saw four ships of about 1,000 tons escorted by four E-boats.

Claim: 1 Me109F Destroyed.

On this June day Neville Duke had broken his duck by destroying his first enemy aircraft. The June intensity of combat continued, Fighter Command taking the air war to the enemy, especially now that the Germans had invaded Russia on 22 June.

The summer 'shooting season', as it was starting to be termed, saw almost daily Sweeps, Circus or Rodeo operations being mounted over Northern France, opposed by just two main German Fighter Jagdgeschwaders; JG2 to the west of the Somme Estuary, JG26 to the east.

That Neville had learned his trade and was not only surviving but starting to inflict damage on his opponents, proved his growing ability as a fighter pilot. Each sortie, each combat, added to his experience. With luck he might survive, but he knew too that luck as well as skill and ability played a good part in any pilot's life. Skill he could hone and work on. Luck was something one just had or ran out of. Only time would tell if luck would stay with him.

CHAPTER II

HIGH SUMMER AT BIGGIN HILL

Pilot Officer N F Duke was fast becoming a veteran having survived a number of encounters with the Luftwaffe over Northern France. His flying hours were almost 250 by this time, each minute increasing his experience.

He flew two operations on 27 June, Circus No.24 to Lille and then a Roadstead sortie against ships off Gravelines. The following day he tested a Spitfire and had a gun panel blow off but he got down safely. However, all was not well and he was beginning to feel under the weather.

Saturday, 28 June 1941
Feel pretty peculiar today—all aches and pains.

Sunday, 29 June 1941
Still feel un-serviceable—don't know what's the matter with me.

Monday, 30 June 1941
High cover at 28,000 feet for Blenheims bombing south of Lille; furthest inland so far. Only saw two 109s look at us then went back into cloud. 609 Squadron got three and the Wing Commander one. George Fraser is now in 609 and so is Dunn whom I knew at EFTS. Was with Fraser at Ternhill and Grangemouth.

I am now off flying for a day or two. Coming down this evening I had terrible pains in my ears and am almost deaf now. Hope I've done no damage. Landed at Hawkinge after tonight's fracas and met Graham Hugill. CO and Wimpy Wade awarded DFCs; Allan Wright a Bar to his DFC.

In fact Neville had cracked both ear-drums as a result of taking evasive action, and was promptly carted off to Orpington Hospital where he languished until 10 July, then took seven days' leave, not returning to Biggin Hill until the 18th. The reason for the ear damage was that Neville had a touch of tonsilitis and a cold and should not have flown. In taking this violent evasive action—half roll and steep dive—he had caused the damage and lost all hearing, but thankfully it gradually returned.

On his return to Biggin, he discovered that Geoff Wellum had also received the DFC, Brian Kingcome a Bar to his DFC, Wing Commander 'Sailor' Malan a Bar to his DSO, while Squadron Leader Michael Robinson DFC, CO of 609 Squadron, had won the DSO.

He also found that Monty Montbron had been lost, and Sergeant Waldern had been shot down into the sea wearing his (Neville's) flying helmet. While Waldern had been rescued, his helmet had 'failed to return'. Allan Wright had also been posted, on rest.

Saturday, 19 July 1941
Some aviation at last. Escort for Stirlings to bomb Lille but bombed Dunkirk harbour as cloud over target area. Sgt Waldern missing. Squadron went down on two 109s. Brian had a squirt but no joy. Wizard night at White Hart, Fox and Hounds and Red House . . .

Obviously Neville was feeling his old self again!

Fighter Command were now escorting small formations of the new four-engined Short Stirling bombers against targets in Northern France. The summer campaign of trying to entice Luftwaffe fighters up to do battle was working up to a point, but as the RAF had found in the latter stages of the Battle of Britain, there was no profit in just engaging fighters, so often the 109s declined to engage Spitfires. Fighter Command and the light bombers of 2 Group had been operating Circus and Roadstead operations during the early summer, thereby enticing the Me109 pilots to 'have a go'.

During the pre-Russian invasion period, the Luftwaffe often chose to ignore pure fighter Sweeps and Ramrods, and only attacked Circus and Roadsteads if they held an advantage. After mid-June Luftwaffe policy had changed. The 109 pilots were now directed to engage RAF incursions whenever possible. In the meantime, with Fighter Command still believing the Germans only attacked bombing formations, they had decided to try a better bait by using the big Stirling bombers.

Whatever the tactics, Fighter Command was losing the battle. Not that they lacked aggression; it was merely that, unhappily, they were not inflicting the amount of damage on the Luftwaffe's day fighters that they either hoped or imagined, while their own losses steadily mounted. As the Luftwaffe had found when operating over Southern England, a downed pilot was invariably lost, even if he baled out, as a prisoner of war. Now Fighter Command were losing pilots over France who also did not get back, and, if they survived they mostly went into a prison camp, although some managed to evade. At least if an evader got clear he might gain help from French or Belgian people. There had been no such luxury for Luftwaffe pilots over England.

For his part, Neville occasionally flew as No.2 to Wing Commander Malan now, which had to say something about his growing ability. Neville once recorded: 'Malan's name and reputation were already by-words to the pupils in our OTU—some of our instructors have served or known him during the Battle of Britain. It was the practice of the Wing Leader to fly with each of the squadrons in the Wing. By July I suppose I was considered a veteran of 19 and respectable to fly No.2 to the great man on many occasions when he led 92 Squadron. It was a daunting prospect and at all costs one was to stay with the WingCo no matter what—not only to ensure his cover but the honour of 92 was at stake! Better not come back at all rather than lose the WingCo. This was all right whilst he was leading the Wing peacefully about our business—he was a master at the art of leading some 36 aircraft in such a manner that the formation could keep station without straggling. He had very sharp eyesight indeed and was constantly reporting enemy aircraft and manoeuvring the Wing into a favourable attack position generally before others had picked up the target. Equally important, he led the Wing in such a way that it was least vulnerable to being 'bounced'.

'He was a great tactician as well, and during bomber cover missions, for example, would not be drawn away by the enemy but might despatch a section, flight or squadron to deal with targets of opportunity. He would always endeavour to give cover to such detached sections. Once engaged, Sailor provided almost a running commentary on the enemy aircraft situation and positions, along with pretty forthright instructions to any squadron, flight or body out of position in the formation. As his No.2 one was, of course, sticking to him like glue whilst at the same time weaving like mad and endlessly scanning above and behind. Once Sailor engaged the enemy things were different—he was a most aggressive fighter, hard on his aeroplane (there was then only one place for the throttle at this stage—fully forward) with both hands on the control column! It was a private dog-fight for a No.2 to stay with him—he fairly

tore into the enemy and I more than once recall pieces of Me109 flying
past, being the first indication of action.'

Wednesday, 23 July 1941
Escort cover Wing for six Blenheims bombing Bethune area;
flying with Wing Commander Malan. Nothing much about.
Sweep in the evening to Hazebrouck. Almost impossible to
tell our position owing to cloud. Some 109s dived underneath
us but did not engage. Sgt Hickman got one.

Neville was now flying QJ-X W3319 as his personal Spitfire V. Two
operations on the 24th brought some excitement. First came a raid on
some shipping off Fecamp and Le Touquet by six Beauforts. Some 109s
were chased but nothing developed. On a later Circus with nine Blenheims to Hazebrouck it was Neville who was chased. He noted in his log
book: 'Top Cover at 25,000 ft—lots of 109s about. Was attacked by a
109 from astern but his tracer went just over the perspex. Climbed up to
a squadron of 109s but was jumped by eight others. Spent rest of the
time dodging same. Also attacked by a Spit!' In the day's Intelligence
Summary his name appeared with the following remark: 'P/O Duke,
when crossing the French coast west of Gravelines was jumped on by 10
Me109s at 20,000 ft, from out of the sun. Only by violent evasive action
was he able to get away, 15 miles out to sea from Gravelines.' A diary
entry for the 28th mentions the name of P H 'Hunk' Humphreys for the
first time. He and Hunk would share a considerable portion of time
together in the North African desert in the months to come, and later in
Italy. They even went out to the Middle East in the same aeroplane.

Monday, 28 July 1941
Squadron set out in pairs at three-minute intervals for
'Rhubarbs'. I led 'Hunk' Humphreys. Everybody turned
back when they encountered sea fog off Beachy. Led Hunk
through it but he left me when French coast at Fecamp came
in sight. Continued on alone but weather was as clear as a bell
all along French coast so couldn't cross and do any damage.
Was back hours after others and they were beginning to
wonder if I had bought it at last!

Rhubarb sorties, while exciting if pilots ran into aircraft or ground
targets, could only be flown in poor weather conditions—low cloud and
so on so that if they got into trouble they could escape into these same
clouds and get away. They were also very costly and later in the war
were mostly frowned upon; pilots were even ordered not to fly them.

Bad weather kept everyone on the ground for the next few days. On 2 August several pilots, including Neville, attended Wimpey Wade's wedding at Oxted. In 1951 it would be Neville and another Hawker man who would break the news of her husband's death to Josephine Wade.

Sunday, 3 August 1941

Aviation at last! Cover in Channel for some Hurricanes beating up a German motor boat. Played about in the clouds with two 109s. CO took a shot but no luck. Four of us took off before dusk and beetled about the Channel and France looking for trouble. Lots of clouds—very pretty.

Thursday, 7 August 1941

Circus to St Omer aerodrome. Biggin Wing escort cover. Lots of 109s about—Sgt Howard missing, Sgt Ahern shot-up. Saw pilot bale out of Spitfire FY-V [611 Sqn]. Supposed to be going on 48 hrs leave all being well.

Afternoon: not going on 48 as Howard is still missing and Ahern is going on sick leave. Show to Lille in evening. Biggin Wing supposed to be high cover but could not find bombers. Lost Squadron when jumped by some 109s and came back alone.

Getting lots more opposition now. The German pilots appear to be pretty experienced blokes. Am getting a little tired of Circuses—am always getting shot at without a chance of shooting back.

In his log book he recorded: 'Nearly collided with a 109 who whistled over our section on his back; lead flying in all directions.' If Neville was getting tired of being shot at without being able to retaliate, he got his chance a couple of days later.

Saturday, 9 August 1941

Fighter Sweep—in at Hardelot to St Omer and out at Gravelines. Engaged immediately we crossed the coast. Attacked by two 109s, and I fired at one from astern with no result. Attacked from astern by another who went past me on the starboard side, gave same a burst and he went into cloud in an inverted spin at 800 ft. Claimed destroyed. Chased to within 2-3 miles of Dover at sea level by two 109s. Damned lucky to be alive. God, what a life!

In a dive from some Huns, in pulling out I was forced forward onto the stick by 'G' and came out of the dive climbing inverted—a horrible moment; feel years older.

Neville described the fight in his log book as a battle royal, also noting that Don Kingaby and Jerry Le Cheminant each got 109s as well.[1]

Combat Report for 9 August
Time: 1800 hrs, Boulogne

Attacked from astern by two Me109Fs at 2,000 ft over Boulogne. I saw the first one approaching to the attack and turned to the left until he was on the opposite side of the circle. I then immediately turned to the right as hard as I could. He went past me on the starboard beam and I gave him a burst from astern at 200 to 300 yards range. At this moment I saw tracer pass over my cockpit and another 109 passed me on the right. I gave him a long burst with some deflection from 50 yards rapidly increasing. The 109 went on its back and did a slow spin in this position into the cloud which was about 800 feet. I did not see it crash into the sea but do not consider it could have pulled out.

I was shortly afterwards jumped by another two 109s just above the cloud. I ducked into cloud hoping they would give up the chase but when breaking cloud, the 109s were still there and chased me down to sea level and to within 2 to 3 miles of Dover.

Their spinners appeared to be painted black and white. Tracer ammunition would have been a great asset as my reflector sight was u/s. I suggest some tracer be used in future.

Claim: 1 Me109F Destroyed.

Neville now got his 48-hour leave. Arriving back at Biggin on the 13th he found the Squadron released and several of the boys went up to London for a night out. That was the beauty of being at Biggin—the fleshpots of London were so near.

Thursday, 14 August 1941

Dawn Readiness after last night! Show after lunch—11 Blenheims bombing E-boats in Boulogne harbour. We were target support Wing. Lots of 109s about but not engaged—most unpleasant trip. My wheels would not lock up, then unable to get them down for about half an hour. I threw the machine about the sky to get them free, while holding long conversations with our ground station as to best means of getting same loose. Damned awful aeroplane and oxygen almost poisoned me. A most unsatisfactory day.

---

[1] Jerrold Le Cheminant came from the Channel Islands; flew with 616 and 92 in 1941, and later with 72 in Tunisia, winning the DFC.

Neville had another unsatisfactory day on the 16th during a show to St Omer. The Squadron jumped some 109s near Gravelines and he got into a good position to hit one, only to find his gun-button stuck.

Wing Commander 'Sailor' Malan became tour-expired in mid-August, succeeded by Michael Robinson of 609. Neville went to one hell of a party for Malan at Biggin Hill on the 17th, which did not help the next morning:

Monday, 18 August 1941

Boy what a hang-over! Show to Lille but did not see any Huns. Sgt Mann missing under very suspicious circumstances. He broke away from the formation off the English coast and has not been heard of since. A mysterious Spitfire joined up with our Wing today. He was wearing the old camouflage—ours was changed yesterday. A Hun in disguise?

On second show [Circus to Marquise] several hundred 109s reported but we did not see many. I had engine trouble—so had to come back alone, a worried man.

Tuesday, 19 August 1941

Biggin Wing as rear support. Ten miles inside Dunkirk at 25,000 feet. Had to escort Phillips back from France as his engine was u/s. Left him at English coast and came across P/O Ortmans of 609 in a dinghy. Circled same with Wing Commander Robinson who arrived on the scene. Fired red Verey lights and eventually a launch came out with a Lysander. Wing Commander thought it was a good show of mine! Was up 2¼ hours.[1]

Started out in afternoon on shipping show but had to return owing to an oil leak. Missed evening show having to leave much later after the others and then unable to find them. Climbed to 20,000 feet looking for them—intercepted a lone Spit over Ashford. Was it our mysterious Spitfire? Very tired and browned off today. Can nothing go right these days?

Thursday, 21 August 1941

Show to Bethune at 8.30 am. Blenheims to go in at Gravelines and out at Hardelot. Bombers turned back inland from

---

[1] Pilot Officer Vicki Ortmans, Belgian, would be shot down again before the end of August, and be rescued again—by the same launch. He became a prisoner on 2 October, being rescued again from a dinghy—but by the Germans.

Dunkirk owing to cloud. Was flying with CO and Archer. Last out and chased by 30 Me109s. Archer badly shot-up and slightly wounded in the legs. CO not hit at all. I was hit by two machine-gun bullets in the wing which punctured my tyre. The second time I've got away with a landing with a burst tyre. Gee whiz, things got hot for a while. They chased us to within five miles of the English coast. Sgt Ahern is missing—I saw a Spit go down, was it him?

Show in the afternoon, six of our machines—all we could muster—patrolled St Omer at 27,000 ft. Nothing seen except three Spits over Kent—strange. Sgt Harrison collided with two aircraft of 72 Squadron when taking off. He later died, poor devil. Gordon crash-landed at Detling, out of petrol. Day's score: four Spits lost and two pilots killed and one wounded. Some day. So tired.

Sunday, 24 August 1941

Went on a Rhubarb this afternoon; led Beake.[1] Crossed French coast at St Valery near Fecamp. Flew about 20 miles inland, almost to the River Seine. Shot-up a factory near Le Troupet, saw tiles and dust come up in clouds. Shot at a tower with a few sand-bags and gun tripod on top. Nothing really worth shooting at. French people waved as we flew over the tree-tops—great fun. Fighter Sweep in the evening, Biggin Wing in at Dunkirk-St Omer, out at Hardelot. Nothing about. I bet the rain comes in that roof tonight!

Tuesday, 26 August 1941

Poor old Phillips missing on a show this evening. He just disappeared and is another of those mysteries.

Wednesday, 27 August 1941

Up at 5 am for a show to St Omer with some Blenheims—target support Wing at 26,000 ft—damned cold. Some 109s about but Squadron did not engage. Three chaps down in the Channel. Did my dinghy rescue act again—circled Sgt Roff in sea 10 miles off Dunkirk as long as possible; he was not picked up. He was flying my old 'X' [W3319].

Squadron Scrambled to patrol Manston and south Kent coast. Two 109s reported over Canterbury. Chased a 109 over Channel at 15,000 ft but he escaped in cloud.

---

[2] P H Beake ended his career as a Squadron Leader DFC.

Friday, 29 August 1941

Circus with Blenheims to Hazebrouck. Extraordinary cloud formations. Some 109s about but not engaged.

Am Flight leader in 'B' Flight now Beake is away. Am leading Blue Section on a show to Rouen tomorrow at 6.30. Hope I put up a decent show.

Saturday, 30 August 1941

Rouen show cancelled! Led convoy patrol—very dull. Led Blue Section on Squadron show—Wing practice flight.

Sunday, 31 August 1941

Very tiring day. Led Blue Section on show after dawn covering some boats in the Channel. Had quite an exciting time with a 109—dog-fought for quite a while. He was quite good and I've never seen a 109 turn so tight before. Took a shot at one and claimed it damaged. Convoy patrol in the evening when my No.2 [Sgt Kenwood] got lost and baled out at Eastbourne. So tired.

Friday, 5 September 1941

Dog-fight with Beaky—gave him quite a tussle. Circus to Mazingarbe with a hell of a lot of fighters. P/O Asselin missing. I saw a 109 beating him up from pretty close range. Also saw a Blenheim go down in flames, hit by ack-ack. Not so good. Dicky Milne now CO of 92 Squadron. Jamie Rankin made Wing Commander of Biggin.[1]

The pace slackened off somewhat in early September, Neville feeling rather browned off by both the inactivity and the acknowledgement that he was tired of all the recent mental strain of combat flying. After all he hadn't had much of a break for three months of intense activity. He was not sorry, therefore, to start a ten-day leave period beginning the 13th.

When he returned, 92 Squadron was about to move from Biggin to Gravesend. When the move came on the 25th, the pilots were billeted at Cobham Hall, the estate of Lord Darnley, which they found very nice indeed.

---

[1] R M 'Dickie' Milne DFC had fought in the Battle of Britain, and had been a flight commander with 92 for several weeks. He would command 222 Squadron later but become a PoW in March 1943, leading the Biggin Hill Wing. Rankin had, by this time, a score of 18 victories, and had received a DSO and a Bar to his DFC.

Friday, 26 September 1941

Flew from Gravesend for the first time. Beating around the sky with Beaky who is getting very worked up about his wedding on Wednesday. Flew in the afternoon leading a section about the sky while Tommy Lund and Beake tried to jump us—great fun. Went into Gravesend in the evening to the pubs. Finished up at Daniel's Den, a hell of a low dive, but good fun. Am drinking too much these days—bad thing, I suppose.

Saturday, 27 September 1941

Flew over to Biggin for a Circus to Mazingarbe. Blasted machine went u/s so was unable to go. Had to leave my plane at Biggin. Squadron had quite a bit of fun. Beake damaged one, CO and Johnston got probables.

Wimpey Wade flew Neville back to Gravesend in a Tiger Moth. He flew back to collect his repaired Spitfire on the 30th and then started out with Don Kingaby on a Rhubarb, but the weather improved, cloud disappeared, so they had to abort. Kingaby was one of the top scoring fighter pilots at this period and the only NCO pilot ever to win the DFM and two bars. Kingaby added another scalp on 1 October, during a cover patrol over the Channel. Neville flew two such patrols this date— searching for men in the sea and escorting an ASR Lysander. Things went sour in early October.

Thursday, 2 October 1941

Fighter Sweep—in at Le Treport and out at Abbeville. Biggin Wing as top cover at 24,000 ft and Blue Section engaged. Poor old Tommy Lund, Sgt Port and Sgt Edge missing and the other member of Blue Section—P/O Bruce—wounded and crash-landed near Ashford. Bad day. Our Section was not engaged. Will want a new flight commander in 'B' Flight now.

Drove down with the CO and some of the boys to Ashford Hospital to see Tony Bruce and bring him back but he is suffering from concussion and has something in his eyes.

The action this day, when it was all pieced together, heralded the arrival of a new German fighter—the Focke Wulf 190.

Friday, 3 October 1941

Circus 105—nine Blenheims bombing the power station and docks at Ostend. Not engaged until out to sea on our way back. We were last squadron out and 20 or so 109s appeared. Eight of them attacked Blue Section. I saw Sgt Close shot down—his glycol went in a second and two flashes of flame came from behind his cockpit and under his belly. He went down in a spin. Sgt Wood-Scawen was shot down as well. We have lost five in two days. Not so good—all five lost on comparatively easy shows and the only ones [the Wing] lost in the two operations.

Whether Neville admitted it, or even knew about it, he was now nearing the limit of his nerves. Well aware of how many of his friends and comrades had been lost over the summer, and with bad weather stopping much of the flying, he was beginning to feel the effects of recent operations. Not surprisingly this was reflected in his diary.

Saturday, 4 October 1941
92 Squadron is not all that it might be. I think it is going to pieces—there is definitely bad form in it. I am now the oldest member except for Sgt Kingaby and the Squadron cannot be compared with the 92 I joined in April.

Tuesday, 7 October 1941
Released for the day. Went up to town in the CO's car with Hunk and Babe Whitamore.[1] Called on Burberry's, visited the 'Crackers' and saw the usual females. Had tea at the Trocadero and then saw *Man Hunt* [film]. Went along to the Ritz 'Rivoli' Bar and had a few snifters. Beetled into the 'Berkeley' for dinner and then staggered along to Hatchett's for a night-cap.

This tender 19-year-old youth had certainly learned all about the places to go to in wartime London! There were, of course, no end of 'watering holes' for the up and coming fighter pilot to find and enjoy—as we shall see.

Thursday, 9 October 1941
Squadron released for the day. Went up to town with Archie, Babe and Hunk in the CO's car. Lunched at Shepherd's and went along to the '49th Parallel'—pretty good show. Had tea at the 'Troc', visited the 'Blue Pencil', 'Tudor Club' and the

---

[1] Squadron Leader W M Whitamore DFC would be killed leading 81 Squadron in Burma in March 1944.

'Crackers'. Indulged in a famous 'Planter's Punch' at the Troc!

Caught the train to Dartford at 8.15 pm and went to the Station Hotel where they were handing over a £50 cheque for the Spitfire Fund. Lots of speech making and I had to give one on behalf of the RAF. It lasted about two sentences. Drunk again—good show!

Sunday, 12 October 1941

Squadron on show to Boulogne. They wouldn't let me go! However, I did not miss anything. Heard this afternoon we are to move to Digby. Hell's bells.

Tuesday, 14 October 1941

Back to Gravesend after two days at Biggin. Evenings and mornings spent at White Hart—good fun. Squadron about to move and life is not going to be so nice in future. The Squadron is getting full of types who think only of practice flying and generally 'bull-shitting' people about. The latest thing is for all pilots to take the squadron at drill in the mornings—Oh God!

I don't much care now what happens to me and I am on at dawn tomorrow so I think I'll prowl about France just after dawn to see what the form is. The more I see of this war the more I fail to see the use of it and the more I fear for Britain.

Monday, 20 October 1941

Arrived at Digby this morning. The place is full of red tape and bull-shit. Don't think we will like this much. Don't think we shall stop here long somehow.

Neville was certainly at a low ebb. Practice flying became the norm and he became so fed up he even contemplated a move to Photographic Reconnaissance in unarmed Spitfires, but fortunately thought better of it. However, within a few days came news of a change, one that was to be the making of Neville Duke.

Tuesday, 28 October 1941

At lunchtime Sandy came in and said either me, Hunk or Archie was to be posted overseas. Archie volunteered for the Merchant Service Catapult thing [MSFU], so Hunk and myself tossed up to decide who should go. I lost the toss so I go overseas! But later in the day another signal came and

Hunk is to go with me. Taking up flight commander's jobs. A hell of a drinks session this evening.

Wednesday, 29 October 1941

Told to get tropical kit, have a medical and be ready to leave tomorrow. Frantic packing and rushing around. Phoned up Dad and then wrote to him. Think we are to fly there.

Friday, 31 October 1941

Came down to London with Hunk. Went home in the evening—bit of a surprise for the folks, who thought I was in Gib. by this time.

Saturday, 1 November 1941

Returned to London and collected tropical kit. Met Hunk and started on a tour of the dives. Commenced at Shepherd's, had lunch, and then went along to 'The New Yorker' with a drunken army type. 'Crackers' next, 'Odd Spot', 'Regent Bar', 'Oddeninos', 'Hatchett's', where I almost passed out.

Dashed back to Digby, only to find we had to return to London same night. Hell!

Time was now short. Within a few days he would be leaving England. For how long he had no idea. Would he ever return? Again, he would have no idea. All he did know was that something of an adventure was about to start and that it would be a very different sort of war from now on. Somehow his tiredness had gone.

Among a number of friends he would never see again was Gordon Brettell. He would be taken prisoner in September 1942 and be shot by the Gestapo following the famous escape from Stalag Luft III in March 1944—The Great Escape. Phil Archer would also be killed, Dickie Milne would end up 'in the bag'—the war would take its toll.

CHAPTER III

TO THE DESERT

Flying Officer Duke's journey to the Middle East began in the first week of November 1941. He had been correct in thinking they would be flying rather than sailing. A four-engined Short Sunderland flying boat was waiting for them. Squadron Leader R B Burrage would be their pilot, the machine belonging to No.10 (RAAF) Squadron (RB-U)—probably W3985.

He and Hunk had been told their overseas tour would only be about six weeks, but this was 'under-exaggerated'! They were, perhaps, naive enough to believe that the 'powers' would make all these arrangements for them to go out to North Africa for just a month and a half.

It was a good 'con' trick. Either that or the postings people really did believe that once the coming battle in Libya had been won, the war in that part of the world would be over! The other 'bait' of course, was the promise that both would be made flight commanders. So genuine did our two heroes think the offer to be that both immediately purchased enough 'thick' braid to put up the double-row flight lieutenant rank on their uniforms in place of their single flying officer braid. Some who saw them, made the odd comment about getting some time in, but it didn't faze Neville or Hunk. They'd been promised! Oh, cruel world.

They were soon to discover that others had been 'sold' the same story, but it did not stop them trying to get back to England, especially once they found how inhospitable the desert was. They did not succeed.

Monday, 3 November 1941
Caught the 10.30 train to Mount Batten with some other RAF types who are going East as well. Had self and baggage weighed, which were, of course, overweight. [The bags— Neville himself could never be termed over-weight!]
Four drinks in the Mess and at 9.30, in brilliant moonlight,

the 14 of us got into launches and scrambled aboard the Sunderland. Had a last look at old England lit up by the moon as we circled Plymouth and set off for Gibraltar. Took a spell on watch as one of the gunners as we were passing Lisbon, which was lit up as per pre-war days.

Landed at Gib at 8 am and rushed up to the Rock Hotel for rooms and brekkers *and* a bath. Probably off to Malta tonight.

Tuesday, 4 November 1941

Spent the day trotting around the town looking at people and buildings—most interesting. Went along to 'The Capitol' with the boys in the evening for a few drinks. There is no black-out here and it's wonderful.

Wednesday, 5 November 1941

Got up at 11 am. Wandered down to see the *Ark Royal* with Hunk after lunch. Was shown over her by a very obliging 'middy'. Also had a look at a ship with a Hurricane aboard on a catapult [CAM ship]. HMS *Nelson* and *Malaya* also in harbour. Were supposed to be leaving at 7.30 tonight but now put off until mid-day tomorrow.

Thursday, 6 November 1941

Left Gib at 12.10 this afternoon—quite a sight to see the Rock from the air. Trip got a bit rough and very boring about eight hours later when it was dark. Landed at Malta in brilliant moonlight and the island looked really beautiful as we went ashore in the power-boat. An air raid tonight but too tired to worry.

Friday, 7 November 1941

Wandered up to Hal Far aerodrome to see the types. There is a Sgt Ream in 261 Squadron based here who I think is the same Sgt who was in 92.

It's quite warm here but the walk was good fun. All the buildings are sand coloured and made of blocks of rock. The whole place looks pretty desolate and Valetta where we went this afternoon, is not awfully exciting—nothing much except women and drink, and both are not much good. Myself and F/O Sulman are left behind tonight and are going on to Cairo later.

Saturday, 8 November 1941

Left Malta at midnight [8/9th] after a day spent wandering

over the island. Pretty uncomfortable trip in a Wellington from Luqa aerodrome. [P/O Wisdom, pilot; an 8½-hour trip.]

Sunday, 9 November 1941

Landed at Feyoum aerodrome [south of Cairo]. Sand and more sand; met the others in Cairo. Staying at the National Hotel—great city; cars a menace though. Met Dickie Milne. [Milne was on detachment to the Middle East but would return to the UK in January to command 222 Squadron in the North Weald Wing.]

Neville listed in his diary the names of the 14 who flew out to the Middle East in the Sunderland, noting too what had happened to some of them. It makes interesting reading:

P/O Masters 250 Sqn, killed in action 20 November 1941
FO J E Sulman 238 Sqn, killed in action 23 November 1941
F/O J F Soden 112 Sqn OTU Aden, December 1941
F/O J J P Sabourin 112 Sqn DFC, killed with 145 Sqn September 1942
P/O G H Ranger 250 Sqn, killed in crash Tobruk, January 1942
P/O R G Marland 229 Sqn, killed in crash Hannish, December 1941—carrying beer
P/O M A Beatty 229 Sqn Malta April 1942; Heliopolis, July 1942
F/L N L Ievers 80 Sqn S/Ldr HQME January 1942; returned to UK
F/O Aldrich 274 Sqn, 33 Sqn, Palestine and then USA, August 1942
P/O I J Badger 94 Sqn DFC, 73 Sqn; back to UK, September 1942
F/O K G Hart 250 Sqn DFC, OTU Khartoum August 1942; killed over Italy in 1944 as S/Ldr
F/O H J Mann 260 Sqn US liaison, August 1942
F/O P H Humphreys 112 Sqn S/Ldr DFC
F/O N F Duke 112 Sqn ....

Monday, 10 November 1941

Visited dentist. Did an enormous amount of shopping. Leaving tonight for the desert—going by train.

Tuesday, 11 November 1941

Arrived at Air Headquarters Western Desert at Sidi Hannish at 4 o'clock this afternoon. Not very impressed with the desert at all. Parked myself in a tent for the night.

Wednesday, 12 November 1941

Saw the AOC—Air Vice-Marshal Coningham—in the morning and he told us all about the push that is coming off. The army expects to travel 80 miles per day as far as Tripoli and then to withdraw. Our job is to knock down the 30-odd Me109s the Huns possess and cover the army from bombing.

Posted to 112 Squadron. Met the CO, S/L Morello, who came to collect us in a car. He was as tight as an owl and I was rather put off and am most unhappy. Met the rest of the Squadron, who are good blokes.

Thursday, 13 November 1941

Saw all the knobs and buttons on the Tomahawk and took one up in the afternoon [AM390]. Promptly crashed when I landed but only got a few bruises. Almost lost my nerve for a bit and felt like running into the desert. If only I could get home again. I hope Dickie Milne tries to get Hunk and self back. When we say we are going back after six weeks everybody laughs and it rather hurts.

This is the first indication they had that perhaps after all they were not coming to the Middle East for just a few weeks. Obviously the old hands had heard this story before, hence the laughter.

After the pleasant Mess living at a permanent RAF base in England, and flying the delightful Spitfire, one can easily imagine Neville's initial panic at finding himself in a tent in an uncomfortable desert, flying a new and strange aeroplane. Having crashed on landing following his first flight in one, it is not surprising he suddenly wanted to go home. In actual fact, Neville had tried to do a three-pointer landing, and ground looped. However, things began to improve—slowly.

Friday, 14 November 1941

More Tomahawk flying—got things OK this time. Don't like them much after a Spit but still can't be helped. Getting to hate this desert more every day.

Squadron moved up to border today, ready for the fun. We are going up tomorrow. Shall be moving all over the place now, trying to keep up with the army. This fight should not last more than 3-4 weeks and then home?

Saturday, 15 November 1941

Moved over to forward base—called LG [Landing Ground] 110—by air. A [German] recce machine came over in the afternoon and AA opened up but without effect.

The forthcoming offensive—Operation 'Crusader'—was to be the biggest operation so far carried out in the desert war, following 17 months of hostilities. In point of fact it was not only the biggest mounted in the desert, but the biggest by any British force so far in WW2.

Great hopes were pinned on its success, for the Malta siege was starting to bite, and Britain's new ally—Russia—was continually asking for the British forces to open another front, or give the Germans something to think about on an existing front, in order to give their own forces some relief from the enemy's onslaught. Britain also need more control in the Mediterranean.

In the Desert Air Force, there were three fighter wings, two of light bombers plus Wellington night bombers and a smattering of Fleet Air Arm Albacore torpedo bombers which would help in night operations.

On the other side, the Luftwaffe were starting to receive Me109F fighters, with the arrival of I Gruppe of JG27 and Me110s of III/ZG26 at Derna. The Italian Regia Aeronautica had two Gruppi of Macchi 202 fighters, while still possessing a number of the nimble CR42 biplanes, Fiat G50s and Macchi 200s. The Germans' bombing force comprised the Ju87 Stuka dive bombers, Ju88s and some Heinkel 111s.

No.112 Squadron was part of 262 Wing, along with 250 Squadron and No.4 SAAF Squadron all equipped with P40IIB Tomahawks, and 80 Squadron flying Hurricane fighter-bombers.

Crusader was due to start on the 18th. Luck was with the Allies as a heavy rain storm on the night of the 17/18th turned the main German fighter bases in the Gazala area into a quagmire.

Sunday, 16 November 1941

Went with Hunk to [recce] Sidi Barrani, Mersah Matruh and got lost coming back across the desert. Just made base— thought a forced landing was in view.

Monday, 17 November 1941

Close escort for 4 Blenheims beating up El Baheira; No.3 RAAF Squadron escorting squadron of ground strafing Naval Hurricanes but Hurricanes did not shoot up the aerodrome as not many aircraft on same. Good fun, like the Biggin days again.

Dust storms all morning—most uncomfortable. Am getting to rather enjoy this life.

The army starts its advance tonight, and tomorrow at 8.30 we are covering the armoured divisions while they refuel. Should get some bombers around.

Tuesday, 18 November 1941
Squadron off on a cover patrol for tanks etc, inside the Libyan frontier. I had to return as my undercarriage was u/s. Nothing was seen however, and a terrific dust storm came up about an hour later and the visibility was almost nil. People were landing in the desert and everywhere. Sand gets in your eyes, ears, nose, mouth, hair, food, clothes, in fact sand everywhere. This air makes me as hungry as an ox. God, I'm looking forward to going home.

Wednesday, 19 November 1941
Wing patrol in Tobruk-Gambut area. Very quiet and not a Hun to be seen—blast. Another Wing patrol in same area in the afternoon and still nothing to be seen except tanks advancing across Libya towards Tobruk to cut off enemy based at Sollum.

Landed back at new advance aerodrome near Fort Maddalena next to the 'wire' marking the Egypt-Libya border. No beds so had to sleep in clothes on the sand, cuddled up with Hunk.

Thursday, 20 November 1941
Up at the crack of dawn (5 o'clock) on another Wing patrol. This time encountered six Me110s south-west of Tobruk. Both squadrons dived on them and created a general mix-up. Spent most of my time getting out of the way of Tomahawks and didn't get a shot at 'em. Sgt Carson got one to himself and rest of Squadron shared another.

No.3 RAAF Squadron, who regularly fly with us, were credited with another two. Shot at by tanks as I came back with the CO at ground level. [Later] Close escort for Blenheims bombing troop positions at El Adem. Pretty bad bombing and little AA from the ground. Feeling a bit tired.

The 110s were from III Gruppe ZG/26, who appear to have lost one aircraft with its crew, and a crew member of another, wounded.

Friday, 21 November 1941
Tobruk relieved. Enormous tank battles going on. Squadron patrolled Tobruk-El Adem area this afternoon. Encountered two Fiat CR42s south of El Adem. Attacked same with P/O 'Butch' Jefferies and Sgt Carson. Did three attacks on one which was flying at about 500 ft. He did a few turns and then

went into land. Turned over, after running a few yards, onto its back and the pilot was out like a shot. Butch and Carson started to shoot the poor devil up but I couldn't do it, so I set the machine on fire.

I went down to look at the pilot who was running with his hands up. His face was full of fear and the next time I saw him he was lying on the ground. There was no need to murder the poor devil as our troops were coming up, and as we came back from patrol we came over the crash and the army had his parachute in pieces.

Saturday, 22 November 1941

Squadron went ground strafing along the El Adem-Acroma road. Whizzing along at telephone-wire height—some fun. Wing Sweep in the afternoon. Engaged by 15-20 Me109Fs. I got on the tail of one and followed him up. Got in a burst from stern quarter and its hood and pieces of fuselage disintegrated. Machine went into a vertical dive and the pilot baled out. Flew round and round the pilot until he landed, then went down to look at him. I waved to him and he waved back. Poor devil thought I was going to strafe him as he initially dived behind a bush and lay flat.

Rejoined Squadron which was going round and round in a defensive circle. The 109s kept diving down on us and I saw a Tomahawk go in with half its wing off after colliding with a 109. The fight lasted about 40 minutes. Longest ever! Force-landed after breaking away from circle by myself, at an advanced landing ground [LG 134].

Combat Report for 22 November
Time: 1615 hrs, south of El Adem

One Me109F Destroyed, own machine undamaged. Pilot baled out after long burst from 100 yards stern quarter. Hood and pieces of fuselage disintegrated.

Pilot had on a German field grey uniform. Unable to strafe pilot owing to presence of other e/a.

The 109s were from I/JG27—and two Luftwaffe pilots were captured. Oberfahnrich Waskott was Neville's victim. JG27 had been very active during the day, and this combat was just one of three major actions. 112 Squadron lost Sergeant Burney, but 3 RAAF lost three pilots with two more shot down, but they got back. Three JG27 pilots failed to return in addition to the two who were captured.

Sunday, 23 November 1941

Flew back from LG134—great excitement at the return of the missing. P/O Sabourin, Sgt Ferguson and Sgt Burney missing. Top cover for some Blenheims but no excitement. Randolph Churchill, Mde Curie, Quentin Reynolds, etc, turned up and I gave a bit of a broadcast on our ground strafing yesterday. Sabby and Ferguson turned up this evening. Sabby cracked his head when he baled out by landing head first. He was picked up by the Indian Division.

In the event, Sergeant Burney also got back. Wing Commander Fred Rosier had seen him brought down and had landed to pick him up. Unfortunately Rosier had a tyre burst and was unable to take-off again, so both men had to trudge the 30 miles back to the front lines.

Monday, 24 November 1941

Escort for Marylands bombing near El Adem. Bit of a mix-up as bombers streamed off without waiting for us. Did not see a thing. The Huns broke through our lines with about 40 tanks and a 100 or so lorries, causing great consternation; all squadrons evacuated and retreated from advance landing grounds and landed here—great panic. Got my stuff packed and put in my machine ready for a quick getaway.

Tuesday, 25 November 1941

Ground strafing Hun tanks, etc, near Sidi Omar. Some of the chaps shot up a bit and I peppered a tank and lorry well and truly, and nearly rammed same. Wing Sweep in the afternoon —70 EA about but no luck. Landed at LG110.

Wednesday, 26 November 1941

From LG110 to base. Did some target practice on the way up and a few aerobatics. Hunk got a CR42 and a 109 probable yesterday. Wing Sweep in the afternoon with 3 RAAF and 229's Hurricanes. The cloud was low, about 6,000 ft, and over the Sidi Rezegh area we saw about six Me109s through a break in the cloud.

Immediately all three squadrons went into a defensive circle! Disgusting show. No.3 RAAF lost two more chaps. That makes about 14 in 4 days. I think Tomahawks are shooting at each other as a Tommy looks very much like a 109.

Friday, 28 November 1941

Close escort for 12 Blenheims who intended to bomb troop positions. Low cloud somewhat disorganised things and the job was finally given up.

Started off in the afternoon with the CO and Jack Bartle for El Adem aerodrome, where six Ju52s had been reported. CO turned back at Sidi Rezegh as cloud cover was not good enough. Weather pretty cold and it's raining today.

Saturday, 29 November 1941

Dawn Wing Sweep with No.3 RAAF—damn cold and nothing doing. Getting a bit browned off with the lack of activity.

Famous last words! Neville should have kept quiet.

Sunday, 30 November 1941

Wing Sweep in El Gobi area. Encountered Circus of 30-40 enemy aircraft including Ju87s, Me109s, Fiat G50s and Macchi 200s. Got into the middle of things, and onto a G50 chasing him west down to ground level where he crash-landed after pumping tons of lead into him.

Jumped on by 2-3 109s and a G50. Damaged a 109. Ran for home and was chased by a 109F; dodged 4-5 attacks and got in a few shots at him but he was too fast. Finally he hit me in the port wing and, I think, the petrol tank. Machine turned on its back at about 500 ft, out of control. Saw the ground rushing up and then I kicked the rudder and pushed the stick and prayed. Got control just in time and the machine hit the ground on its belly. Hopped out jolly quick and then darted behind some scrub and lay on my belly about 20 yards from the crash.

The Hun came down and shot-up my machine, which was already smoking and set it on fire. Horrible crack and whistle of bullets near me and I thought I was going to be strafed but the Hun cleared off. Started off to walk across the desert home but saw a lorry coming my way. Lay down behind another bush thinking they were Huns but as they went past I recognised the uniforms and popped up and gave 'em a yell.

A Lysander came over and after much waving, landed. Got a lift in the back seat with a General and flew over to battle H'Qtrs with them. Later returned in Lysander to my own

aerodrome. Feel very lucky to be alive and a bit browned off
with the war!

Combat Report for 30 November
Time: 0830 am, El Gobi

EA dived down and went westwards at ground level. Little evasive
action except for a switch-back action. EA crash-landed after a long
chase. Was then attacked from astern by 2-3 109Fs and a G50 or
Mc200. Turned into a 109F and gave a short burst and observed
glycol stream as he passed overhead. Pursued home by 109F and
was finally hit in port wing and rear petrol tank by EA.

My machine went onto its back at about 500 ft and hit the ground
as it pulled out, on its belly. Machine took the air again and I had
sufficient control to crash-land. EA strafed my machine which was
already smoking and set it on fire.

Claim: 1 G50 Destroyed;
       1 Me109F Damaged (Probable).

At this stage of the land battle, the German Afrika Korps was counter
attacking the British at Sidi Rezegh and had recaptured this area, once
more making Tobruk an isolated port under siege.

On this early Sweep, 3 RAAF and 112 Squadrons had run into Ju87s
of II/StG 2 with large German and Italian fighter escort, that were about
to attack the New Zealand Division. The Allied fighter pilots claimed
some 15 aircraft shot down, 12 by the Australians, three by 112. The
Italian fighters, from 20 Gruppo, had one pilot killed, one bale out and
another crash after being wounded.

The 109s—of II/JG27—had got in amongst the Tomahawks, and
Oberfeldwebel Otto Schulz had shot down Sergeant A C 'Tiny' Cameron,
who baled out and was picked up by Wing Commander P Jeffrey and
flown back. Considering that Cameron was by far the largest pilot in the
Squadron, getting himself and Jeffrey into the cockpit was some effort.

After downing Cameron, Schulz had turned his attention to the P40
flown by Neville Duke. Otto Schulz was a seasoned veteran fighter
pilot, having flown with JG27 since August 1940, gaining his first victory
during the Battle of Britain. He had also seen action in the Balkans and
in Russia before JG27 moved to North Africa. He had around 30
victories at this date. Neville had been shot down by one of the best air
fighters in the business, despite being 30 years of age.

Schulz would go on to win the Knight's Cross in February 1942 but
he was killed in action on 17 June 1942 near Sidi Rezegh, having brought
his overall score to 51—42 of them in the desert.

Monday, 1 December 1941

First trip after yesterday—don't think I have suffered any ill effects except for a sleepless night!

Squadron patrol in Sidi Rezegh area during the morning but only saw about ten Macchi 200s very high above and going home. Jerry [Westenra] says he saw some 87s but there was too much cloud about to make contact.

Squadron patrol with 80 Squadron (Hurricanes) to pick up Blenheim at Tobruk and bring the GOC back. Bit of a mess-up on the way back when the Blenheim went down through cloud and things became a bit hectic with Tomahawks and Hurricanes whistling by each other in the cloud.

Thursday, 4 December 1941

Oh, Boy, another! Encountered the Hun Circus of Ju87s, 109s, Macchi 200s and G50s. Got stuck into them. Came across five Ju87s flying in close formation and sprayed them all. One broke away and went down in a gentle dive, smoking a bit. Couldn't watch him as some 109s appeared and I don't like them!

Pounced on a Macchi 200 and had a pretty good dog-fight. He started beetling off home and I chased him. Once he did a complete roll in front of me. My guns were all haywire and in the end only one cannon was going and I had to keep cocking that. Finally that stopped just as we came roaring over Tobruk at nought feet. The Macchi was still showing fight however, but he suddenly spun in off a steep turn and crashed. I was hoping he would land on the aerodrome as he had put up a good fight—nearly always at ground level, and once we went chasing out to sea. I was making dummy attacks on him as my guns had packed up.

I landed at Tobruk and had lunch. It had bucked the boys up no end to see the fight. One Macchi destroyed, one Ju87 Probable. Makes the bag 5⅓ destroyed, 1 probable and 3 damaged. Feel a bit tired now and am not going on the next show today. I was posted as missing as I did not turn up until the afternoon. That's the second time!

Combat Report for 4 December
Time: am, El Adem / Sidi Rezegh

A Ju87 broke away from other 87s smoke coming from the nose. Did not observe it crash but last seen going down in diving turns to the east of Sidi Rezegh.

Mc200—attacked from astern, Maachi turned, climbed and dived. Chased him to Tobruk where he spun in off a turn about 1-2 miles from Tobruk aerodrome.

Claim: 1 Mc200 Destroyed; 1 Ju87 Probable.

Friday, 5 December 1941

Oh dear, shot down again. Met the Hun Circus again and all the types piled in and got 10 down. I stayed up to stave the 109s off but got hit in the right elevator which was carried away, and in the starboard wing where all the trailing edge up to the aileron was shot off.

Spun down from 10,000 ft to about 2-3,000. Undid the straps, etc, preparatory to baling out, but it seemed to fly OK. Made north for Tobruk at ground level. Crash-landed at 150 mph as I could not keep nose up at slower speed; got thrown about the cockpit, and found I'd been hit in the right leg by cannon shell splinters. Hopped out pretty quick. Pinched the compass and clock from the machine as spoils of war!

The chaps were pretty surprised to see me again at Tobruk. I was whisked off to the hospital and X-rayed but the wounds were not very bad. Lucky enough to get a lift back in a Blenheim same evening. Shot down twice within five days—so flying down to Cairo for a few days' leave.

Saturday, 6 December 1941

Flew down to Fayoum, Cairo, in a Tomahawk, stopping for lunch at Sidi Hannish. Very nice trip along the coast to Alex and then down to the Pyramids. Circled them and had a look at the old Sphinx. Only drawback, sand-storm all the way.

Got to Cairo about 7 o'clock but couldn't get a room at the Continental, but finally got one at the National for the night. Leapt into a superb bath and soaked for an hour, then had the odd drink and ate solidly for the next hour. Boy, this is the goods!

Monday, 8 December 1941

Brekker in bed and an enormous bath. Staggered around Cairo buying things and met a chap by the name of Ferguson who I had met on Malta. Arranged to have lunch with him. Had the biggest shampoo, shave, face massage etc, in the world. Spent the afternoon yelling to Ferguson on the telephone. Prowled around the hotel after tea—drinking pretty good too.

Tuesday, 9 December 1941

Tottered around with Fergy today. A most amusing chap but he does talk and talk in a slow Canadian drawl for hours on end about some obscure tale.

Spent the afternoon hiring a car to take two Egyptian girls out this evening; most high class Egyptians apparently. Bowker, a Rhodesian, who drinks more than is good I fear, [That's calling the kettle black, Neville! Ed.] turned up from the Squadron for a spot of leave. Very pleased to see him and we started out on an enormous drunk. Visited Tommy's Bar, The Dolls, and Mogadu. Had to leave at 10 to meet Fergy and these girls. Was in pretty good form by then too. Took them to Shepherd's for a dance.

Wednesday, 10 December 1941

Started a day of real solid drinking and Bowker and myself got amongst it about 11 am and kept it up on Rye Highballs. I got to bed at 4 am. We started at the Continental, then a spot of drinking in my room this afternoon and after a few more at the Hotel bar, went along to the Trocadero and spent the rest of the night there chatting with the females. Ended up by finding myself climbing out of a back window of a house near the Pyramids 10 miles from Cairo!

Quite obviously Neville's severe bar, restaurant and 'dive' training in London while at Biggin had not been wasted effort.

Thursday, 11 December 1941

Today I feel like nothing, repeat nothing, on earth or elsewhere. I feel terrible. A pretty quiet day!

Cairo is all right for 3-4 days, but a week is too long. I feel now that my nerves were in a pretty shaky state before this leave but they seem a lot better now. This city is so noisy, so smelly (some good, some bad) and full of people trying to swindle you or else people in cars intent on running you over.

Friday, 12 December 1941

Cash situation is getting very difficult. Went out to the Mena House near the Pyramids for lunch with Bowker and Jerry. Came back to the Continental for tea and found an enormous box left by Mrs Stephens, wife of the CO of 80 Squadron [Squadron Leader M M Stephens DFC] whom I'd met last Wednesday. Wants me to take it to him—hope I can find him.

Met one of the types who came out from England with me in the bar, but I can't make this a good last night as I'm broke. Must even go without dinner tonight—and brekker tomorrow. Understand the Squadron has moved now to somewhere near El Adem. Suppose I shall tour about the sky looking for it.

Saturday, 13 December 1941

Hired a car from the Continental to get me to the airfield. Stopped at the Pyramids for breakfast. Took off about midday and arrived at Sidi Hannish for lunch. Arrived at El Adem at tea time. Squadron is very short of machines and three pilots are missing from yesterday when they had a dust-up with 109s and Mc202s. Hunk was flying a new 'F' that was meant for me. I think 'F' is unlucky as this is the third time it has been shot-up. (He was pretty badly shot-up too). And its numbers added up to 13 as did the 'F' before! [Neville was shot down in AN337 on the 5th]

Led five machines in a prowl around below cloud near Derna and Gazala. Met some 109s and had a dust-up in and out of cloud—no results.

CHAPTER IV

'CRUSADER'

Neville may have used up all his money, but he had at least had a good break from the war, even if he'd not had a break from the Middle East. There is absolutely no doubt that he hated almost every moment of his time here. Only when he was stuck into the enemy did he see any good in his surroundings, but that was often short lived. It comes through in his diary, however; if he was in action things were not so bad, out of action, things were bleak.

Fighting in the desert required a very special breed of man and few really got used to it. Like men who would later fight in the jungles of Burma, there were so many other problems to face, without dealing with the enemy too: sand and flies, poor food, bright cloudless skies that could and did conceal 109s, living under canvas, primitive sanitation, the constant desire to bathe; the list goes on. One even had to take off with the cockpit hood closed, unlike in England, otherwise the slipstream would suck in sand, and sand over the perspex would make it almost opaque. Yes he often hated everything about the desert.

And he was not alone . . .

Monday, 15 December 1941

The Squadron is in a very poor state of morale. Everybody has had enough of the war. I know I have.

Led the Squadron on a Wing Sweep in the Gazala-Derna area, but nothing encountered. Sat at stand-by in the cockpit this afternoon in a hell of a dust storm; no fun at all. Drove out to Air HQ at Sidi Rezegh with the CO and Ambrose[1] at tea time. Went through an area where a tank battle had taken

---

[1] C F Ambrose DFC had fought in the Battle of Britain. He later became a Group Captain and retired with a CBE and AFC in 1972.

place. Hun, Italian and British tanks all over the place. Several graves around too.

Got a bit tight tonight—nothing else to do and it helps the old nerve.

Tuesday, 16 December 1941

Nothing for me this morning so trotted around taking some photographs. Went off on a Wing Sweep this afternoon but I had to return with my airscrew control u/s. I think I was looked upon with suspicion as so many people come back nowadays saying their machines are u/s.

The CO told me Hunk was to get a Flight here and he is sending Soden and Sabourin[1] (who came out with me) home as he thinks they have 'had' it. Ambrose is also going home. I could have cried on the spot when I heard that as I know I have 'had' this war good and proper. Got good and drunk tonight with the CO and Ambrose. Hunk told me in confidence tonight that I had been put up for a 'gong'!

Wednesday, 17 December 1941

On stand-by in the cockpit this morning but did not have to take off. Close escort to 10 Blenheims in the afternoon. Finished up leading the Squadron again, when Jerry [Westenra] dropped out. One Blenheim dropped its bombs in the sea and turned back with engine trouble.

On the way to the target, which was transport at Mechili, we passed 12 Ju87s and a couple of 109s but could not attack them. We were in a pretty good position, above them and in the sun.

The most enormous drinking session this evening. Got really stinkers. In fact I got really ill. CO had a little chat with me in our drunken state—thinks perhaps I should go home but wants me to stay. What is a chap to do? Hunk tells me I should pack up.

Thursday, 18 December 1941

Squadron off to do some ground strafing near Mechili with 250 Squadron, who were picked up after landing at Tobruk just after dawn. CO could not find the Huns who were not in the position stated, so did not strafe anything. Another show in the afternoon on the same thing and the boys strafed our

---

[1] J J P Sabourin, a Canadian, in fact went to 73 OTU Fayid as an instructor; later won the DFC but was killed in action in September 1942 with 145 Squadron.

own troops. The army admitted it was their fault as they had moved further west than they should have done.

Took the parcel given to me by Mrs Stephens in Cairo to 80 Squadron at Tobruk. Found Stephens was on leave in Cairo so as the box had fallen to pieces, and oranges and a couple of bottles came to light, Soden and myself partook of one bottle of champagne and split it in the Mess tonight.

Operation 'Crusader', which had opened in mid-November, appeared to be going well, with the British army pushing westwards, making it necessary for the air force boys to move up too. The day fighters were starting to go down and to strafe the retreating Axis forces on the ground.

Friday, 19 December 1941
Up early and packed things for our move to Gazala today, from El Adem. Took off as escort for 10 Blenheims who bombed some transport west of Mechili after stooging along at 150 mph for 2½ hours. Landed at Gazala aerodrome which was recently occupied by some 109 boys. Wreckage of some still remain there. Squadron told to move on to Mechili and I left by road with the advance party.

The army is moving forward some and is now well past Derna I think. There has been no Hun opposition in the air for some time now—thank God. It's rumoured he has withdrawn all his air force from this part of the world. However, spent the night in the middle of the desert, sleeping 'neath the stars. Have got a hell of a bed.

Saturday, 20 December 1941
Moved on for Mechili at dawn but the staff car broke down for an hour and the rest of the convoy moved on. Got things going and arrived about mid-day. Very tired and very dirty.

Went up to the fort of El Mechili with Jerry and Bart and saw where two Italian ammo trucks had been blown up. There were several dead bodies around which shook me a bit, never having seen any before. Blast the war—why fight for this god forsaken part of the world?

Sunday, 21 December 1941
Went on scrounging expedition with Bart and Jerry. Got a lot of stuff off wrecked Italian lorries.

Monday, 22 December 1941

Squadron arrived from Gazala this morning and we went on a Sweep with 2 and 4 SAAF and 250 Squadrons. [Six of 112, six of 250 with SAAF boys flying cover.] Ran into Ju87s taking off and flying around the aerodrome of Magrun, near Soluch. Attacked an 87 and think I hit him. Carson, my No.2, gave the same one a burst and he thinks it went in. Shot at three 87s landing. Then saw a 109F taking off and flew across the aerodrome at 100 ft after it. Chased it for quite a while and it finally crashed. I pulled up into cloud and started beetling up the coast for home.

South of Benghazi I ran into 15 Ju52s escorted by 110s. Attacked a straggler and it started to go down with smoke coming out. I was then jumped by the 110s, so buzzed off.

Combat Report for 22 December
Time: 1030-1100 hrs, Magrun

Attacked Ju87 circling aerodrome from left quarter. Observed Me109 taking off—pursued same across 'drome. EA crashed W of Magrun near coast. Climbed up into cloud and flew north up coast. Saw 15 Ju52s off coast, S of Benghazi. Dived on Ju52 at rear of formation and observed smoke come from fuselage as EA started to go down. Did not observe same further as attacked from the rear by Me110 escort. Observed six Me110s in all. Climbed up into cloud and cleared off. One Me110 was desert brown and another dark blue-grey sea camouflage as were the 52s.

Claim: 1 Me109F Destroyed;
      1 Ju52 Probable;
      ½ Ju87 Probable shared with Sgt Carson.

The Me109s of JG27 were in evidence and a couple managed to take off, one being Leutnant Rudolf Sinner, one of their up and coming aces, but the III Gruppe lost Feldwebel Erich Wassermann of the 7th Staffel on this date, which was the 109 pilot Neville shot down. 112 Squadron's Jerry Westenra and Jack Bartle claimed a Stuka, with 250 and 4 SAAF pilots also claiming an 87 each. Two Ju87 pilots of II/StG.2 were killed.

The Ju52s were flying in urgently needed drums of aviation fuel, which enabled Luftwaffe fighters that were virtually grounded by lack of petrol, to take off and retreat to Arco Philaenorum—known as Marble Arch by the Allies, and to Sirte. The fuel arrived just in time, as advancing British tanks were a mere 30 miles away.

Tuesday, 23 December 1941

Wing Sweep. Bit of a tank battle going on 50 miles SW of
Bengers [Benghazi]. Saw no enemy aircraft. Went out in the
afternoon with Ambrose to find our trailer, stuck somewhere
on the Derna road. Found the swamp where it had been stuck
but it had got out again and arrived at the 'drome about 10
mins after we had left. Got our car stuck in the mud and had
to leave it there for the night.

Met Ken Sands at Fort El Mechili. He had been missing for
three days and had been walking around with Bedouin Arabs.
Eventually picked up an armoured car [patrol]. [Sands had
been brought down by JG27 on the 20th.]

Do not feel things so nerve racking these days and hope,
and want, to see this show through. Off ground strafing an
aerodrome tomorrow early.

Wednesday, 24 December 1941

Flew down to Msus landing ground with Jerry and four other
pilots to escort some Blenheims on a bombing raid on El
Aghelia aerodrome and road. 2 and 4 SAAF machines got
lost so they called the thing off and kept us there until 2.30
when we went off to ground strafe the aerodrome and road.
Got a good burst into a lorry. Saw three Me109s on the way
back darting around a cloud. Furious weaving for a while but
12 Hurricanes put them off.

Thursday, 25 December 1941

Christmas Day. The first Christmas I have not spent around
the old home fire. Breakfast of bully beef and egg plus
porridge in the cookhouse tent. Five of the chaps off on a
Sweep with 250 and 2 and 4 SAAF Squadrons. It takes four
squadrons to make up a wing of a score of aircraft now as our
serviceability is very poor. All we can muster are these five
aircraft and 250 Squadron has only two! However, we do not
expect much more opposition in the air and they hope to be in
Tripoli by February. (Home by March?).

Had an enormous hot bath to celebrate Christmas. The
first wash for three days! Lunched on bully soup, steak and
bully pie and biscuits with ham and tea, plus one tin of
beer!

Got amongst the liquor at 250 Squadron in the afternoon
and met Les Harris who is a friend of Gordon Brettell, and
who was at FTS with me. A small world. Had a few with our
CO in the evening and then bowled over to 250 again and got

down to some drinking whilst talking over old times with Les. Heard we are to get Kittyhawks.

Friday, 26 December 1941

Boxing Day. Wonder how and what the folks are doing at 82? Getting over the enormous feed of turkey etc, of yesterday no doubt. Oh, to be there. Still, a war is on I'm told and the sooner we get this business over out here, the sooner we will get home. Rumour of [going to] Singapore? Golly.

Blasted sand storm this afternoon which prevented any shows. Spent the afternoon chatting in the tent with Jerry, Bowker, Bart, Soden and Hunk. Talking of this and that.

Saturday, 27 December 1941

No aviation to-day. Flew from El Mechili to our new base at Zeit Msus. Went off ground strafing with the other 'Tommy' squadrons. Hundreds of Hun lorries along the Aghelia road and we got a good deal of return fire. F/O Bowker (12 destroyed) was hit and crash-landed near the Huns. Last seen running east. No news of him yet.

Monday, 29 December 1941

No aviation for the last two days. Off to get Kittyhawks today or tomorrow.

Wing Commander Rosier was trying to post me to an OTU at Aden but the CO would not have it.[1] The Wingco had a shot at it the other day but the CO gave Soden's name and now he has given Sabourin's as well. Both Soden and Sabby (and Ambrose) have left the Squadron and were expecting to go home.

Tuesday, 30th December 1941

Went by Bombay to Heliopolis. Into Cairo for the night; stayed at the National. Had a wizard bath and the most enormous feed at the 'Kursal'. Visited 'Dolls' and steamed along to the Continental Hotel where Hunk and myself met Ambrose and Soden. Had a terrific drunk in their room with Burney and Leu (two of our sergeants). Stirred up the Continental a bit too!

---

[1] Wing Commander Fred Rosier had seen action in France and in the Battle of Britain. Posted to the Middle East in October 1941 to command the Wing he was about to receive the DSO. Staying in the RAF after the war, he retired a Knighted Air Chief Marshal.

Sergeant R M Leu hailed from Australia, known to everyone as 'Blue' Leu. In fact he was born in Canada, spent some of his childhood in South Africa and Madagascar before coming to England to be educated. He then went to Australia in 1934, joining the RAAF in 1939. He won the DFM in early 1942 but became a prisoner of war in June.

Wednesday, 31 December 1941

Flew from Helio to Kasfareet on the Suez Canal to collect our Kittys. Had a short fly in one—they seem OK. Spent night in the Mess. Feel a trifle u/s after last night.

Nev recorded this empassioned resume of his flying life so far, at the end of his 1941 diary: 'So ends this year. A year as has never been seen before and, I hope, never to be seen again. From the serene days of FTS in January I went to an OTU in February, from there I went to my first Squadron in April, the famous 92nd Squadron, where I had my first combat a week or two after I joined. Later taking part in over 60 Sweeps and Circuses over France where I had some enormous frights dodging angry 109s, but enjoyed the war and lived from day to day to the best of my ability.

'Surviving several months of this the Squadron went north for a rest and started to get split up. Was posted overseas expecting a Flight which did not materialise however. Arrived in Cairo and was posted to the Western Desert with 13 others who came out in the Sunderland with me. Of us 14, only 8 remain. P/O Masters and F/O Sulman are missing; F/O Ranger spun in at Tobruk on a training flight; P/O Marland spun in near Sidi Hannish trying to pull off a forced landing; F/O Soden and P/O Sabourin are posted away to an OTU at Aden, having had enough of the war.

'I joined 112 Squadron with Humphreys, Soden[1] and Sabby; crashed the first time I flew there. Have shot down 6⅓ EA to date, two probably destroyed, and three damaged. Wounded once and am awfully tired of war. Want to go home and expect to go home at the end of this campaign. Have been recommended for the DFC which was my ambition to get before I was 20. Still have 7 days left for it to come through. Have lived highly and fast in Cairo, and lived like something not human in the desert.

'So ends this year. Soon to be home, I hope. I think long and lovingly of England, of home, and of Biggin and friends. I face this new year with

---

[1] J F Soden was, in fact, the son of Group Captain F O 'Mongoose' Soden DFC & Bar. A fighter pilot in the Great War, Mongoose had commanded RAF Biggin Hill in 1941.

some trepidation and have had enough of air fighting, out here at any rate, where there is no rest or respite from continuous fighting. Fighting for your very life each time you go up in a machine which is not equal to the enemy's.'

Thursday, 1 January 1942

Collected a new Kittyhawk from the MU at Kasfareet, then flew up to Mersah Matruh with five others and landed there to refuel. Donkin 'pranged' his machine when he taxied out to take off, running into a soft patch. Sgt Hoare got bogged down and we remaining four took off as the sand started to blow. After about 1½ hours flying, we ran into a sand-storm and the others turned back. I climbed above it and struggled along. Got pretty lost and ended up nearly at Derna.

After three hours flying, made El Adem and landed in a sand storm without a drop of petrol left. The only one to get here so far. Spent the night sleeping on the desert floor!

Had a pretty uncomfortable trip. My coolant temp. was off the clock, warning lights kept going on, the windscreen was oiled up and I couldn't see ahead. The rudder pedals were stuck back and I was cramped to hell—and getting unhappy.

Friday, 2 January 1942

The CO arrived this morning at El Adem; the only other one to turn up so far. The others rolled up during the morning except Sgt Johnson who is missing after yesterday's sand storms. All took off for Msus after lunch except P/O Sands and myself as our machines were u/s. Spent another night on the desert floor. Quite a raid on Tobruk to-night.

Saturday, 3 January 1942

Left El Adem with P/O Sands, Sgts Donkin and Hoare in a DH86 for Msus. Wizard trip in a wizard machine. 3 RAAF have run into the angry Hun again [on the 1st] and got a couple of 109s and a few Ju87s.

The war is held up a bit near Agedabia by Hun tanks. We expected to get to Tripoli by 15th this month but I don't think that will happen now. I had hoped to be on the way home by March!

Old Hunk is a flight commander now. CO—S/L Morello—is leaving the Squadron. I don't think this a good thing as he was all in favour of Hunk and myself going home after this blitz and the next CO may not be so keen.

Sunday, 4 January 1942

Flew down to El Adem with P/O Sands, Sgts McQueen, Donkin and Hoare in the Bombay to collect some Kittys ferried up for us. Met the CO there who had been to see Air Commodore Embry[1] re: going home. He brought up about Hunk and self, and Embry said there was every chance we would be going home. Easy to say!

Left El Adem pretty late with Sands and McQueen. Was afraid I would not make Msus by dark but steamed along and got here in 40 minutes, breaking all records, just as dusk fell.

Old Sands could not keep up with me but he got here OK. Sgt Crocker was killed this afternoon in a Kitty; he crashed after taking off.

Monday, 5 January 1942

Spent the morning pottering around with Ken Sands taking some photographs. Hunk is off to Cairo for a few days' leave. Sgt Johnson, who has been missing on the ferrying trip, was reported killed in a crash. He apparently hit some telephone wires in the sand storms which we were caught in.

Three Kittyhawks have been lost to date and two pilots killed on them! Not so good. We should be operational in them in a few days though.

Heard today that F/Lt Caldwell of 250 Squadron is to be our new CO[2]. I don't like it much as I don't think he is in favour of us going back to England after the show. I was hoping Jerry would be the CO.

Spent the afternoon getting my new machine organised. She's quite a beaut.

The Curtiss P40E Kittyhawk (I) was an improvement on the P40D Tomahawk in that it had a more powerful engine, a 1,600 hp Allison, rather than the 1,090 hp engine of the Tomahawk IIB. There was a new cockpit design and rather than the six guns of the earlier model (2 × .50s above the engine and 4 × .3″ in the wings), the Kittyhawk carried six .50s and could carry 1,000 pounds bomb-load, usually one 500 lb under the belly and two 250 lb'ers under the wings. Visually it was bigger—two feet longer—with a larger air intake, although its service ceiling was lower, 30,000 as opposed to 35,000 feet.

---

[1] Basil Embry had been AOC 2 Group Bomber Command, but had been sent to the Middle East on a fact finding tour.
[2] Clive Caldwell DFC and bar, from Sydney, Australia, currently had 18 victories, flying with 250 Squadron. He died in 1994.

It would eventually equip 94, 112, 250, 260 and 450 Squadrons RAF, 5 and 7 SAAF Squadrons and No.3 RAAF Squadron, in the Middle East.

Neville's 'beaut' was AK595 GA-Y. By this time, Neville had flown 134 operational sorties accumulating 180 operational flying hours. Of these, 94 had been from Biggin Hill, and 40 in the desert, covering 120 hours in the UK and 60 in North Africa.

Wednesday, 7 January 1942

The weather is much better today [wind and sand storms on the 6th]. It is nice to sit on the ground under a clear blue sky but bags of cloud is the thing for operational flying these days. 109s have a habit of sitting up high in the sun and whistling down on you and back up again into the blue before you can even see them coming. We have no hope of dealing with 109s when they do that as they can climb away from us like a lift. They say the Kittyhawk can hold them in a climb but that remains to be seen.

Took my machine up this afternoon to test the guns and generally get the feel of things. Did a spot of shadow firing and aerobatics. These machines are a definite improvement on the Tomahawk in climb and speed and the six .5 machine guns are pretty good fun. Still don't think they can cope with the 109 though. So roll on bags and bags of cloud.

Thursday, 8 January 1942

Flew up to Barce, near the coast, where they have hills and trees and green valleys. It makes you want to jump out and play on the grass. Went from Barce down to Benina and Benghazi. Lots of ships sunk in Benghazi harbour and the place is fairly battered by bombs.

There are scores of Italian aircraft on these aerodromes, some seem repairable and a party from each squadron has gone up to see if they can get something serviceable. We want something big to bring the beer from Alex to us beleaguered folks in the desert.

There are some scares regarding parachute troops these nights and guards are put on everything. I sleep with my revolver under the pillow.

Friday, 9 January 1942

A Me110 came over at brekker time this morning and lobbed a few bombs around. All the AA in the world opened up but, as usual, it was miles behind him.

The Squadron is about operational now and we are standing by for a show at any time. We are to fly as a Wing with 3 RAAF again who also have Kittyhawks. Yesterday 3 Squadron ran into some CR42s who were bombing, escorted by G50s, Mc200s, Mc202s and two Me109s. They got seven confirmed with the loss of one Kitty. [The Australian pilots considered after this battle, that the Macchi fighters could out-turn the P40.]

Rommel is still withdrawing from Agedabia and we should move up any day now. Squadron put eight aircraft up this afternoon with 250 Squadron. No.3 RAAF were top cover. They [seven Marylands] bombed enemy troop positions near El Agheila but the bombing was not very good. A 109F jumped us on the way back and took a shot at Sgt Carson, my No.2. The Hun appeared to come from nowhere. I took a shot at him as he pulled up but saw no result. He came back later on and I did a head-on at him, again with no apparent result. This Hun was pretty good; he attacked the formation three times and got one of 3 Squadron. Sgt Carson had to force land on the way back.

The German pilot was Oberleutnant Gerhard Homuth of I/JG27—one of the big aces of the desert war. He had already scored 15 victories before coming to North Africa as Staffelkapitän of 3/JG27 in April 1941. In June he was awarded the Knight's Cross. By June 1942 he would be Kommodore of I Gruppe JG27. His score rose to 63 before his death in combat on the Russian front as leader of I/JG54, on 3 August 1943.

In fact, Homuth scored against two of 3 RAAF's aircraft. Flying Officer G Chinchen crash-landed near Msus and Sergeant R H Simes DFM failed to return. Ronnie Simes had claimed three of the Squadron's kills the previous day. As Carson had to force land due to damage from Homuth, he had managed to pick off three of the Wing's pilots.

Saturday, 10 January 1942
The beer lorry arrived yesterday so we polished off our ration of three bottles last evening. I saw Hart and Les Harris of 250 last night and hear that Hart and Ranger have got the DFC.

Blasted sand and dust storms wrote off flying for today. We were to escort some Blenheims on a spot more trouble making. This Wing has now got 200 EA destroyed since this push started. It is made up from about a dozen squadrons. We have got 37.

Sunday, 11 January 1942

My Birthday—20 today! And what a day. Took off this morning as bomber escort. No sooner off the ground with my section than smoke filled the cockpit from under the instrument panel. Closed throttle hastily and started to go down. Switched off and crash-landed after dodging army trucks and nearly hit a trench with piles of earth round it. Got out with some haste (a movement which I have now got used to, having done it on previous notable occasions), expecting things to go up in smoke, but they didn't—rather disappointed. A funny thing was that I said to my tent mate (one Jock Crawford) this morning, that Sunday had been an unlucky day in action for me, having been shot down a couple of times on Sundays. Another funny thing was that I had fastened the catch of my safety straps up, just before I opened up to take off, a thing I always forget to do. I only had a bump on the forehead, like a ducks egg.

The same thing as this may have happened to Sgt Crocker the other day, when he was killed as he turned back to the 'drome after something (perhaps the same trouble) went wrong.

Monday, 12 January 1942

Our advance party moved on this morning to Antelat, near Agedabia. We shall probably move tomorrow or the next day. The new CO, S/L Caldwell DFC and bar, came back from leave today with P/O Eric 'Dicky' Dickinson, who was at FTS with me. They brought some new Kittys with them and Hunk is following with another.

Had quite a talk with old Jock Crawford [Squadron Equipment Officer] in the tent last night after turning in. He is most concerned about me and doesn't want me to take chances. He thinks I am too young for this racket and that I should pack up. He is a most fatherly old bird to me.

Wednesday, 14 January 1942

Off on a Wing patrol with 3 RAAF this morning over the troops west of Agheila, but nothing about. The Hun appears to be diggin' in along a road west of El Agheila, running south. These marshes around Agheila are the worst part for us. Once we can shift him out to Sirte we should be OK.

He is using CR42s escorted by G50s and Mc200s etc, to stuff our troops. They always come up after our patrols have gone so he must have a pretty good RDF system [radar] or some means of knowing our movements.

Escort with 250 and 3 Squadrons this afternoon, for a Tac/R Hurricane prowling about. 250 engaged a couple of 109s but we had no fun. The sky was absolutely clear, with a blazing sun and we were up for 2½ hours. It was jolly tiring.

Friday, 16 January 1942

The AOC—AVM Coningham—is going to look us up today, so everybody is having a wash! Some even going so far as to comb their hair!

He gave us quite a talk but there was not much to really go on. I think it was a pep-talk to keep the old morale going. He did say two Spitfire squadrons were almost here; I thought he was going to say 92!

It has been raining like fury this afternoon and everything is mud. Tents are flooded and everything is wet and soggy—what fun.

Saturday, 17 January 1942

Squadron patrol over our advance forces south-east of Agheila led by Hunk. Nothing seen, but Sgt Burney, who took off late, ran into a 109F fitted with a long range tank. Took the odd shot at each other and then the 109 went into cloud.

Several aircraft went up on their noses in the mud after this patrol. We have three aircraft with bent props. More rain today.

Monday, 19 January 1942

More rain last night and the place is more like a bog than ever. It is not possible to fly until the runways dry up a bit. Hope the Hun is in the same predicament.

About lunchtime a Ju88 dropped a stick of bombs on the other 'drome about 5 miles from us and damaged a Hurricane. He was only at about 5,000 ft but the AA, as usual, was miles behind. There is a bit of flap on now and we are to stand-by to take off the fighters from the two 'dromes if they start bombing. The Hun may think—and rightly so—that we can't get off and send some Stukas over. Wing is prepared to lose a dozen aircraft getting off rather than lose them by bombing.

In fact, most of the Luftwaffe airfields, nearer the more sandy coast, drained far quicker, and the RAF commanders guessed the Germans would be less troubled than the RAF units further south in the desert.

LIBYA — EGYPT

Tuesday, 20 January 1942

More rain last night and still no prospect of flying. I'm getting pretty fed up with sitting around. Let's get cracking and get this war over and go home.

We are withdrawing to Msus tomorrow. Don't like this retreating but it is impossible to operate from here and the army is getting peppered by the Stukas.

Wednesday, 21 January 1942

Moving today. Luckily the rain kept off and with the help of the army wallahs we got a strip of runway more or less usable. The worst part was taxying and people were bogged right and left. The army did some good work by towing people out of the bogs but it was no fun as the ground looked quite firm until you taxied over it, then you disappeared up to the wing tip in mud.

The strip of runway was not too long and there were some pretty hair-raising take-offs, chaps just staggering into the air and waffling over the top of lorries. Things were not improved when a 'shufty kite'[1] came over when about 20 machines were congested at one end of the runway. Poor old Group Captain Cross was running around in small circles.[2]

However, we all got off except four who are coming on tomorrow. I was the last to take off and got blinded by the sun—swung a bit off the runway and went over an enormous pile of scrub and churned through about a dozen shovels. Shovels flew right and left, but the old kite flew!

Thursday, 22 January 1942

Bomber escort this morning to eight Blenheims. Quite good bombing on some trucks. On the way out we passed about 20 to 30 Ju87s and some Italian machines about a quarter mile on our left, who dive bombed some of our troops. We could not tackle them as it would have left our Blenheims without escort. On the way back some Huns came roaring by heading for home, having been mixed up in a dog-fight with 3 Squadron. I do wish these Blenheims were faster; we don't have much of a chance if we are jumped with only 150 on the clock.

S/L Morris of 250 Squadron is missing after mixing it with

---

[1] Enemy reconnaissance machine.
[2] Group Captain K B Cross, later Air Chief Marshal Sir Kenneth Cross KCG CBE DSO DFC.

Top left: 'AC Plonk' – No. 4 ITW Paignton, Summer 1940.

Top centre: No wash day blues for Neville – he would soon be flying.

Top right: Squadron Leader Jamie Rankin DFC, OC 92 Squadron 1941.

Middle: No.2 Course, 58 OTU, Grangemouth, February 1941. NFD front right.

Bottom: Three 92 Squadron stalwarts in 1941: Tony Bartley DFC, Allan Wright DFC and Brian Kingcome DFC. The latter would be NFD's boss in Italy three years later.

Top left: Ron Bary – he was killed as a Wing Commander in 1945.

Top centre: Flight Lieutenant W L 'Red' Chisholm RCAF; 92 Squadron.

Top right: Squadron Leader J M Morgan DFC, CO 92 Squadron, December 1942.

Middle left: Back at the front. 92 Squadron pilots at Nogra, December 1942. There was little luxury in the desert.

Middle right: Spitfire V (Trop), 92 Squadron.

Bottom left: Flight Lieutenant C J Samouelle DFC and Bar, 92 Squadron.

Bottom right: Flying Officer Paul Brickhill, 92 Squadron, taken prisoner in March 1943.

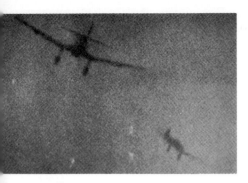

op left: Ju87s in NFD's camera gun, Castel enito, 21 January 1943.

op right: Trop Spitfire Vc, 92 Squadron, on ne of the Bir Dufan airstrips.

1iddle left: NFD and Red Chisholm, flight commanders, 92 Squadron.

Middle right: Squadron Leader W J Harper and NFD.

Bottom: Abandoned Italian transport aircraft.

Top: But he wasn't the only one to fail –
GA-D also eating sand.
Middle left: Otto Schulz of JG27.
Middle right: The Shark's mouth; NFD,

Western Desert, 1942.
Bottom left: The P40 cockpit.
Bottom right: For some, this sight in a rear-view
mirror was their last.

Top left: Captured opposition – the Italian
Macchi 200.

Top right: Captured opposition – the German
Me109F, El Adem, December 1941.

Middle left: Jerry Westenra, 112 Squadron.

Middle right: CO's trailer, 112 Squadron. Note
Squadron code letters on cab.

Bottom: Re-arming a Tommy, 112 Squadron.

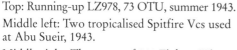

Top: Running-up LZ978, 73 OTU, summer 1943.

Middle left: Two tropicalised Spitfire Vcs used at Abu Sueir, 1943.

Middle right: The cream of 244 Fighter Wing just before NFD joined it: (l to r) Stan Turner, CO 417 Sqn; Hunk Humphreys, CO 111 Sqn; Wg Cdr W G Duncan-Smith, Wing

Leader, Gp Capt Brian Kingcome, OC the Wing; Lance Wade, CO 145 Sqn; Maj Osler SAAF, CO 601 Sqn.

Bottom left: Spitfire VIII, 145 Squadron, Italy 1944

Bottom right: Frankie Banner DFC, 145 Squadron Italy 1944. Later killed with Supermarines testing a Seafire.

op left: Me109G, shot down over Arezzo, 13 ay 1944.

op right: Successful 145 Squadron pilots, after e combat on 21 May 1944: (rear) Jeff ilborrow, NFD, Jock Wooler; (front) Joe xbury, J S Anderson, James Colin Stirling.

iddle left: Squadron Leader Graham Cox FC, OC 92 Squadron, 1944.

Middle right: NFD, Graham Cox, Brian Kingcome and Stan Turner, 244 Wing, Venafro, June 1944.

Bottom: Hunk Humphreys, CO 111 Squadron, with Barrie Heath, Wg Cdr Flying, 324 Wing. Note Heath's personal initials on his Spitfire IX, and Wing Commander's pennant by the cockpit.

Top left: The gang: Caldwell (Aus), W Carson (Aus), Andy Taylor (Aus), NFD, Humphreys, Drew (KIA, on wing), Burney (Aus, KIA), Donkin (NZ, KIA), Leu (POW), Dickinson (KIA) and K Carson (Aus). The Carson boys were brothers.

Top right: Squadron Leader C R 'Killer' Caldwell DFC RAAF, in his 'Don't mess with me' stance. Many Germans, Italians and Japanese did – and came second.

Second down left: Kittyhawks of 260 Squadron – note long-range fuel tanks.

Third down left: The Blenheim IV – Desert Air Force.

Fourth down left: If they're clean they must be in Cairo: Jerry, Neville and Hunk.

Above right: DFC – 11 March 1942, two months after his 20th birthday; Sidi Hannish April 1942.

some Stukas. Heard tonight a Hun flying column has broken
through with 2,000 vehicles, including tanks. We had to burn
a Kitty we left at Antelat.

Erwin Rommel, against orders from Berlin, had made a limited thrust
against the British 13 Corps which had been forced to retreat to a line
from Agedabia to El Haseit. This coincided with the Wing evacuating
Antelat due to the waterlogged conditions.

Squadron Leader E J Morris, and another pilot, were both brought
down by anti-aircraft fire, but both returned on foot.

CHAPTER V

RETREAT

Despite the precarious and tentative advance made by Rommel, he found in fact a weakened Allied force falling back before him. As the Axis forces moved eastwards, across Cyrenaica, Msus soon came up on the horizon, much to 112 Squadron's consternation.

Friday, 23 January 1942

Dawn patrol south-west of Agheila. Passed over a Hun column at Antelat. They appear to possess bags of Breda guns. We are all prepared to move back again to Mechili. Blast the Hun and his column.

33 Squadron lost six out of six machines yesterday, when they ground strafed this column. They will probably get us on the job sometime!

Squadron patrol in the afternoon around Antelat-Haseit. Three aircraft passed us which I swear were Ju88s. If they were, we lost a wizard chance of getting 'em. We are under orders to move at the crack of dawn tomorrow, moving to Mechili.

Alarm and despondency reigns. The six machines of 33 Squadron reported missing turned up, and Teddy Morris, CO of 250 Squadron, who was missing, also turned up OK.

Saturday, 24 January 1942

Squadron dawn patrol of Antelat area looking for the dreaded Hun. Jumped one Hurricane but nothing else. The ground people moved off at dawn for Mechili and we landed back there after the patrol.

Nobody really seems to know what is going on—the situation one moment is in hand and the next it's critical. Oh, to be in England.

Another one of the 14 of us who came out together has packed up. F/O Hart of 250 Squadron has retired—'bout time I did too!

The beer lorry arrived with our people tonight, so we can expect a good beer up.

Sunday, 25 January 1942

Flew escort for 9 Blenheims in the afternoon. They were to bomb any target they could find and it was not until they had wandered all over the desert that they bombed near Agedabia. The road from there to Antelat was packed with Huns and after bombing, the Blenheims went down to 2,000 feet along this road, getting all the AA available! I saw three EA take off from Agedabia and as I took a pot-shot at them, Sgt Leu hit one head-on and shot the wing-tip off. It was seen to go in near Msus. The rest of the 109s left us about there.

Our advance party has moved back to Gazala and we may go there any time if the Hun gets any further. The Hun is certainly making a mess of us now. We seem to be completely disorganised by his advance.

Monday, 26 January 1942

We are on half an hour's notice to quit this place now and may leave for Gazala any time.

Ground strafing this morning. Hunk led the Squadron off before lunch and we started strafing along the Antelat road and up to Msus. I was to stay above with a section and attract the AA. They were doing a good job of work too.

I went down around Msus and shot up a truck which was seen to catch fire. Got quite a bit of AA fire all to myself. Poor old Hunk has not returned yet and neither has his No.2, Sgt Donkin. They may have got lost and gone to some other landing ground.

Tuesday, 27 January 1942

Hunk turned up this morning. He had got lost and he and Sgt Donkin had landed at El Adem.

More ground strafing this morning. Beat up the Huns along the Antelat-Msus road. I attacked three 'Blitz' buggies out of the sun and they never saw me coming. They were full of troops. My four guns stopped after beating up another couple of lorries, so stooged along and watched the others mess about.

The most enormous dust storm this afternoon. The worst I've seen so far. It's starting to rain now.

Wednesday, 28 January 1942

Still more ground strafing. Four of us went out in the afternoon to strafe at Sceleidung, between Msus and Soluch. Think we came upon the Huns when they were at tea. Peppered them quite a bit but the tanks opened fire when we made a second run.

Came across three lorries by themselves and everybody strafed them one after the other. I saw a big flash of flames from one of the lorries when I fired and thought it was going to blow up in front of me.

Met a 109F on the way back under the cloud. I got two long bursts at him and tried to follow it up and nearly stalled. I think something must have hit it but he seemed to keep going. Landed at Mechili to pick up my blankets and then went on to Gazala, our new base.

Thursday, 29 January 1942

Back to Gazala by the sea. Very nearly back where we started from three months ago. Greeted by more sand and dust storms this afternoon. This blasted dust is bloody awful—what a country.

Spent the morning getting organised and went over to Gazala No.3 to look at a 109F the South Africans have got flying there. I can't get into the thing properly as I am too tall and don't like the restricted vision. But it is a really wizard little machine. Perfect flush riveting and only essentials are put in it. Looked over some of the Hun and Italian aircraft left here last month. The Macchi 200 is a rather nice little machine.

Friday, 30 January 1942

No shows at all today. Organised a bath in the afternoon and felt a lot better for it, so much so, that I felt I just had to fly. Took my machine up at sunset and did a few aerobatics and beat up the aerodrome.

Apparently I am to go to 94 Squadron for a few days to tell them how to fly the Kittyhawks.

Saturday, 31 January 1942

Set off in one of the lorries for Sidi Barrani and then on to LG110 where 94 Squadron are, and also our base party now. Made pretty good time along the coast road via Tobruk, Bardia, Fort Capuzzo, Halfaya Pass and on to Sidi Barrani; all the historical places.

Spent the night about 10 miles south of Barrani in the desert. Cooked up some tea and bully stew on a petrol fire along with Sgt Edwards and six airmen who are going to 94. Slept under the desert sky, my roof the stars. It was a really wizard night with a full moon and clear sky. I lay in bed and just looked up at the sky and thought of things for a while.

End of month résumé: 'We have not done well this month. The Hun has broken through from Agheila and has got as far as Msus and retaken Benghazi. Rather squashed our hope of getting to Tripoli for a while.

The Squadron has done quite a bit of strafing lately. It is good sport if gone about it the right way. None of this going back afterwards over a column. One run Dookie, they call me.

It is a terrific thrill to come pelting down out of the sun to let rip at the Huns with the .5s. To see your bullets making little spurts in the sand in front of a truck and then pull the nose up a bit until the spurts no longer rise and your bullets are hitting home. Pulling out just before you hit the target, as the tendency is to be so engrossed in your target that you forget the ground. Then making your escape, taking advantage of every little rise in the ground and dodging the hate thrown up by the swines.

You can't help feeling sorry for the Jerry soldier when you ground strafe them. They run, poor pitiful little figures, trying to dodge the spurts of dust racing towards them.'

Sunday, 1 February 1942
Arrived at our base at LG110 this afternoon. Of course, my presence at 94 is not required as they already know how to fly the Kittys!

Tuesday, 3 February 1942
The CO and Jerry turned up this afternoon with the news that this campaign is about over and that the Squadron will soon be back at Sidi Hannish where we started from in November. The army is going to hold, or try to hold, the boundary wire including Bardia and Sollum.

Now that the campaign is over, I wonder if promises will be kept and will Hunk and myself go back to England? This new CO is not in favour of people going home after a couple of months in the East and of people retiring from Ops when they have had enough. If we stooge around and stay in this bloody desert I shall go mad I'm sure.

Thursday, 5 February 1942

I am going back to the Squadron tomorrow. F/O Peter
Brunton is missing from some ground strafing yesterday
around Derna. He has only just been married too, poor devil.

Mechili was evacuated on the 3rd. 112, 238 and 3 RAAF Squadrons
moved to Gambut and 250 went to Gazala No.1. Neville travelled back
by road, and then learned that he and Jerry Westenra were to go to
Cairo on leave. They would fly out in a German Junkers tri-motored
transport plane.

Saturday, 7 February 1942

Just caught the Ju52 this morning by the skin of our teeth.
Had a pretty dull trip of five hours to Heliopolis [pilot W/C
Fenton]. We took a room at Heliopolis Hotel as we figured
Cairo would be packed out. It was. Had a cold shower as the
hot water was not on, and then sped into Cairo and had an
enormous feed at the St James. Wandered around the pubs
and got pretty good and tight.

Neville spent the next few days in a bit of a haze. He and Jerry were
supposed to fly back on the 10th but found the Junkers was u/s, which
pleased Neville, as he was feeling like death and felt sure he would have
died on the trip. Wing Commander Fenton piloted them back to
Gambut on the 11th.

Wednesday, 11 February 1942

Back to the toil today. Arrived back and found we had lost
three pilots the day before yesterday: Sgts Donkin, Hoare
and Elwell. 109 trouble when escorting some Blenheims to
Derna. Sgt Holman was shot down today when two of them
were attacked by eight Me109s and Mc202s. We have got half
a dozen Poles in the Squadron now.

The Axis forces had now reached Tmimi and began to dig in. They had
now recaptured the greater part of Cyrenaica, and the line was set over
which the two opposing forces would look at each other for several
months, while they regrouped and built up strength for another
offensive.

The three NCO pilots had in fact been shot down on the 8th. The
fighter force from 112, 3 RAAF and 73 Squadron had escorted the
bombers to Derna and met JG27's 109s. A 3 Squadron Kitty went down
to Oberleutnant Keller, then he shot down a second, but its pilot baled

out and he was later picked up. One of 73's machines also crash landed. 112 fought a rearguard action against JG27, the latter claiming four victories—three of 112 and one of 73. The victors were Oberleutnant Homuth, Leutnant Hans-Joachim Marseille (two) and Leutnant Friedrich Körner.

The reference to Polish pilots was because a group of Poles flying transport aircraft, or delivering aircraft from the West African base at Takoradi, had arrived. Wishing for a more warlike duty, several of them volunteered to fly fighters, at a time when fighter pilots were short. Eventually 12 flew with 112 Squadron for a few months, two being killed and two others wounded.

Thursday, 12 February 1942

Six of us were Scrambled in the afternoon and after climbing to 18,000 ft over El Adem, the remaining two out of the six, Jerry Westenra and myself, saw lots of AA over Tobruk and El Adem. We could see some bombing going on but damned if we could see the bombers.

We eventually jumped—repeat, jumped—two 109s out of the sun head-on. They never saw us but we did not get them. After attacking, we climbed away above them and came down behind them again but couldn't get very near. Contented ourselves with the odd long shot. Jerry broke away and I was left following these two which I did not think was good enough, so broke off for home. Met another 109 over Tobruk under the cloud but we just looked at each another and went on.

One of our Poles was killed this afternoon during a practice dog-fight; he went in from about 800 ft.

Saturday, 14 February 1942

Great Day. Best engagement yet. Got 16 Italian and Hun aircraft without a loss to ourselves.

We intercepted some Macchi 200s and Breda 65s ground strafing south-west of Acroma. Sighted them just as we came out of cloud at about 9,000 ft on our left. I was leading the left section and attacked 10 Macchis just below us. Got on the tail of one straggling a bit and gave a long burst. He was hit around the engine and he spun away. This was seen to crash by Sgt Evans.

A general dog-fight started and I enjoyed myself more than I have ever done before. The cloud was just right and we dived down, had a squirt and climbed up into cloud again.

109 tactics! I finished up at ground level chasing a Macchi 200 with a chappie of 3 RAAF Squadron. After two or three attacks the Macchi crashed and burst into flames in an army camp where they had been strafing.

Led the Squadron on a Scramble from El Adem in the afternoon but the R/T was all haywire and no contacts were made with the enemy.

Combat Report for 14 February
Time: 1215 pm, south-west Acroma

Astern attack on Mc200 on left of formation. Saw hits around engine and Macchi spun down. Seen to crash by Sgt Evans. Second Macchi attacked at ground level from astern. After 2-3 attacks with aircraft CV-W (Sgt Reid) of 3 Sqn, e/a hit ground and burst into flames. Several e/a's evasive tactics consisted of rolls and dives down vertically to ground level. One e/a had one wing bright green, and was seen to crash.

Enemy adopted strongly defensive action and made no attempt at attacking. Superior speed of our a/c enabled us to dive from cloud base, attack and climb back to cloud again.

Claim: 1 Mc200 Destroyed;
          ½ Mc200 Destroyed, shared with 3 RAAF.

In total there were ten Kittyhawks of 112 Squadron and eight of 3 RAAF. When the scores were totted up, every pilot but one of 3 Squadron had claimed something. The air battle, which lasted for half an hour, took place over heavy ground fighting, the downed aircraft falling in the battle area.

Sunday, 15 February 1942

Squadron moving up from Gambut to El Adem. On stand-by all morning. Scrambled with 94 Squadron but told to land soon after taking off. On stand-by again in the afternoon. Two 109s dive-bombed the aerodrome apparently aiming for the machines lined up on stand-by. The bombs landed near our tents but nobody was hurt.

Led the Squadron on a Wing Sweep with 94 Squadron, over Martuba area. The CO of 94 took us right over Martuba aerodrome and we got all the AA going and watched the 109s taking off. I left him there and went south under the cloud, watching two 109s climbing above us in a clear patch but we did not contact them. Patrolled Tmimi-Mechili-Martuba area under the cloud and saw nothing except 73 Squadron's Hurries who came out of cloud on top of us.

The CO of 73 was apparently shot up by Sgt Burney who was leading a section. It appears a 109 was on top of the Hurries and the Hurricane ran into Burney's fire. Sgt McQueen left the formation on the way home to look at some fires on the ground. He was then left behind and went down to ground level to catch me up again. A 109 jumped him and he nearly got shot down although he was below us. It was impossible to see him because it was nearly dark. *Do not* leave the formation!

94 Squadron rather foolishly went down on Martuba and lost four pilots, including the CO, S/L Mason, to the 109s.

Once again it was Otto Schulz in evidence. He had attacked the Hurricanes of 94 Squadron after they and 112 separated and shot down all four! He then spotted McQueen, and although McQueen got back—wounded—Schulz was credited with a fifth victory.

Squadron Leader E M 'Imshi' Mason DFC was an experienced fighter pilot and pre-war airman. He was among the top scoring pilots of the Middle East campaigns at the time of his death.

Monday, 16 February 1942
On Readiness all day today. I was to lead the Wing if we took off! The 109s visited us again this afternoon and two of them dive-bombed the aerodrome, writing off five Hurricanes and damaging a sixth. Good bombing. We are moving back to Gambut again tomorrow.

Tuesday, 17 February 1942
Promoted to Flying Officer today. Stand-by all day at El Adem. The parties moved off and I was left to lead the Squadron. We stood by all the afternoon but did not have to take off at all.

Flew back to Gambut at dusk. Chatting with Hunk in the Mess tonight over the odd beer and the pipe. When you get to know him he is a very decent and kind hearted fellow. He is about as fed up with this desert as I am, and wants to get out. We probably will have a chance if we go to the Delta for a rest. He seems to think I am in line for a Flight.

Wednesday, 18 February 1942
Old Hunk is not feeling so well today. I think he has done

enough in this war; he's got nearly 300 Op hours. He is the level headed type who, if told to fly in pretty foul weather, would not take off if he didn't think it was good enough.

I am acting the instructor today and showing a new sergeant pilot the knobs and things on the Kitty. Have got the patter weighed up now.

Hunk and I went over to 450 Squadron at lunchtime to see Ken Sands. He seems in good form and is coming over this evening for a beer up. Some beer up I'd say—really got amongst it.

Saturday, 21 February 1942

Today dawned bright and clear. After breakfast this morning a 109F flew round the aerodrome at about 2 to 3,000 feet and waggled his wings. Blasted fellow had a nerve. Of course, all our AA missed him.

Squadron Scrambled in the morning and met seven 109Fs over Gazala. The CO got one down in flames. One of our Poles, F/O Jander, was wounded but got down allright and crash-landed. Sgt Elliott crash-landed after getting a cannon shell in the engine. Another Pole sergeant [Sgt. Derma] crash-landed out of petrol near El Adem. Not such a good exchange I reckon.

Once more it was JG27. Marseille and Homuth claimed two and one respectively. Leutnant Hans-Arnold 'Fifi' Stahlschmidt crash-landed but got back to his base that evening. He would eventually achieve 59 victories before being lost in September 1942. A few days after this event, Stahlschmidt was shot down and taken prisoner, but escaped back to the German lines.

Sunday, 22 February 1942

Moving from Gambut to a new aerodrome 5 miles east of here. On stand-by in the afternoon and Scrambled to intercept a raid on Tobruk. It was a pretty good mess-up too. The call to take off was six minutes late and then Bart's engine would not start. People started taking off in ones and twos. Eventually got my section in the air. We then started going around in circles with 94 Squadron following. I broke away and started for El Adem and the rest of the Wing followed. Enemy fighters were up to 24,000 ft so even if we had got there in time we would have caught a packet. Feel pretty browned off and everybody keeps on about this show.

Monday, 23 February 1942

The AOC turned up for lunch. We went off on a Wing Sweep after taxying about in thick dust and after climbing to about 10,000 feet my engine cut and I force landed at El Adem, nearly killing myself again! I think my old machine has just about had it [AK578 GA-V].

I hear we are to move from here back to Gambut. My God, the people at Wing are the dimmest crowd imaginable. It was obvious that this 'drome was unsuitable owing to the dust, and furthermore, it shows up as well, if not better, than Gambut for the Hun bombers.

Wednesday, 25 February 1942

Interest was aroused when it was learnt the CO had force-landed and busted the Magister belonging to G/C Cross. Poor old Doc was in the front and thought it was the normal way to land I think.

The beer flowed pretty freely after this and after it had sunk in a bit, Bart and the CO started making bets regarding revolver shooting. Quite a good display ensued and the CO hit a 40-gallon drum from 100 yards several times. Pretty good shooting. Bart had bet him he wouldn't do it in three shots but he hit it the first shot!

Thursday, 26 February 1942

I've got a new machine as my old 'V' is a bit teased out. I've had 'Jäger' put on the side, which is German for fighter or hunter or chaser! Also put up eight strikes on the tail plane!

Friday, 27 February 1942

Boy what a day! Squadron of 12 aircraft went over to Gambut for stand-by in the morning. They were strafed by several 109s and two of our machines were burnt out and five others just about written off. My new machine was shot up as well.

The 109s shot down a Boston and a Hurricane in their stride too. Next thing was, a patrol of four went up with Dicky leading—he decided to practise some turns in formation and Sgt Jackson spun off a turn at 10,000 feet and never got out of it, poor devil.

Everybody at Gambut was a bit nervous of noises in the sky for the rest of the day. Two of our machines came down from patrol in a hurry causing everybody to streak for holes like rabbits.

Got pretty good and oiled in the Mess with Dicky and

Leu—my word. People gradually passed away quietly, finally leaving us three holding great converse in serious tones up to 2 am, when we aroused the anger of some bodies, by chasing about the desert after our Alsatian, Wilber-Rex.

Saturday, 28 February 1942

Staggered out of bed at a late hour. Went down to the coast with Hunk, Jerry and Jeff Carrol in the staff car in the afternoon and scratched about round the old Jerry tanks. It is raining and quite cold. The weather seems to change a hell of a lot here.

Monthly résumé: 'I have not done a great deal of flying this month. Have put the old score up to 8 and got the 200 hours up and 150 sorties. The Macchi show was the best yet—my God it was some fun. The Squadron has had bad luck lately and lost quite a lot of pilots—Sgts Donkin, Hoare, Elwell, Jackson, and F/O Brunton and one of our Poles. Sgt McQueen has gone away wounded and so has F/O Jander.'

Sunday, 1 March 1942

Up at the crack of dawn and on stand-by. Did not have to take off. On stand-by again in the afternoon until relieved by Dicky who had a Scramble a few minutes after he took over. I had sat in the cockpit for four hours and he gets a Scramble after three minutes!

The Squadron is supposed to be moving out within a fortnight to Sidi Hannish for a 'rest'. Pilots are also supposed to get a fortnight's leave. If we get out of the desert I vote I don't come back.

Monday, 2 March 1942

Chatting with Hunk in the evening over the odd whisky. He says the CO does not expect Jerry Westenra, Bartle, Hunk or myself to come back with the Squadron into the desert. He isn't far wrong as far as I am concerned.

Wednesday, 4 March 1942

Raining like stink and everywhere under water. One day we nearly suffocate with dust, the next day we nearly drown in mud. Clouds right down. I wanted to prowl around the lines in the cloud looking for the odd Stuka, but Ops would not see eye to eye with the idea. Hunk tells me to be careful every time I go up. I really think he is most concerned for me somehow.

Thursday, 5 March 1942

What a day and what a night. It rained and blew like hell all night. The tent leaked all over my bed and I lay there all wet and soggy. Shall probably die of rheumatism or whatever people die of. God I feel fed up today. The rain does not drain into the sand but just lies on the top making things pretty grim.

Saturday, 7 March 1942

Aerodrome not yet good enough to use. Very pleasant day, lots of sun and blue sky. The odd 109s over high-up and also the usual recco Ju88.

Things are getting a bit much in the Mess now. Some of these Australian types can't get away from the subject of English versus Australians, or British aircraft versus American. Am getting fed up with these people.

Sunday, 8 March 1942

On stand-by at 8 o'clock this morning and took off to intercept six fighters but made no contact. This is one of those bad flying days with not a solitary cloud in the sky. I hate this bowl of blue where 109s can lurk and not be seen.

Great fun and frolics this afternoon. Six 109s came whistling down on Gambut No.2 where the Hurricanes dwell and did some strafing—knocking out the odd Hurribus. I knew there were some 109s about by the way my hair started to crinkle on the back of my neck.

Eight more 109s, just after this, bombed Gambut Main and then four of them jumped a Hurricane which was flying serenely along near here. The first 109 closed to about 100 yards and let him have it but missed, and by the time the second and third had attacked him, he had got wise and started going round in terrific tight turns at '0' feet over his aerodrome, in and out of a pretty AA barrage. Sgt Simpson coming back, also ran into a 109 near here and chased it past us at about 200 yards, going like the clappers. The 109 just flew away from him.

Jerry led the Squadron around Gazala late in the afternoon while Stukas were bombing Tobruk. They ran into two Mc200s and Jerry shot one down into the sea. They unfortunately missed the Stukas except for Sgt Evans and a Pole—P/O Kuapik. Sgt Evans got one and then left owing to the presence of something above. Kuapik came in and hosed all 15 Stukas without success and then buzzed off for the same reason.

The Hurricane pilot was Sergeant Persse of 274 Squadron. He crash-landed having been wounded in the leg.

Monday, 9 March 1942

More early morning interludes. 109s in evidence all morning. Sgt Elliott killed, damn shame when he was to leave the desert in a few days. Suppose it's just one's luck. Elliott apparently was not shot down but spun in for some unknown reason. This is happening too often. Led a Sweep over Gazala way but only saw eight 109s in the distance going north. Patrolled around Tobruk where they were plotting us as 'Bandits'—the AA went as far as to give us a few rounds. Moved forward to Gambut Main this afternoon.

Wednesday, 11 March 1942

Surprise this morning! The CO sent for me whilst I was in the process of taking some photos of Kittys and in stern tones asked me if I had anything on my conscience—he really took me in for a bit and I was just beginning to get worried when he produced a DFC ribbon and said the Group Captain asked him to give me this.

So I've got the DFC. I wanted it more than anything to please the folks back home. I hope they will be. It is costing me an awful lot of beers this lunch time and I shudder to think of the awful beer-up there will be tonight. Still, I've got Sgt Leu, who has just come back from leave with the DFM, to help me out.

I remember the first day at EFTS when a friend of mine who was put off flying 'cos he couldn't take the air, said, 'I don't mind; I bet I'll see Duke with a gong in the end.' I hope he made it too.

Thursday, 12 March 1942

Golly, what a session it was last night! I faded away at 1.30 but it was still going strong then. I just couldn't get my glass empty. No sooner had I taken a sip than it was topped up again, by some passing, staggering body.

The CO rather put up a 'black'. We had been drinking good and hard since lunchtime and at sunset he announced he was going to drop a bomb. He took off and it appears he dropped it on Martuba. He landed and when taxying in put the machine on its nose! Then at dinner time he was sitting at the head of the table, chattering away, and he suddenly disappeared from my sight. I thought I had had one too many but no. He had gone over backwards and a sepulchral voice from the depths enquired as to the whereabouts of his bloody beer. Oh, yes, it was a good session.

Led the Squadron on a Sweep, Bir Hacheim-Gazala way. Low cloud and lots of rain. Did not see anything but it's all experience. There is a terrific line in the Egyptian Mail about F/O Neville Duke!!

Friday, 13 March 1942

The odd 109s were busy strafing and bombing most of the day. In the morning our people met up with some 109s and Macchi 202s covering some Stukas who had bombed Tobruk. We were too late to get the Stukas but ran into the odd 109 and 202. Sgt Burney got a 202 and Sgt Rozanski was shot down by a 109. He crash landed and burst into flames but is OK. He was lucky—his rudder was shot away and the cockpit was pretty well shot about.

Rozanski was shot down by Otto Schulz, who bounced both him and Bartle from heavy cloud cover.

Saturday, 14 March 1942

Bunged an application in to the CO to go home and back to 92 or else go to Rhodesia or South Africa. I hope it comes off as I've had this desert pretty well. I don't mind going back on Ops in England and if there is to be a blitz on, then that's where I want to be.

Sunday, 15 March 1942

Out of the desert! And like a shot. Flew down to Sidi Hannish at 9 o'clock—never to return!?

I didn't get off with the formation as I thought something was haywire with the controls when we started to take off, so closed everything and stood on the brakes and managed to dodge barrels and slit trenches etc. Thought I was going to prang on the last take-off!

Nev was lucky—this time.

CHAPTER VI

INSTRUCTOR

Neville Duke and 112 Squadron went on rest. However, 112 was soon back in the fray, where it began fighter-bomber sorties in earnest, but for Neville, it was leave in Cairo and Alexandria. So pleased was he to be finally rid of the desert that he neglected his diary over the next several days. Days blurred together in eating and drinking sessions, sharing the activities with Caldwell, Hunk, Jerry Westenra, Dicky Dickinson and Bart Bartle.

However, on 22 March he and Hunk ran into Babe Whitamore, whom he had last seen at Biggin Hill. It was then he discovered that 92 Squadron had now arrived in the Middle East. Neville continued to try for a posting home or to Rhodesia (as an instructor), but he wasn't getting anywhere with Middle East HQ. All he could discover was that he might end up at a Conversion Unit for Kittyhawks, so he thought he'd try to get to 92 Squadron.

Neville was also beginning to realise that his experience of the Desert Air War was also working against a return to England:

Monday, 23 March 1942
I don't know if joining the Spits is a wise move or not but I should hate to get stuck on that conversion job forever. I had promised myself that I had finished Ops for a while because at times I felt I had really 'had it'. However, if they can't give a chap a decent job after he has done a bit—well damn them.

So I suppose I shall go back to the desert. Shall tread pretty warily though, might take the old score to double figures. I don't suppose the folks will be very happy because of this but there is a war on they say, although by the number of 'Pongos' in Cairo, you wouldn't know it.

Wednesday, 25 March 1942

The CO says seven picked pilots are going to the Spits and that he could get me in OK. (Later.) The CO has seen the Air Marshal and I am apparently one of the types picked to go on the Spits. Quite an honour I think, as everybody is clamouring for them.

Again Neville neglected his diary until after the Easter weekend—3/6 April.

Tuesday, 7 April 1942

Back to the flaming desert. Arrived feeling pretty despondent about all things connected with war and the desert. I enjoyed my leave in Cairo and am sorry not to have kept a record of it. Each day was much the same, though. Up about 11 am, drinks on the Continental terrace from 12 to 1 pm. Then lunch at Ghezira or some place. Perhaps watch the polo or swimming, or some sports. Drinking in the Continental at 6.30, followed by a tour of the cabarets: the Dug Out, Dolls, Continental, Trocadero, etc., arriving in bed about 2 am.

Wednesday, 8 April 1942

I am seeing the postings people tomorrow about getting away from here. This Spitfire racket keeps changing. The idea now is to have half a dozen picked crack pilots to fly polished Spits and shake the Hun a bit. The CO is to lead them and I am now one of the half dozen 'crack' types!! This will take a month or two to materialise and I should like to rest until then at least.

Thursday, 9 April 1942

Went to see the postings people at Air HQ this morning with Hunk. They told us that going home was washed out. Pity, I get jolly homesick at times.

We have been put up for a rest with a suggestion from P-staff that we are posted to Rhodesia. I should like that very much but expect Middle East HQ will stick us at the Kitty conversion school.

Friday, 10 April 1942

Things are getting a bit grim in this Squadron now. Bartle has been made Flight Commander in place of Hunk. Think most people expected me to be [promoted] but as I intend leaving, I suppose the CO thought otherwise. Besides, I am not Australian. The CO tells me I am going to 92. That would not be so bad really but I am not going to stooge around with this Squadron for another 2 to 3 months.

After a couple of days stooging about, 112 moved back to the satellite at Gambut. At least it was near the sea and the boys could get in a swim, but the weather was still pretty grim with dust storms a particular irritant.

Friday, 17 April 1942
Signal came through for me to report to base landing ground. I suppose a posting has come through. So I've finished Ops for a while. I have rather mixed feelings about it. Have been on Ops for just over a year and it has been the most exciting and (on looking back) I think the most enjoyable. No more fighting for existence in these clear, hot blue skies. No more nearly breaking my neck trying to look over the tail, no more spasms of fear as white streams of tracer lance at you out of a white spinner. I shall miss the excitement of mixing it with the Stukas and Italian machines. Still, every dog has his day and I feel I have just about had my day for a while. You can't be lucky for ever and one day I should probably not have skidded away quite quick enough—but enough of this. See what the future holds.

Sunday, 19 April 1942
Left Gambut for Sidi Hannish in a lorry. Bade the types farewell in good form. Hope I shall see some of them again. Had a seven hour run, arriving at tea time to find Hunk i/c Base Party! F/L Costello was there, on his way to the Squadron. He used to be with it some time ago. Hunk and I are posted to the Fighting School at Ballah to teach the younger generation.

Monday, 20 April 1942
Left Marten Bagush in a Bombay in the afternoon. 'Pissy' Darwen[1] brought a Kitty down to base so had the odd beer at lunchtime to celebrate. Pretty dull trip to Khanka in the old Bombay. Got transport into Cairo and had some trouble finding a place to stay, finally putting up in a dead-beat room in the National.

---

[1] Wing Commander John Darwen, later OC 244 Wing DAF, and succeeded by Ian Gleed DSO DFC (see later). Darwen was killed leading 239 Wing in Italy later in the war.

Tuesday, 21 April 1942

Just a day in Cairo—women, beer and food, etc. Doesn't change much. Moved into Shepherd's, thank God, as the National is pretty grim. Saw the postings people at HQ. Hunk and self are apparently going to the Conversion School at Ballah. Not very keen on it—first time I've been out of a squadron in 12 months.

After a couple of days and several drinks later, Neville made his way to Ballah (El Ballah), situated just north of Ismailia by the Suez Canal, about 60 miles to the north-east of Cairo. He was greeted by Jerry Westenra. He arrived in good form on the 23rd after a watering stop(!) at Ismailia.

Friday, 24 April 1942

Wandered around the place called Ballah. It seems stinking hot here and very damp. Not very nice at all. Hunk and self are joining the Conversion and Refresher School, converting people on to Kittys via Harvards and Tommys [Tomahawks].

We are supposed to give them dual landings and such things in the Harvards. Must learn to fly one myself sometime.

We appear to start flying at 6 o'clock and pack up at 12, starting again at 5 to 7 pm. In the afternoons we go into Ismailia and swim in the United Services Club by the Suez Canal. You can sail on it too which is good fun.

Saturday, 25 April 1942

Went up in a Harvard with Jerry to get the form on these jobs. They are nice and easy to fly. Talking of flies, there are plenty here.

Sunday, 26 April 1942

Got up quite early with Hunk and took him up before breakfast in a Harvard to show him how it's done! Rolled and looped him about the sky from the back seat and then pulled off the odd landing. Took the Harvard up by myself later in the morning to do some aerobatics. They are nice little machines and I like flying them about the place.

Got amongst the beer in the evening I'm afraid, at the US Club [Ismailia], then The Greek Club and The French Club. Quite an enjoyable day except that I hear I am to be the Sports Officer for the Station.

Tuesday, 28 April 1942

Took a Tomahawk up this morning to jump old Jerry who was

leading a formation around the sky—did jump him too! Pulled off the odd aerobatic—had a grand time. I think I like a Tommy much more than a Kitty. You can handle it much better.

Saturday, 2 May 1942

Tested the odd Kitty this morning. Sgt Dalton took off in a Kitty at 9.30 for local flying and has not been seen since. I went out in a Harvard to search for him but no find. Reports from the Suez Canal north of the Bitter Lakes say a Kitty was seen to be flying along the canal at 100 ft and wobbling, but we can find no trace.

Sunday, 3 May 1942

Seems we have found the wreckage of Dalton's machine east of the Bitter Lakes—nothing left of it.

Thursday, 7 May 1942

Took a Kitty down to the Kitty Repair Unit at Ismailia for repair. Stopped there to see a demonstration of types: Fulmar, Lodestar, Blenheim, Boston, Maryland, Baltimore, Tommy, Kitty and a Ju87. A Beaufighter flown by W/C Stainforth[1] put up an amazing show doing rolls and loops and rolls off the top from the deck, also doing a figure of 8 within the aerodrome boundary. He is a wizard pilot.

Had lunch at Ismailia Mess and returned in a lorry for the usual swim in the canal. We duly sunk the dinghy half a dozen times and awed the 'pongos' to silence with our rowdiness. Temperature 114 degrees yesterday!

Wednesday, 13 May 1942

Last night the place was raided by bods unknown. Two officers had all their stuff taken—everything, and a corporal was left with a pair of shorts and a shirt. Blighters. Getting my .45 out—time some of the people were shot.

New Course about to start although we have not yet got rid of the last Course yet! Took up P/Os Atkins and Chisholm for some dual in the evening.

---

[1] Wing Commander G H Stainforth AFC, won the King's Cup Air Race in 1929 and was then a member of ther Schneider Trophy Team. In 1942 he was commanding No.89 night-fighter Squadron, flying Beaus from Abu Sueir.

Thursday, 14 May 1942

Collected a Tommy in the evening after our swim. F/L Bary[1] flew me up to Port Said in a Harvard to get it. Port Said is just about surrounded by sea and just as I got off the deck the coolant temperature went whistling off the clock. Some fun—thought it would seize up or something any minute.

S/L Powell had a close shave tonight. A cloud of smoke was seen out in the desert and as he was slightly overdue, Jerry and Hopkinson went off in a Harvard to have a look. Sure enough, our Tommy on its belly and burning away merrily with Powell alongside. Jerry came back and reported same and dropped Hoppy and flew over and picked Powell up. Powell was burned in the back and had his head cut quite a bit. He was concussed so doesn't know what happened except that the plane caught fire in the air.

Saturday, 16 May 1942

Took P/O Chisholm up for a bit of dual in the Harvard after tea. Saw a very silly crash about 7 this evening. AFS Hurricanes had been out escorting General Smuts in his Blenheim around the sky. Coming back, their CO, S/ L S-- brought his three very low across the 'drome and pulled up and broke away in a Prince of Wales thing. The chap on the left tried to do a roll but obviously had not enough speed and spun out of it. He had got it out of the spin but he was still sinking and hit the deck a hell of a crack and burst into flames. The pilot, F/O Russell, was thrown out of the cockpit but was burned to a cinder. Poor old Russ. This place is getting a pretty bad name for crack-ups now.

For some reason the 'powers-that-be' had decided to convert the Spitfire pilots of 92 Squadron on to Kittyhawks, and so in an indirect way Neville once more was in close contact with his old Biggin squadron, as the pilots came through Ballah. The Spitfire, of course, was in short supply to overseas commands, and 92 had arrived in the Middle East without aircraft. After a while, however, they were attached to 80 Squadron—Hurricanes—until August 1942, at which date Spitfires arrived and they went back to their more usual fighter type. Nevertheless, in view of Neville's as then unknown future, it was fortuitous that he became acquainted with the present batch of 92 Squadron personnel at this juncture.

Later Wing Commander R E Bary DSO DFC, from New Zealand. Killed in Action 12 April 1945. In 1941-2 he had flown with 250 Squadron.

Tuesday, 19 May 1942

Took Sgt Novak up for some landings in a Harvard which he pulled off OK. Novak had twice ground-looped Harvards when he was doing dual with Jerry Westenra and had been grounded by the WingCo. However, Chisholm[1], a P/O in 92 Squadron, and an extraordinarily good type, asked the WingCo to let me take Novak up and give him a chance which was duly done to the satisfaction of all parties.

Novak is a very keen type and worries over the least thing. I'm taking personal care of him as I don't want to see any of 92 'scrubbed'.

Wednesday, 20 May 1942

Tested the odd Harvard. Later tested a Tomahawk and had some fun chasing around the clouds and 'jumping' pupils in Kittyhawks. Numerous rolls and dizzy aerobatics.

Sunday, 24 May 1942

Arose about 10.30 [at Heliopolis visiting 92] with the news that Hunk and I were to take two Spitfire Is—ex-Turkish Air Force—back to Ballah with us. Flashed around trying to organise some notes on Spits for the ground crews but didn't have much luck.

Took my Spit off in the evening, Hunk staying behind to get some paper work done. Caused a terrific stir at Ballah when I arrived. In the news again! Very pleasant to fly a Spit again but it is all in Turkish and it has a push-pull prop control (VP).

Wednesday, 27 May 1942

I've just about had this place and most of the dead-beat types here who haven't a clue and who just don't want to get mixed up in the war again.

Two Baltimores arrived this afternoon! We are going to convert types on to them. A Blenheim or Maryland is supposed to arrive soon and perhaps some Hurricanes. Some school this!

Saturday, 30 May 1942

[date of the first 1,000 bomber raid from UK]

The 92 people left today and a new Course of folks arrived from ADU to be converted to Spits and Kittys; Poles among them.

---

[1] W L 'Red' Chisholm RCAF, later DFC and Bar and a squadron leader.

Flew Bary down to Wadi Natrum to get a Blenheim along with Chubb and Hunk in another Harvard. Saw Jerry Westenra there and apparently he likes it a lot at Helwan. He told me Dicky Dickinson is missing from a Kitty bombing show. Poor old Dicky—shared a tent with him for a long time.

Gave dual to a couple of blokes in the evening. Getting pretty hair-raising at times. Chappies putting their flaps down on take-off instead of wheels-up!

Sunday, 31 May 1942
Some day. Two Kittys pranged one after t'other. One broke a leg of his undercart and had to land on one wheel, thereby causing some damage to said Kitty. T'other chap opened up to take off but didn't like the sound of his engine so closed throttle again and swung—swiping off undercart.

Wednesday, 3 June 1942
Another 'prang' today. One of my pupils—F/L Franklin. He burst a tyre on take-off and then damaged his undercart on landing—having to go round again and land wheels-up. So another Tommy bites the dust.

Saturday, 6 June 1942
More Harvard flying with a pupil this evening. Nothing exciting although every trip in the back of a Harvard is an adventure!

Another Tommy pranged by another of these ferry pilots we are training here. He ground looped. Another taxied into in a barrel with a Kitty! Nice types.

Sunday, 7 June 1942
Flew back from Wadi Natrum at nought feet and beat-up all the wogs in the Delta. Some of them threw stones at us as we went over—after they had climbed out of the ditches again.

I hear tonight that the period of service of operational people is 32 months in this command. That leaves me about two years to go—could be worse I suppose. Might even stick it out—June 1944!

Thursday, 11 June 1942
I hear the Spits will be coming through in force within the next fortnight and that 92 should be getting them. Suppose Wedgewood [92's CO] asks for me shortly, am I to say 'yes' and go to the desert with them, or say 'no' and perhaps miss

my chance of going on Spits again. I might even find myself
back in the desert on Kittys if I pass up Spits now.

Sunday, 14 June 1942

Flew down to Kasfareet in a Harvard with P/O Morris and
brought a Kitty back. Very nice to fly this Kitty as it had no
guns aboard. Aerobatted for half an hour after which glycol
started to leak, oil covered the floor of the cockpit, smoke
appeared in the cockpit and engine started cutting. Oh, nice
machine. Engine stopped as I landed. [Sunday again,
Neville!]

Monday, 15 June 1942

Took two pupils up this morning—very hot and tiring. Having
difficulty keeping my temper these days but must maintain
my reputation of calmness.

Getting a bit drunk tonight. Having another of my homesick spells. So to bed—a bit under the liquor but still mobile.
Must get on Ops and shoot at things.

Friday, 19 June 1942

Heard that poor old Dicky Dickinson has [indeed] been killed
by AA fire on one of these ground strafes and dive-bombing
raids. Poor old Dicky[1], he was awfully good.

Position in the desert does not seem as good. Understand
old Sammy Saunders[2], ex-92, is out here with 74 Squadron.

In the desert the Battle of Gazala was on, with Rommel pushing east
again back towards Tobruk. By the 14th of June the Allied troops were
retreating from Gazala, the RAF retreating too. On the 17th, Neville's
old antagonist, Otto Schulz of II/JG27, was shot down and killed
moments after gaining his 51st victory.

Then, on the 21st, Tobruk surrendered, which gave Rommel the
incentive to push on towards Egypt, rather than hanging-fire at the
Egyptian border. Three days later, his Panzers crossed into Egypt. By
the end of the month, the British forces were back at a line running
south from a place called El Alamein. It was here that the Afrika Korps
would be held, the southern flank edging onto the impassable (for heavy

---

[1] Flight Lieutenant Eric Dickinson was shot down by ground fire on 27 May but got back
the next day, the 28th, only to be shot down and killed on this date by 109s of II/JG27.
[2] Flight Lieutenant C H Saunders DFC, 92 Squadron Battle of Britain. Later flew with
145 and 1 SAAF Squadrons. Commanded 154 Squadron in Italy in 1944. Retired as a
wing commander in 1958.

armour) Qattara Depression. From this position the Allies built up their strength for another push west later in the year, while Rommel's supply line was badly disrupted by Malta-based aircraft and submarines.

Neville was suddenly keen to get to the front to try and do something about it, but wishing and being allowed to do things are very different. And there was a sudden panic to produce more pilots through the system, in order to replace losses. Their target was now to have 50 to 75 Kittyhawk pilots operational a month.

Friday, 26 June 1942
Same dreary old round, same dead-beat non-operational types! Same heat, same everything. However, with the Hun pushing as he is we may get some action and excitement here soon. He is around Barrani now and still going like a bomb. Soon be having 109s beating us up again—oh, happy days.

Everything going smoothly on the Kittys until this evening when a type held off about 10 feet and stalled into the deck, busting his undercarriage. Came down a hell of a wallop but didn't hurt himself.

This evening I flew over to chaps in the desert in a Harvard, working on another Kitty crash out there. P/O Morris dropped food and tea over the side as I flew along about 10 feet with flaps down. He also dropped his watch over by mistake so we had to go back and drop a note. They found his watch OK!

Saturday, 27 June 1942
Flew the odd type around in a Harvard, then took up a pupil of Bary's to test him as he was thought to be no good by Bary. Flew me around the circuit and then ground looped in the middle of the runway; couldn't stop the swing at all. Think he had his feet planted on the rudder. However, it doesn't matter now. This pupil says he doesn't want to fly Kittyhawks anyway! Too many of these unkeen types about these days. The Harvard's number was 805, adding up to 13, as all other do's!

Sunday, 28 June 1942
The damned Hun is around Mersah Matruh now! Our last line of defence. If he comes through there I think we've had this part of the world.

Monday, 29 June 1942
War news very bad today. The Huns seem to have taken

Mersah Matruh. Have we had it out here? Bags of flap on this evening, people running around with maps of Palestine. Is this to mean anything? Soon to leave I suppose. Bits of odd air raids in the distance tonight, so things may become exciting once more.

Tuesday, 30 June 1942

Terrific panic today. We are moving to Palestine shortly. Flew the WingCo down to Cairo and collected my kit from Shepherd's and cleared the bank of my money!

More panic—all our operationally serviceable Kittyhawks are to be flown to squadrons tonight. I was to take one down to 239 Wing with Sgt McQueen and to stay there and operate with the machines as the Huns came getting damned close and this is our last line of defence. Every aircraft is to be made serviceable and to get bomb racks on.

The situation is really serious now. If he breaks through we've just about had it. He is only about 60 miles from Alex at the most. However, couldn't make LG91 tonight so put down at Amiriyra for the night and quite pleasant it was.

Wednesday, 1 July 1942

Up at dawn and on to LG91 where 239 Wing is located. We handed over the two Kittys to them and then wanted to know what I was to do. They did not appear to know or care, so went over to 112 Squadron Mess. The CO, Billy Drake, wanted to know if I would like to come back to them but I said nothing doing pal—no more Kittys for me if I can help it.

Thought of trying to get into 145 Squadron with Spits, but no go. So went off to Cairo to get the form from the 'horse's mouth'. Saw W/C Honor at Air HQ. Started off at 2 o'clock with Tom Morgan and Babe Whitamore in the staff car and did not arrive at Mena until 10.30. The road was simply packed with army transport going south. They were clocking 700 [vehicles] an hour yesterday. Stayed the night at Mena—very nice.

Billy Drake had taken over from Clive Caldwell who had completed his tour in North Africa, and was sent to England prior to returning to Australia to form No.1 Australian Fighter Wing at Darwin. He had about 20 victories in the desert, adding another eight Japanese aircraft over Darwin. He died in August 1994 aged 83. Billy Drake DFC had seen action in France with No.1 Squadron in 1939-40, then 91 Squadron in late 1940. After commanding 128 Squadron in West Africa he took over 112 Squadron in April 1942. He would become another high-scoring fighter pilot in the desert air war with the DSO and Bar to his DFC.

Dudley Honor DFC and Bar, had seen action flying Fairey Battles in France, then been on fighters in the Battle of Britain. Fought with 274 Squadron in the Western Desert and then commanded No.258 Wing. He was now in MEHQ and would later command 17 Sector at Benghazi.

Thursday, 2 July 1942
Went into Cairo this morning and saw Wing Commander Honor. I am to go back to METS. Chubb came down in the Blenheim with Hunk, who was pleased to see me back. Had lunch at 92 Mess—all the pilots have gone up front to fly Hurrys or Spits. Flew back to Ballah; we are moving on Saturday now. Looking forward to seeing Palestine.

Friday, 3 July 1942
No news from the front. These are pretty tricky days. The pongos think if we can hold up Jerry's advance for three days while we get our own stuff organised, we shall be OK, other-wise we've had it. That was three days ago!

Saturday, 4 July 1942
Off to Palestine today like a shot. All aircraft moved up in a bunch—myself in a Tommy. Wizard country—simply magnificent after that damnable Egypt. We live in a valley surrounded by hills about 2,000 feet high. Everything is green and golden. Birds sing and the air smells sweet again. Almost like England. The Mess is not finished yet but it is a nice roomy brick building with a tin roof. We live in rooms now—Hunk and myself together still.

Despite the nice surroundings, the new place was really unfit for flying training. After several days of deciding whether to stay, move some-where else or go back to Ballah now the main flap seemed over, it was finally decided to return to Ballah, which they did on the 31st. Neville flew back in a Kittyhawk with the wheels down as he had a bad hydraulic leak.

Neville was starting to agitate about moving on and was beginning to contemplate almost any flying job. During August he seriously contem-plated trying for Beaufighter night-fighters, and then the high-flying Spitfires going after recce Ju86s, but he did not get very far. He seemed doomed to stay an instructor until he'd been off Ops for the obligatory six months.

Saturday, 8 August 1942

Nine Spitfires flew down the canal this afternoon. I hear they were 601 Squadron going back to Kilo 8 after a swim at Port Said. Bisdee, ex-609 Biggin days is the CO. Wish I could join 'em.

Squadron Leader John Bisdee DFC, had fought with 609 Squadron during 1940-41, when Nev was at Biggin. Bisdee flew 601 off the US carrier *Wasp* to Malta, first cannon-armed Spitfire Vs on the island. He then brought the Squadron to the Western Desert in July. Kilo 8 was also known as LG219—Matariyah, situated north-east of Cairo.

Sunday, 16 August 1942

Wrote to S/L Wedgewood, 92 Squadron, to see if he could use another pilot, as I've 'had' this place.

Squadron Leader J H Wedgewood had flown with 253 Squadron during the Battle of Britain. He took command of 92 Squadron in the summer of 1942 just as it was moving to North Africa. He was about to receive the DFC.

Wednesday, 19 August 1942

[date of the Dieppe Raid in Europe]

Brassed off again! Got a good bit of flying in, which is the only compensation. Showing some pupils how to work the guns on a Kitty tonight and two of the damned guns started firing, causing some panic and sucking of teeth.

Monday, 24 August 1942

Two neat crashes this evening—a Kitty whose undercart was not locked and a Hurricane who had one u/c leg not locked. The WingCo's fairly dancing around.

Friday, 11 September 1942

Afraid I have not kept up my diary for the past couple of weeks. There is nothing really interesting to write about these days. Still at Ballah giving types dual in Harvards and dog-fights with them in Kittys or Tommys—generally imparting my knowledge to them so that I may in some way prevent them from being easy meat for the Hun. I fear for many of them as the standard seems lower these days, and 109s are doing all the work up at the front, escorting Ju87s with about 40 109s at a time. The Spitfires, however, are the saving factor—doing interceptions and covering the Kitty-bombers who are pretty easy meat if jumped without top cover.

Saturday, 12 September 1942

Staying in bed under Doc's orders—temperature of 102 yesterday. Bary, the boss of C & R, is now a Squadron Leader and almost unapproachable.

Received a reply from S/L Wedgewood 92 Squadron. Apparently he had asked for me to join the Squadron but was told I had to stay off Ops for six months, so I may be able to get back the end of next month—I will have been off six months on 23 October.

A period in a hospital bed took care of mid-September, and then, with his continued life at Ballah depressing him further, Neville left his diary until 17 October. On that day he approached Ron Bary about leaving, asking Bary to mention it to the WingCo. Hunk Humphreys has put his spoke in regarding 92 as well.

Saturday, 24 October 1942

The 'Big Push' started in the Western Desert last night. This will be, in all probability, the decisive push in the Middle East. If it succeeds we will have North Africa to ourselves—if it fails we may lose Egypt!

Had words with the WingCo this afternoon re. leaving for a squadron. He says he is prepared to let me go if he has a replacement for me. Also that it could be arranged for me to probably go where I wanted (92) if I got the CO to ask for me.

Things got pretty busy over the next several days, but gradually things began to sort themselves out.

Friday, 13 November 1942

Flew up to see 92 to get things fixed up. Wing Commander said I could take the Tomahawk. Pretty good fun—left Ballah early and flew way up to the south of Barrani calling at Sidi Hannish on the way, seeking the elusive 92.

Monday, 16 November 1942

Flew to Heliopolis in the Blenheim with Chubby en-route to

92. Farewells over at lunch time. Good types most of the Ballah boys. Hunk said goodbye very sorrowfully. Poor old Hunk—hope he gets up here soon.

Organised myself into Shepherd's and went along to get some air transport laid on for me on the 18th. Some trouble about the weight of my kit but managed to be allowed a bit more after some hard talking.

Wednesday, 18 November 1942

Up at 4.30 to get the Lockheed from Almaza. Arrived at Gambut and was picked up by Squadron Leader Wedgewood in the 'jeep'. Good to be back with 92. The desert has not changed much from last April. Same dust, same grime.

CHAPTER VII

FORWARD FROM EL ALAMEIN

Bernard Montgomery's Battle of El Alamein began, as Neville recorded in his diary, on the night of 23 October 1942. Over 1,000 guns had opened up on the German positions, the greatest barrage since the grim days of WW1. Twenty minutes later, at 2200 hours, British troops began to advance, supported at first light by allied aircraft.

Since then, allied forces had kept up a steady advance and the air fighting had been intense. As well as their old adversaries in JG27, JG77 were also in the desert to reinforce the Luftwaffe fighter force. By 19 November, 92 Squadron were at Gambut West, having moved westward with the advance—LG 173, LG 21, Sidi Haneish, Gambut West. But the Germans were retreating so fast, 92 were still some way back.

Not that 92 had not been in the recent actions, far from it. On the first day of November, Pilot Officer Ted Sly, who would fly with Nev on several occasions, an Australian, was hit in a fight with JG27 and had to crash land in the desert. Feldwebel Gerhard Keppler of I Gruppe claimed him but his 'victory' remained unconfirmed. The following day, Pilot Officer Carpenter (in BR521) shot down a 109G flown by Leutnant Bruno Kolthoff of I/JG77, who baled out near Bir el Abel.

On the 9th, Flight Sergeant Blades, in EP616, was shot down 15 km east of Buq Buq by one of the top German aces, Major Joachim Muncheberg, of JG77—his 117th victory! It was now that Neville arrived on the scene.

Thursday, 19 November 1942
First Ops with 92 on my second tour. Patrol of Tobruk harbour with the CO. The Huns are way up around Benghazi and west of there. Hope we move up soon and start some flying. Dust storms and high wind all day.

Sunday, 22 November 1942

Called on Sammy Saunders this morning along with Tony Bruce. Sammy was pleased to see me and we talked over the old days at Biggin when he was in 92. He is in 74 now. Also called on Babe Whitamore in 601. Had a look at their [liberated] Stuka and 1 SAAF's Me109.

This Squadron is not too well organised at the moment. Hope it improves later on.

Tuesday, 24 November 1942

Squadron moves from Gambut West to Msus. I led the short range Spits to Gazala to refuel but had to stay the night there as the rest of the Squadron were scattered about.

Friday, 27 November 1942

Party arrived from Gambut at last with our baggage. 1 SAAF Squadron tangled with 20-odd 109s over Agheila this morning and lost one chap who spun in from 7,000 ft. No 109s shot down although a couple were damaged. In the evening the same Squadron was again engaged by 109s over the same place—lost two more types and got one 109. Not good enough.

We did a Sweep over the Agheila line in the afternoon—six of us with six of 145 as top cover. Led Blue Section and Sammy [Samouelle] led the Flight. Nothing seen and 145 eventually lost us.

I always fly with the hood back now—am getting to like it and can see lots more. Must not get jumped this time!

Saturday, 28 November 1942

Raining this morning and things getting muddy—shades of Antelat last year! Cloud wizard for beating up the Huns. Too far away from the lines here though. The 109s are getting organised again now and we may expect to meet big 'gaggles' of them any time—also this talk of FW109s is not funny either. Sweep in the afternoon over Agedabia and Agheila for two hours but saw nothing.

Sunday, 29 November 1942

Stripping our Spits now to try and cope with the 190s when we come across them. Taking out such things as IFF, one oxygen bottle, etc.

This lightening of the Spitfire was in response to the arrival in North

Africa of the Focke Wulf 190. It was well known, by this time, that in Europe the Spitfire Mark V was no match for the 190, and although the squadrons in 11 Group in England were starting to get Spitfire IXs which could cope with them, there were no IXs in the Desert Air Force.

Tuesday, 1 December 1942

S/L Wedgewood's last day with the Squadron. Sorry to see him go as he is an extremely good type. Red [Chisholm] flew six cases of beer up from Cairo and we got stuck into it this evening. Tony Bruce got amongst the whisky as well and made himself ill so I put him to bed in my cot. Result—I had to sleep on the floor.

First party moved off to Hassiet today. We shall shortly go down there to operate I suppose. It is about 30 miles south-east of Agedabia and about 50 miles from the front line.

Wednesday, 2 December 1942

Red Chisholm went over on his back landing and was lucky to get away with it almost unhurt except for concussion. Picked up our Tac/R Hurricane [tactical reconnaissance] of 40 SAAF Squadron and escorted same on a recco of the enemy lines. No EA seen except for one 109 in the distance behind us. Nearly squirted at some Kittys we met head-on. Some heavy ack-ack from large Hun concentrations west of El Agheila.

S/L Morgan took over the Squadron from S/L Wedgewood this morning.[1] Red Chisholm would appear to be the new flight commander although nothing has come out about it. Feel rather disapppointed and not a little brassed off regarding this.

Thursday, 3 December 1942

Am acting 'B' Flight Commander until Red comes operational again, which will be about a week. The Squadron moves down to El Hassiet today—about 50 miles east of the lines. Piled blankets, sleeping bag, ground sheet, 'lilo' and water etc., into the old Spit. Amazing what you can get in especially now we have taken a lot of equipment out of them.

Left Msus midday and did a Sweep of the Mersa Brega area

---

[1] Squadron Leader J M Morgan DFC, had previously flown with 238 Squadron in the Western Desert before becoming a flight commander in early 1942. Posted as a flight commander to 92 in the summer, he then took command. He would go on to command 274 Squadron in Italy but became a prisoner later.

east of Agheila. Nothing about at all—things are very quiet these days—both sides storing up for the next push which we expect within a couple of weeks.

Saturday, 5 December 1942

Enjoying myself as OC 'B' Flight. Can't deny I should have liked the Flight but 'Red' is a good bloke and will handle things OK. I do feel a bit stooged though, but I am told I am taking over 'A' Flight when Samouelle goes.

Sunday, 6 December 1942

Wing escort of us and 601 Squadron to Kitty-bombers bombing Mersa Brega point. Not bad bombing on troop concentrations. One direct hit on the inn at Brega. Was a pretty cold trip as we now fly with hoods taken off completely. You can see everything which is the main thing but it is a bit cold and uncomfortable especially at high speeds.

We have a little liquor now which is rationed to two tots a night! Previously we have had no drinks at all. The food is a bit better now but still don't get enough. The water is a brownish colour and tastes awful. I haven't had a good wash for two weeks but I am enjoying life. I think after a while, the quiet and loneliness of the desert gets you. I know when I left it last time I said I'd never come back—but here I am.

Operating with the cockpit canopy off, was, says Neville, a momentary fit of desert madness and the hoods were soon put back on (see later this month). It was an experiment, for the problem was sand and dust stuck to the perspex on take off which reduced visibility at times.

Monday, 7 December 1942
[first anniversary of Pearl Harbor]

Was to have led the Squadron this morning on a 109 delousing sweep for the Kitty-bombers, but unfortunately the Kittys have run out of bombs!

Two 109s came over early and had a good look at us from way above. Later a Hun prisoner had lunch with us. He was in one of the 109s that came over this morning—shot down by 601 Squadron.

On a Sweep this afternoon and ran into lots of 109s—about 30 in all I think. I got three good shots—the first one just climbed away apparently unhurt—second one I think I maybe got as I pulled up under him about 320 and gave him several bursts closing quite close until the speed chopped off and I fell away. He was seen by my No.2 and 3 (which was Tony Bruce) to roll over and go down. Making no claim until I hear if any other chaps claim, as three fires were seen—one may be mine.

Third attack was made by three 109s out of the sun. We did a turnabout and broke them up. I got a good squirt but nothing happened. Joerns was shot down and baled out at 2,000 ft or so. [All this] ran us pretty short of petrol and four chaps are missing.

This action was against JG77; Joerns baled out. The German guest was a 109 pilot of 4(H)/12, shot down by Pilot Officer Laing-Meason of 145 Squadron, who claimed one and the other as a probable.

Tuesday, 8 December 1942

Off at dawn to look for the missing blokes. Found Tony Bruce and Colin Sinclair at Agedabia. Hendrich Smith is down in the 'bundu' and Joerns was shot down by two 109s. With his tail shot off and his engine on fire, he got out only just in time. Near thing.

Led the Squadron on a delousing patrol near Marble Arch, the 109's base. Engaged by 109s twice but not much doing. Very low on petrol and Charlie [Lt Charlie Hewitson SAAF] was caught lagging by a 109. We were unable to go back and help. The 109 left him, however, after waggling his wings to Charlie!

The ack-ack was something terrific. Several chaps holed and it got past a joke. The Kittys bombing Marble Arch and shot down five or six 109s.

Wednesday, 9 December 1942

Squadron moving forward to El Nogra, about 15 to 18 miles from the front. I led the Squadron from Hassiet on a Sweep to Marada looking for the King's Dragoon Guards who were supposed to be in the middle of the desert north of here but we did not see them. Swept north and crossed the coast and went out to sea between Agheila and Mersa Brega. Little ack-ack this time, and we landed at Nogra. Shall have to watch our step here; it's a bit close for the 109s to jump us in the circuit.

Friday, 11 December 1942

Dozens of Kitty-bombers dropped in on us this morning on

their way to bomb Nofilia aerodrome, about 120 miles west of here. We provided top cover for them.

Led the Squadron in the afternoon to Sweep up to Nofilia with 601. Cloud was about 6,000 ft and raining quite a bit. Attacked in feeble manner by six Me109s in all, who worried us for some time. Could not get at them as they would not play at all.

Jackie Joerns who baled out the other day after being shot down by two 109s, went over on his back when landing this morning but did not hurt himself. Right out of liquor tonight except for a bottle of whisky supplied by Brickhill—a new pilot.[1]

Tuesday, 15 December 1942

Jerry is withdrawing from Mersa Brega and Agheila without putting up a fight except for this rear-guard of the Afrika Korps. A New Zealand Division has been moving up from Marada towards Marble Arch to cut off Jerry and get his rear-guard in a box.

Suspect the Hun will move about 2 to 300 miles back to Misurata and make his stand in the very strong natural defences there; also it will stretch our lines of supply to breaking point.

Wednesday, 16 December 1942

We hear the New Zealanders have pulled it off and done a wizard show by blocking the road near Marble Arch and cutting off the retreating Hun rear-guard. Should be a terrific fight there.

We are flying standing patrols over them all day. The Bostons, Baltimores and Mitchells are going over continuously and the Kittys are doing grand work.

Friday, 18 December 1942

Saw 'Topsy' Turvey have a nasty crash as I was going round the circuit. He took off straight into a 601 Spitfire which was parked in the middle of the runway. His wings were torn off and his engine torn out, the fuselage smashed up but all he got was a bashed face. I'd say he was lucky. Couple of

---

[1] Flying Officer Paul Brickhill; after the war he became a well known aviation author, with such books as *Reach for the Sky* (the life of Douglas Bader), *The Dam Busters* (the story of 617 Squadron) and *The Great Escape* (the escape from Stalag Luft III in March 1944).

machines went up on their noses today. My machine caught fire in the cockpit as I taxied in but I put it out with my gloves without much damage.

Monday, 21 December 1942

Squadron moved up this morning to new base west of Marble Arch. The Huns had heavily mined all this area including the 'drome. Our losses in men so far have been chiefly due to mines.

This is a pretty small aerodrome for four squadrons and is in a pretty bad state really. Hope we can remain here over Christmas though. The WingCo —Darwen—led us up in his new clipped-wing Spit. He has also taken all four machine-guns out. His idea is for speed which I agree with but he goes excessively fast and some types are going to have to use their emergency boost +16 to keep formation.

Tuesday, 22 December 1942

Pep-talk this morning by Air Commodore Broadhurst [Later Air Chief Marshal Sir Harry Broadhurst GCB KBE DSO DFC AFC]. Pretty good chat too. We are all getting tuned up for the Beurat fight. We expect 109s and bombers—88s and 87s—to be pretty active.

I think I shall use my hood in future. Without the hood visibility is perfect but your speed is cut down and when travelling very fast you can't see very well owing to the terrific slipstream. With the new bulge hood which have started to arrive, you can see quite well over the tail but it gets scratched by sand, and then, sun on these scratches makes it hard to see out. I may take out the two outboard machine-guns too but don't like this move much.

No.92 Squadron were flying the Spitfire Mark Vb, which had two 20 mm cannon and four .303 machine-guns, two in each wing outboard of the single cannon in each wing. Contemplating the removal of two guns would give added manoeuvrability in combat. As Neville recalls, another problem in the desert—apart from scratched cockpit covers—was that particles of sand also tended to stick to the perspex which could make it opaque, and, if one wasn't careful, make one assume a speck to be a distant enemy aircraft.

Friday, 25 December 1942

Christmas and in the Western Desert again. A much better Christmas than the last though. Made a round of the

Squadrons—601 and 145 in the morning. Fed the airmen their lunch. Jerry Westenra rolled up with Bartle in the DH86 Ambulance plane so I got pretty merry with them and some more visitors in the Mess. Had a great Christmas dinner of turkey and pork, wine, Christmas pudding, etc.

Sunday, 27 December 1942
Jerry Westenra turned up again. He is posted to 601 Squadron so had the odd drink with him in the Mess in the evening.

Monday, 28 December 1942
Saw Jerry over to 601. He would rather stay with us but I think he will be getting a flight over there.

Three 'prangs' today. Tony Bruce put one of our Spits on its nose taxying; a 601 chappie dropped one in from about 20 feet and shoved the wheels through his mainplane, and one of 145 hit some barrels taking off and took most of his under-cart off and his oil cooler—causing some little embarrassment.

Tuesday, 29 December 1942
S/L Wedgewood has been killed at night on Malta in a Halifax with a Polish crew. One of the cruellest blows of fate. He had been through two tours of operations and was on his way home to take his well earned rest. Those whom the gods adore . . .

In fact it was crueller than Neville knew, for the 138 Squadron Halifax had been accidentally shot down by Malta AA fire (17 December).

Thursday, 31 December 1942
Moved from El Merduma to Alem El Chel this morning. Seems a pretty good spot—nice big square 'drome—but still almost out of range from the front which is around Beurat now and moving towards Misurata.

Air Chief Marshal Tedder came round and gave us a farewell chat. Sholto Douglas is taking his place as C-in-C Middle East.

Shooting this afternoon and bagged a couple of gazelle. Chased them in the jeep doing a steady 40 mph for quite a while before we got them with .303 rifles. Types were blazing away in all directions.

Once again Neville wrote-up an end of year résumé in the back of his diary: 'So ends this year 1942. Perhaps not as exciting as the last year but still a good year that sees me back on Ops again and back with good old 92. Or rather the new Western Desert 92. The coming year will, I think, prove a pretty exciting one with unbounded possibilities.'

Friday, 1 January 1943
This year starts pretty cold and bleak on the flat desert south-east of Sirte. Nothing to do this morning. Some of the types off on another gazelle hunt and returned with a fair bag but pretty cold and dusty. Gazelle for dinner again and very nice too.

Wonder how things will fare this year? My 21st year too. Think it will probably find me at home at any rate—if I survive.

Sunday, 3 January 1943
Squadron at Readiness at 8.30. Sand got up about 9.30 and wind blew like hell. Continued to rise in some volume until dusk. Sand was really thick at times. Our tent came down, of course, and everything covered in sand and dust. I think most everybody's tent was down—wizard shambles.

Poor old accountant's tent came adrift at Wing and all his 'akkers' blew for miles around!

Monday, 4 January 1943
Wind continues with unabated fury. More tent troubles but the sand is not so bad; wonder where it all blows to?

Pep-talk by S/L Harper this afternoon in the Mess which was quite well appreciated, on the subject of officers and men and attitude towards same. Standard of officers seems to go down out here, probably because the officers and men live such similar lives.

Squadron Leader W J Harper was soon to be the new CO of 92 Squadron. He had fought over Dunkirk and in the Battle of Britain with 17 Squadron before being wounded. He later commanded 453 Squadron in Malaya at the start of the war in the Far East, later leading 135 Squadron in India.

Tuesday, 5 January 1943
Trying to make a fire in the Mess this noon; poor old Ted Sly in his keenness, nearly had a nasty accident. Everything was set and very nice, all we had to do was light it. He strikes a

match, peers in, drops the match—and woof! Hair, eye-brows, eyelashes and moustache go in one big blast of petrol. It was really funny—for us, but not for Ted, although he is much better now and running around covered in blue ointment.

I flew up to Sirte and had a look at the place. I love just flying around doing nothing in particular. One minute nipping along the deck at nought feet and then, with just a gentle pull on the stick and a little more motor, soaring up and up for hundreds of feet, feeling the immense power that you have got just at your fingertips. Feeling that you are a part of this fine machine, made by a genius. It is said the Spitfire is too beautiful to be a fighting machine. I sometimes think it's true but then, what better fighter could you want?

The weather was pretty bad along the coast to Sirte—rain and low cloud. Wizard to go rushing through the rain and cloud and yet be nice and dry and comfortable inside your cockpit that just fits around you so snugly.

Thursday, 7 January 1943

Squadron took off at dawn for forward landing ground at Tamet where our advance party is already established. We arrived there as the 109s finished their breakfast bombing and strafing, and landed amidst some confusion. 109s have been bombing Tamet three times a day lately so we looked forward to some fun. We got it.

We were on stand-by in our cockpits when we were Scrambled. I led the formation and we climbed up westwards to 12,000 feet where we engaged some five 109Gs at our own level. I saw them coming and got round into the sun. They saw us and started climbing with us into the sun and we engaged them head-on. One took a pot at me but it went over the top. General mêlée started and I engaged two 109Fs and started a climbing and turning match with them. Chasing round behind this pair we climbed to 20,000 ft. I found I could climb and turn inside them with no trouble. When they found I was getting inside them first one and then the other rolled over and dived away. I didn't follow as the 109s were becoming embarrassing.

From this show Sgt Paterson was shot down and baled out. Sgt Broomhall was also shot and baled out being wounded in the foot. The CO shot down one of the 109 bombers into the sea and F/O Nomis shot down one also. At stand-by again in the afternoon and Scrambled for some 109s but did not engage, although I saw bombs bursting on our own 'drome. Clouds gave cover to the 109s. Nearly shot down by our own AA. A change from our recent inaction. The future holds more excitement I feel.

These first 109s were from II/JG77, and the pilots claimed three Spitfires shot down this date; Hauptmann Anton Hackl, Oberleutnant Lutz-Wilhelm Burckhardt and Leutnant Ernst Wilhelm Reinert. These three would achieve 192, 61 and 174 victories respectively. The two 92 pilots appear to have been the victims of Reinert at 1303 pm (his 105th kill) and Burckhardt at 1305, (his 54th). Unfortunately for Burckhardt, he stepped on a mine later this day and was wounded.

Friday, 8 January 1943

Field Day. Once more to Tamet for stand-by. Scrambled in the morning and came across Stukas and 109s bombing our forward troops. Got stuck into the top cover of Macchi 202s at 13,000 ft. The boys had a pretty hard fight as the Macchis stayed and fought. I dived on two slightly below, with F/Sgt J Sails. We were well placed and in the sun—they never saw us until too late when they put their noses down for home but we were on them. The one I chased went down almost vertically from 10,000 feet to the deck, clocking 400 plus. Gained on him easily along the deck and drew smoke from him with a cannon shell in his radiator and oil cooler. He finally hit the ground and burst into flames after some more hits from my cannons which were working well this day! The aircraft dissolved into flame and small pieces. His parachute somehow came out and was lying open on the ground and was billowing in the breeze with something on the end of it which was once the pilot. Poor devil. Seems a pity.

I dived and took a few photos with my camera gun and then tore back at nought feet for home—only to find there was no camera film aboard. Would have had some good pictures. From this show, Red Chisholm, Lt Smith and Sails got probables. Quite a scrap. The enemy fighter boys seem pretty clueful these days—perhaps we shall find the going a bit hard.

Combat Report for 8 January
Time: 1100 hrs, Zidan

I dived on two Macchi 202s from 13,000 feet (Macchis at 10,000 feet). Enemy aircraft dived earthwards. Sgt J Sails, my No.2, engaged the second Macchi. I chased enemy aircraft to deck level and observed hit with cannon shell on radiator, or oil cooler under fuselage, from which grey-black smoke started. Enemy aircraft continued along the deck for some time, finally being hit by several cannon shells and DeWilde in rear fuselage. Enemy aircraft struck the ground and burst into flames. I observed pilot's parachute open on the ground after the crash.

I was easily able to hold enemy aircraft in speed along deck without using full throttle. I overtook enemy aircraft fairly rapidly in dive. No evasive action from enemy aircraft apart from dive.

Claim: 1 Macchi 202 Destroyed.

Later that day, 92 Squadron were in a fight with JG77, and although Leo 'Chief' Nomis (he was an American with Sioux Indian ancestry) shot one down into the sea, 92 and 601 lost pilots: Pilot Officer Geoffrey W Rose, an Australian, was the 92 pilot. I/JG77 claimed three—Leutnant Heinz-Edgar Berres, Staffelfuhrer of 1/JG77 (26th), Oberfeldwebel Ludwig (32nd) and Oberfeldwebel Walter Schumann (11th).

On the 11th, 92 engaged a large formation of Italian fighters, comprising 17 Mc200s and 202s from 13 Gruppo, with an escort of 23 more Macchis from 18 and 23 Gruppi. Nine Spitfires of 92 were Scrambled at 1630:

Monday, 11 January 1943

21st birthday—some birthday! Up at dawn and on stand-by. Squadron Scrambled but a bit of a shambles when the CO's R/T packed up. Finally got going with Sammy leading. Vectored around a bit by Ops, but saw nothing, except for a lone 109, which everybody had a crack at except little self who went down by himself to chase something he saw low down. This lone little 109 is only, however, a probable.

Off again after a quick lunch with my No.2—P/O Brickhill—to intercept two 109s near Tamet. Saw the damn things all right, way below us but lost them in the dive. Nearly passed out with lack of oxygen.

Off again after tea, leading the Squadron up to 13,000 feet east of Tamet 'drome and there saw bombs bursting on the airfield. Put the speed on a bit and spotted five aircraft coming in from the sea. They turned west and we gave chase. Four of 'em dived and one climbed—I went after this one—closed to a couple of hundred yards—gave a short burst and hit him—a Macchi 202—behind the cockpit and pieces flew off in abundance. He rolled over and I had a glimpse of the pilot pulling himself out of the cockpit. Saw his 'chute open nicely and his machine go down—pieces still coming off. Confirmed by rest of Squadron. This pilot was taken prisoner. He was the CO of a fighter Group—some catch!

Squadron was split up then and I and my No.2—P/O McMahon—stooged about for a while until I spotted a single aircraft low down—another Macchi 202 . Dived after him at considerable speed and caught him after fairly long chase in and out of cloud down to ground level. Made numerous attacks and he put up quite a fight. Saw my hits along his fuselage and he put flaps down and hastily crash-landed, after about a 10-minute dog-fight. He was out of his cockpit before the dust had settled. I sympathised with him, having had the same experience. I gave him a wave!

Combat Report for 11 January
Time: 1645 and 1700 hrs, NNW of Tamet and WSW of Beurat

Five enemy aircraft approaching coast. Enemy aircraft turned west and dived except one Macchi 202 which pulled up. I closed on enemy aircraft astern and fired a short burst; hits observed in fuselage. Pieces flew off and enemy aircraft rolled over and the pilot baled out.

I observed one aircraft flying west at low altitude. I dived on the aircraft from 8,000 ft. A stern chase for some considerable time. Attacks were chiefly made from astern. The Macchi 202 finally crash landed and the pilot got out. The pilot made use of cloud cover and threw his machine about to some extent.

F/O B McMahon, my No.2, also made several attacks on this machine.

Claim: 2 Macchi 202s Destroyed.

The Intelligence people interrogated both Italian pilots following their capture and several things were revealed and noted in their report. The first pilot was Second Lieutenant Telleschi, who baled out. The second was Maggiore Gustavo Garretto, the CO of No.18 Gruppo (3rd Stormo), aged about 35. This day his unit had been escorting about 20 Macchi 200s which were to bomb the landing ground at Tamet, these aircraft carrying two 50 kg bombs. They were on their return when engaged by 92 Squadron. Maggiore Garretto had been in Africa for about 15 months, having been in his present command position for the last three. The Major also stated that he appreciated the sportsmanship of the Spitfire pilot who came down to have a look at him—but did not open fire!

The Italian noted that his machines had poor R/T communications; indeed, his own aircraft's R/T was u/s on this day. Therefore, the pilots generally signalled to each other by waggling wings if danger was imminent. He was described by his captors as '. . . a good Italian type and politely secure.'[1]

For their part, the Italians claimed four Spitfires and two P40s, with nine more damaged, in a fight with 25-30 Spitfires!

Tuesday, 12 January 1943

Visited by 109s early this morning, who dropped bombs and things around about. 145 Squadron got amongst some Macchi 200s and shot down five of them. S/L Marples of 145 went into the sea but was pulled ashore by two army officers who swam out a mile to him.

Called on Jerry Westenra in 601 this afternoon. He is pretty brassed off as they've had no luck lately.

Wednesday, 13 January 1943

Dawn Readiness. Squadron off about 9.30 to meet B25s and Kittys coming back from bombing show. Met them crossing the coast NW of Beurat. We split up and myself and Tony Bruce diced with a Mc202 which we would pretty sure have clobbered if our guns hadn't packed up. This Macchi pilot could certainly throw himself about in no mean manner and we had grand fun there for a while until he rushed off home— a moral victory at any rate. Six Kittys missing from this morning's show. Tough.

Thursday, 14 January 1943

Off after lunch escorting 18 Kittys to bomb Jerry. Two 109s passed under us on way out almost at target. Went after them but I only got one burst at one of them as they rolled over and went down. Some dive. Squadron was split up and I snooped about with Charlie Hewitson for a while but nothing doing.

Big push for Tripoli starts at midnight. We expect to be there in seven days. Hope to God nothing goes wrong. Hear I've been put up for bar to DFC.

---

[1] Garretto later went on to become a Generale in the post-war Italian Air Force.

CHAPTER VIII

ON TO TRIPOLI

The British 8th Army began its assault and push against the Beurat line on 15 January, with the 7th Armoured Division and the 51st Highland Division. Not wanting a fight here, Rommel immediately began withdrawing his forces to the Homs-Tarhuna line.

No.92 Squadron had a quiet day, just flying one top cover sortie to Kitty-bombers and then a freelance patrol over the forward troops. Tank battles and much shelling could be seen, with lots of movement on the ground.

Saturday, 16 January 1943
Escorted Yankees on strafe of Hun forward elements. Two Yanks collided—saw one bale out OK. They left some MT burning.

Air Chief Marshal Sir Sholto Douglas called on us this morning, having taken over from ACM Tedder. Wing patrol this evening with 1 SAAF over forward troops.

Sunday, 17 January 1943
Putting our overload tanks on again as we are almost out of range of the forward areas now. Escorted some Warhawks [P40F] to Dufan aerodrome where they strafed. On the way back we saw about eight 109s dive-bombing some of our troops but couldn't get anywhere near them. Our 'A' party moved off for Dufan this noon. We shall probably go in a few days.

Squadron moved on the 20th, but beat the ground party to it!

Thursday, 21 January 1943
Squadron patrol Tripoli-Benito area in the afternoon at about

10,000 ft. Bloody accurate flak from Castel Benito area causing some panic. Grand party this afternoon when I spotted Stukas bombing our troops while we were patrolling Tripoli area led by Wing Commander Darwen. Squadron did not spot them so I dived after them and caught same near Castel Benito aerodrome. Broke up their vic formations and shot at one without doing much damage apart from a few strikes.

Attacked second one and closed, fired and hit him in starboard wing root which burst into flames. Ju87 went down in spirals and exploded on hitting the ground. Observed by most of the Squadron. Amazing sight when I broke up the Stukas by myself—they gave me some return fire and carried out stall turns and turns all around me until the rest of the Squadron rolled up. They were Italian Stukas. My 12th victory.

Appointed Flight Lieutenant of 'A' Flight. Got legless with CO and 3 RAAF and with WingCo Darwen in his trailer.

Combat Report for 21 January
Time: 1400 hrs, south of Castel Benito

I dived after eight Ju87s in two vics of three and a two. I closed astern of starboard vic and attacked extreme starboard Ju87; he broke away as I closed before I opened fire. I changed attack to the No.3 and opened fire at 100 to 200 yards. I observed DeWilde strikes but make no claim. The Ju87s then completely broke up making steep climbs and stall turns and dives.

I attacked one Ju87 from astern at 100 yards slightly to starboard; I observed cannon shells burst in the starboard wing root which caught fire. The enemy aircraft went down and I saw it crash and burst into flames. I observed two Me109s attack a Spitfire. The Ju87s were Italians.

Some considerable return fire was experienced.

Claim: 1 Ju87 Destroyed.

In fact the Stukas were aircraft of III/St.G3; ie: German not Italian. The pilot of the Stuka Neville shot down baled out but his parachute failed to open. Two other Stukas came down, their crews safe, these being the victims of Flight Lieutenant Samouelle and Flying Officer Jowsey, who each claimed one. Two others were claimed as probables.

This was the last sortie of Sammy Samouelle DFC, who had risen from Sergeant to Flight Lieutenant with 92, gaining seven confirmed victories with others damaged. As promised, Neville took his place as commander of A Flight—hence the additional celebrations.

Friday, 22 January 1943

First day as flight commander. Led patrol over Castel Benito-Tripoli area in the morning without event. Led a top cover to some Kittys to Zuara in the afternoon where they bombed and strafed. Got some pretty nasty ack-ack crossing the coast west of Tripoli—can hear the stuff exploding these days.

Fires burning in Tripoli—probably Huns burning stores. Our boys nearly at Tripoli now; they should make it tomorrow.

Saturday, 23 January 1943

Think we are just about to occupy Tripoli at last. The Hun Panzer Division (90th Light) is still putting up a fight on the outskirts of the town. They have put up a good show so far throughout all the campaign out here. Big convoy on its way to Tripoli now. We may move again pretty soon.

Things became quiet for a few days, but on the 26th, Ted Sly returned from a trip to Castel Benito aerodrome talking of an almost serviceable Italian tri-motored Savoia Marchetti 79 bomber he had found there. This was too good to miss.

Wednesday, 27 January 1943

Flew to Castel Benito along with Ted Sly early this morning to get going on the '79'. It seems a pretty feasible job. Spent the morning looking over CR42s, and Macchi 200s, 202s and G50s, etc. The 'drome is packed with all types of Eyetie and Hun aircraft in various states of disrepair. The Kitty Squadron stationed here have got 42s etc. flying.

Friday, 29 January 1943

Took four aircraft to Castel Benito at first light this morning for Readiness. Had one Scramble and patrolled around Tripoli harbour for a while but nothing doing.

Did our Readiness in 112's Ops trailer with Jeff Carroll, their Ops officer now, and talked of the old days. Invited over to 260 Squadron for a second lunch and had a noggin of Chianti.

Big conference today. We are to stay here for a week and then move to Surman for a month or so. The push is not coming off for another two months. Shall try to get home after this I think. Hundreds of aircraft on Benito—three Mosquitos arrived—damned nice machines. Our SM79 is coming along well.

Squadron Leader Morgan and Flight Lieutenant Samouelle finally left after a boozy evening; Harper took over 92. Things remained quiet after the recent advance. Red Chisholm received the DFC, and a new wing commander came on the scene—Ian Gleed DSO DFC, a former Battle of France and Battle of Britain pilot. News was also received that the Germans had 60-odd Focke Wulf 190 fighters at Gabes. Then Neville was notified of the award of a bar to his DFC, on 13 February.

Thursday, 25 February 1943

Started writing up my diary again after a lapse of a couple of weeks—not much has happened. The Squadron moved up from the desert of Wadi Surri to the comparative green paradise at Castel Benito. We did a little flying but made one or two Scrambles after 'shufti' kites, which however, we did not intercept, although 145 was lucky and damaged two.

Our days are spent in a bit of flying training, and drinking. Liquor being brought up from Cairo. Tony Bruce has had the Savoia 79 up—and down—in comparative safety.

Today we are all set to move up to Medenine just, but just, this side of the lines. The Huns have given the Yanks a beating and we have to push a month earlier than we intended. Visited Tripoli a couple of times too.

Monday, 1 March 1943

Led five aircraft on a Scramble from Medenine during the morning. Climbed up to about 15,000 ft and spotted three aircraft in vic formation below us at about 10,000 ft. Dived on same out of the sun and closed right astern before I was spotted. They were three Macchi 202s stooging along near Bord Touaz. Hit one of them in a climbing turn and saw my shells exploding all over his fuselage. The pilot baled out as the machine spiralled down.

The second engaged in a dog-fight and after a few bursts in turns he was hit by machine-gun bullets—my cannons having stopped. Aircraft went over and the pilot baled out. Saw both parachutes going down almost together side-by-side. The third got away although one of the boys had a shot at him.

Terrific panic in the evening when we were shelled by the Huns from the hills north-west of the landing ground. All aircraft were evacuated in a hurry and the ground parties left en masse.

Combat Report for 1 March
Time: 1130 hrs, NE of Medenine

I was leading five aircraft at 15,000 ft after being Scrambled. I observed three Macchi 202s below at about 10,000 feet flying north in vic formation.

I dived after enemy aircraft out of sun, and closed astern to about 300 yards, when I was observed by the port enemy aircraft which broke away to port. I attacked the starboard Macchi 202 which went up in a climbing left hand turn. I observed cannon strikes in the engine, and behind the cockpit. The enemy aircraft went down in a spiral dive and the pilot baled out.

I engaged the second Macchi in a dog-fight and after several short bursts with machine-guns, I observed hits in fuselage. The enemy aircraft turned on its back and went down. The pilot baled out. Enemy aircraft showed keenness to engage in dog-fight.

Claim: 2 Macchi 202s Destroyed.

These Macchi fighters, along with others, were escorting Macchi 200s who were to strafe vehicles south of Ksar Rhilane. While it was believed that both came down inside Axis lines, it is now understood that at least one, Second Lieutenant Antonio Reglai, became an Allied prisoner of war.

Wednesday, 3 March 1943

What a day! Up at dawn leading a section on a 'Suicide Four' [top cover section] job with 145 Squadron to Gabes area. A misunderstanding on take-off and Lt Smith collided head-on with one of 145. I thought Heindrich was killed for sure and I took off feeling like death, myself with the remaining two. One of these turned back with a ropey engine leaving two of us.

I climbed to 22,000 ft and flew to the north of Gabes and came back across the sea. As we were crossing the coast near the Mareth Line, spotted a lone 109 below us at about 10,000 ft—we were then at 14,000 ft. Pounced on same and saw strikes all over his fuselage. Smoke and glycol poured out and he went vertically down, crashing near the coast. Sgt Paterson confirmed the fireworks all over the 109 and also he saw it crash although I didn't.

Combat Report for 3 March
Time: 0800 hrs, Pisida, Libya

I was leading two aircraft on a roving top cover to 145 Squadron in the Gabes area at 20,000 feet. Set course for home from north of

Gabes in a gentle dive at 14,000 feet, crossing the coast north-east of Mareth. In Square Z.71 saw one Me109 at 10,000 feet. I dived down and closed to about 250 yards. The enemy aircraft turned sharply in a climbing turn to the left. I observed strikes with cannon in the fuselage and wings. After the second burst the enemy aircraft went down vertically with smoke coming from the fuselage. F/Sgt H Paterson confirms seeing it crash.

Claim: 1 Me109F Destroyed.

This appears to have been a 109 from III Gruppe of JG77; this unit lost Unteroffizier Werner and Feldwebel Herbert Schwarz on this day. However, Unteroffizier Willi Streba of 9/JG77 also crash-landed north west of Mareth in a 109G, which was a write off.

The collision on the ground was between Smith and Flying Officer P B Laing-Meason; both survived the experience.

Thursday, 4 March 1943

Another big day. Yet another prang when Sgt Ott collided with P/O Wilson, who was parked on the runway, as he took off. Nobody was hurt fortunately—our guardian angel works very very hard.

I took eight aircraft on stand-by up at Medenine at midday and we were Scrambled late in the afternoon. We climbed up to about 8,000 ft and I spotted two Me109s coming our way. The AA opened up and gave us a pounding. Had to fly thro' the ack-ack to get at these Huns!

I attacked the first from the port quarter and astern—a big explosion behind the cockpit and he rolled over and went down—pilot baled out. Attacked second one which dived straight down—we pounding along behind. Chased him for some time on the deck, seeing strikes on same. I broke away thinking I was hit by AA fire but Sergeant Askey saw him go in a little further on. Five in four days. Took some cine film shots of chap in his parachute and the crash on the ground.

Combat Report for 4 March
Time: 1735 hrs, Pisida, Libya

While leading seven aircraft on a local Scramble I observed two Me109s when at 8,000 feet, slightly above us. I closed on the leading Me109F and fired from port quarter and observed strikes. I fired a second burst from astern at fairly long range. The enemy aircraft exploded in the fuselage and went down. The pilot baled out and the enemy aircraft crashed near Medenine. I turned above the second enemy aircraft and closed astern, the enemy aircraft dived steeply to ground level, I chased him for some while and observed strikes on aircraft.

This enemy aircraft was seen to explode on the ground after I broke away, by Sgt M Askey. No evasive action was taken by the enemy aircraft apart from a straight dive. I experienced extremely accurate fire from our own AA.

Claim: 2 Me109Fs Destroyed.

From an Intelligence Report, it appears that both German pilots were from I/SG2 (First Gruppe Schlachtgeschwader Nr.2), based at Gabes West airfield. According to the one captured, their assigned task this day was for four aircraft to bomb a landing ground east of Medenine, four 109s from another staffel providing top cover.

However, the prisoner said he was delayed from taking off due to dust blown up by the others leaving the ground, and once airborne he and his wingman failed to meet up with the others. At about 5.30, while near Medenine, he saw the other aircraft bombing what appeared to be some tents and MT, and at the same time saw flak coming up. He bombed the same place from 5,000 feet but owing to intense ground fire results were not observed.

As he turned away eastwards to avoid further ground fire, he was attacked by the Spitfires although he had not seen them coming, so did not take any avoiding action. His engine was hit and burst into flames and he rapidly baled out.

Friday, 5 March 1943
Red Chisholm got tangled up with seven Me109s on a dawn Sweep this morning and had a pretty tough doggers by himself. Poor old 'Happy' McMahon was killed on this show. He laughed his way through life. 601 were tangled with twenty plus 109s at midday and two of 601 were shot down. Both pilots baled out.

Huns are putting up 109s in no mean manner now. Dust put a stop to any more Ops for the day.

We may get Spit 9s. Had the WingCo over to lunch and impressed upon him we were the right people. Been delving into 'bumph' all day—who would be a CO.

Once again 92 were providing a roaming top cover, to Spitfires of 1 SAAF Squadron, what they called a Suicide Four. Chisholm and Co were attacked by JG77, and it was Hauptmann Heinz Bär who shot down McMahon (who was flying ER646). It was Bär who also got one of 601's pilots, bringing his score to 166.

Saturday, 6 March 1943
Red Chisholm took 10 aircraft to Medenine for stand-by at dawn but was not there long. The Huns have started a push and the aerodrome was shelled necessitating another hasty withdrawal from the landing ground. Parties were ready to move up forward today but this looks like being cancelled.

Sunday, 7 March 1943
Intense operations continue. Led six of the boys on a patrol of the Medenine area at 18,000 ft. Spotted three 109s pass below us at a couple of thousand feet. Dived and caught same, who split up and then it was every man for himself. I closed on one and saw cannon shells exploding on the fuse-lage as he went up in a climbing turn. Another burst and the 109 seemed to lurch as if the pilot was hit. It went down in a slow spiral near Medenine.

On stand-by in the afternoon at Medenine. Scrambled for a raid and climbed up to about 20+ 109s. Engaged them and chased them to their target—7 SAAF's home at Noffatia. Closed behind one 109F, in the thick of our AA, to about 100 yards and saw his hood blow off, top of his tail shattered and lots of pieces of fuselage flew off. His machine caught fire and the pilot baled out.

Returned to land at Hazbut but we were shelled out again and had to return home. Squadron score 5 destroyed; Hunk and 'Chis' each got one.

Combat Report for 7 March (No.1)
Time: 0800, Nr Medenine

Leading a Sweep of six aircraft on patrol of forward troops, at 17,000 feet over Medenine, saw three Me109s flying east in line abreast at 15,000 feet five miles east of Squadron.

Squadron turned about and dived on the 109s. I closed on the port 109, and observed strikes on the fuselage as enemy aircraft turned; with second burst enemy aircraft seemed to lurch violently.

The aircraft went down in a wide spiral dive, as if the pilot was hit and crashed. The enemy aircraft did not explode on the ground.

Claim: 1 Me109F Destroyed.

Combat Report for 7 March (No.2)
Time: 1450 hrs, Nr Noffatia

I led four aircraft of a Scramble from Huzbub at 10,000 feet, and
engaged 5-plus Me109Fs above us. The enemy aircraft dived east
and I followed firing bursts at one 109 on which I observed strikes.
At 6,000 feet over Noffatia aerodrome I was engaged with
numerous 109s. I closed to 100 yards astern of enemy aircraft and
observed top of tail, hood and large pieces of fuselage disintegrate.
The enemy aircraft caught fire, and the pilot baled out.

Claim: 1 Me109F Destroyed.

In the first combat, Red Chisholm and Flight Sergeant 'Cash' Sails each
claimed a 109 probably destroyed, Hunk Humphreys a damaged.

In the second fight, Ted Sly claimed a probable and Flight Sergeant
H Paterson a damaged. These latter 109s appear to be more of SG2's
aircraft, Leutnant Heinz Schiedat baling out to become a prisoner.
However, II/JG51 had been in action, four 109s escorting bombers,
during which they reported meeting 20 Spitfires 25 miles south-west of
Medenine. They claimed two Spitfires but Feldwebel Heidenreich
baled out and later reached the German lines, while Leutnant Heinz
Föhl was lost. Thus Neville's victim might have been Heidenreich.

A possible candidate for Sly or Paterson was Leutnant Karl-Heinz
Krieger of 1/JG77, who crash landed his badly damaged Messerschmitt
109 at 1400 hours German time.

A feature of this combat was that it brought 92 Squadron's total
victories to the 250 mark, or to be precise, 254½ destroyed, 101 probables and 134 damaged. The day's score was 5-3-4, with Neville two
destroyed, Chisholm 1-1-1, Hunk one destroyed, Sly and Sails a
probable each, Flying Officer M Jowsey one damaged, Flight Sergeant
Paterson two damage. It also brought Neville's personal score to 19
according to 92 Squadron's records.

Monday, 8 March 1943

Very quiet after the storm of yesterday. Led a patrol of our
lines in the early morning but nothing doing. Hunk came
across what he thinks may have been FW190s on a patrol this
morning!

The Hun appears to be withdrawing now, thank God. A
few days like yesterday and I've had it in a big way.

The pilot of the 109 I shot down on 4 March and baled out,
came to see me this morning. He was very anxious to see who
had shot him down. He was 24, an NCO with the Iron Cross.

Seemed a pretty good type. Am trying to get my last victim along!

Neville took photos of 'his' German, one being taken as he stood in the cockpit of a Spitfire. The German, his right arm in a sling beneath his tunic, presented Neville with his flying badge, which he still has as a memento of their two meetings—one in the air, the other at 92's base airfield.

Neville's comment that he hoped to meet his most recent victim would not have been something 'higher authority' would have condoned in the light of events. The German NCO, fresh from his visit to 92 Squadron, managed to effect an escape! However, he was quickly picked up—still in his pyjamas.

Wednesday, 10 March 1943

Up before dawn and took off for Medenine. Escort to tank-buster Hurricanes to beat-up a Hun column which had knocked hell out of the Free French Forces. Led Squadron on a Scramble in the morning to 18,000 ft around base and dived down over Hun lines after some 109s, but got jumped by the flak!

Led Squadron on close cover to Kittys bombing and strafing Hun column. They made a good job of it too. Led Squadron in the evening to intercept Huns near this same column. Came across 109s in low cloud at 5,000 ft—diced around for a while but they all got away in cloud. Landed back at [Bu] Grara by the sea. This new 'drome is right on the sea shore. Just a flat salt flat which I don't trust much—the machines are sinking in a bit already. Pretty fresh and healthy here, which is a consolation.

Sunday, 14 March 1943

Things were quiet all morning. Replied to my friend Group Captain Atcherley, who wrote the other day congratulating me on my recent doings and also hinting at a DSO. Big time!

Boys up covering some Kittys and damn if they didn't run into some 109s, and without me. Simpson got one and Baker and Savage damaged one each. Good effort. 601 got a Macchi 202 this morning.

Grand news tonight, we are to get Spitfire IXs and to collect them from Algiers ourselves. Cheered the boys up no end. Strange that we were the first squadron to get Vbs in England—now first again.

Big feast tonight. Invited W/C Gleed, Major Moodie and some of his SAAF boys over. Had a wizard steak and lots to drink. S/L Harper came back from Cairo with a hang-over.

Wing Commander I R Gleed DSO DFC had taken over from Darwen as CO of 244 Wing on 31 January. He had seen considerable action with 87 Squadron in 1940, headed a detachment of his Squadron on the Isles of Scilly in 1941 and in 1942 had led the Ibsley Spitfire Wing. Major D D Moodie commanded No.1 SAAF Squadron. Harper had been CO of 453 RAAF Squadron at Singapore in late 1941, and 135 Squadron in India the following year. He had previously fought in the Battle of Britain with 17 Squadron.

Group Captain Richard Atcherley was one of the two Atcherley twins in the Royal Air Force (the other was David). Richard, or 'Batchy' as he was universally known, had been a member of the Schneider Trophy Team in the early 1930s. He had commanded Kenley Sector in England in 1942. His letter read:

Dear Duke,   211 Group, 9/Mar/43
Please accept this tardy letter of congratulations on behalf of your magnificent efforts during the recent operations. They will be immediately rewarded, as no doubt you must be aware.

The Hun seemed occasionally to put up quite a spirited show in the air and it will be increasingly important to show him, by examples like yours, that he is butting his head against a stone wall. The FW190's debut here went a bit flat as far as I can see—which is good news for us and bad news for him.

A bloody good show old boy and a bloody well deserved DSO—I hope to be able to let you know you have been awarded one very soon.

Yours sincerely,

R L R Atcherley.

Tuesday, 16 March 1943
Glendinning and friend arrived in their Cant 100, an Italian biplane like a Tiger, at lunchtime, so I flew the thing in the afternoon. Good fun.

Put on the usual line-shoot for a movie type who would insist on taking shots. Have at last got a new pair of pyjamas donated by Harpy. My old ones were consisting only of a collar holding two sleeves on.

Wednesday, 17 March 1943
Up awfully early and on stand-by later in the morning.

Scrambled and ran into about 20+ 109s over Mareth. Tony
Bruce and Hunk got a damaged but damned if I could get
near any. They would buzz off home or into cloud as soon as
you turned after them. Bags of very accurate ack-ack—how
I detest AA.

The 'battle' is due to start tomorrow—pretty tough going
probably too. Gave Red Chisholm a send off tonight. He
might get home to Canada if he is lucky. Incessant rumble of
guns all night.

Oddly, Neville does not mention the loss of Paul Brickhill in this action.
Brickhill's Spitfire was hit in the wing which exploded his ammunition
bay, forcing him to bale out and become a prisoner. He was shot down
by Leutnant Berres of JG77—the German's 35th victory. Brickhill used
his PoW time constructively, and was later to write three books on
prisoner of war escape stories. His *The Great Escape*, which was later
the basis for the equally famous film; *Escape to Danger* in 1946, and
Escape—Or Die in 1952. Another of his books which became a film was
The Dam Busters.

In the event, the 'battle' did not start on the morrow. In fact it was fairly
quiet for several days. 1 SAAF Squadron landed on the 20th following
a fight with some FW190s, having shot one down with three more as
probables. It was the first 190 shot down on this front.

Tuesday, 23 March 1943
Flew off to Algiers at dawn in a Hudson to collect some twelve
Spitfire IXs from Maison Blanche aerodrome. Very interesting trip—mountains, green fields, trees and farms. Hope to
have success with these 'niners' and finish my time soon. Then
get home!?

Neville flew EN147 back to Bu Grara via Gabes, but on the next sortie,
on the 24th, he was back in his usual Spitfire Vc—ER821 'R'.

Wednesday, 24 March 1943
Show with W/C Gleed leading, so was a bit hairy. Covered
Kittys and tank-busting Hurrys strafing lines north of the NZ
forces. Flak'd a lot but no 109s until on the way home when
they powered down behind us but didn't stay around; thank
goodness, 'cos I had my windscreen oiled up and the armour
plate headrest had come undone. Couldn't see a thing.

Thursday, 25 March 1943

Up at dawners and on an early show in the Spit IXs. Scrambled and gave top cover to the Squadron in our IXs at 25,000 ft, and very nice too. Patrolled over the New Zealanders uneventfully.

Second show I led the Squadron on patrol between Gabes and El Hamma at 20,000 ft. Patrolled without incident for a good while, and almost as we were turning for home saw a Ju88 in front and above us about 21,000 ft. Climbed and engaged him, and when he saw us he dived right down to ground level doing a good 380 to 400 mph. I got a good burst in before he drew away and hit his port engine and drew smoke which didn't seem to slow him any. He brought us right over his landing ground at nought feet so I broke the chaps off. I shouldn't think he has slowed down yet! The 88's gunner put some good shooting in on me. A bullet through the tyre, one thro' the airscrew, two thro' the leading edge.

Strafed some Italian trucks on the way as we crossed the coast road and caused no little panic and casualties. Show with the IXs in the evening with the Wing Leader but didn't see anything. Tony Bruce put a Spit IX on its back landing with engine trouble. Hunk takes over 'B' Flight!

Combat Report for 25 March
Time: 1100 hrs, 15 miles west of Gabes

I was leading 8 aircraft on patrol between Gabes and El Hamma at 20,000 feet when I observed one aircraft in front at 21,000 feet. I identified the aircraft as a Ju88 and climbed and closed to 300 yards. My approach was observed by enemy aircraft which dived away steeply going north.

The enemy aircraft dived at very high speed. With first burst I observed strikes on the port engine which threw out smoke. Accurate return fire from rear gunner in lower gun position.

The enemy aircraft dived over Tabaga at nought feet.

Claim: 1 Ju88 Damaged.

Oddly enough, No.244 Wing's Diary noted this Ju88 as 'destroyed'.

Everyone was beginning to realise there would be no retreat this time and that the Germans were not only on the run but would soon be pushed into a corner. The end seemed to be in sight.

CHAPTER IX

THE BATTLE FOR TUNISIA

For the men of the Desert Air Force, the final battles of North Africa were about to begin. After more than two years of see-saw actions back and forth across the desert of North Africa, Rommel's forces, along with their Italian allies, had finally been squeezed into the Tunisian peninsula. Attacked from the east by Montgomery and pushed from the west by the combined Anglo-American forces that had landed in Algiers in the previous November, the Germans now faced defeat.

Rather than contemplate any form of offensive action that might once more bring advances against the Allied forces, Rommel was now faced with a holding action, while seriously contemplating a wholesale evacuation of his men from Tunisia.

The island fortress of Malta, with its attacks on Rommel's sea lines of supply had finally brought the German forces to the brink of disaster. Without fuel, especially, his Panzers were powerless to strike or defend, while his aircraft were grounded and vulnerable to air assault upon their airfields. What supplies were coming in were mostly in transport aircraft, themselves highly vulnerable to air attack, both from Malta and from the DAF and USAAF fighters in and around the Tunisian ring.

Meanwhile, the DAF fighters were daily patrolling the air over Tunisia, harrying the retreating enemy, and combating whatever German aircraft were able to take off.

Friday, 26 March 1943
A busy day. Up at crack o'dawn and got in a show before brekker. I gave top Suicide Four cover in the Spit IXs to Hunk leading the Squadron. Nothing doing but a pleasant trip.

Just time to snatch very hasty brekker then on Readiness and another show before midday. Led the Suicide Four again with the IXs but uneventful, although we intercepted a [US P38] 'Lightning'.

No time for lunch as big push starts this noon so led another lone four over Matmata-Hamma, where the NZ forces are pushing thro' to Gabes. Big strafing do's by the Kittys and bombing by the Bostons, etc.

Saturday, 27 March 1943

On Readiness. The AOC 'phoned up whilst I was on Readiness and said he had a DSO for me! I'm certainly very pleased with it and I am sure it will buck the folks up a lot.

Squadron show covering Kittys strafing El Hamma-Gabes road. Gave the Squadron top cover in the Spit IXs—my usual job. Weather extremely thick and Squadron was a bit lost coming back after a long patrol. Sgt Symes could not make the 'drome by half a mile and had to crash-land. Brad Smith [F/O Bradley-Smith. Ed.] had a near one when a Breda shell scored a direct hit just behind his cockpit.

Army did a good show last night by pushing right through and are now on way to Gabes.

Sunday, 28 March 1943

Bad show yesterday evening when the boys were jumped by a 109 and Flight Sergeant 'Cash' Sails was shot down. One of our best types.

It cost me a lot in liquor last night to celebrate the 'gong'. Good party tho', and Jerry Westenra, who came over to indulge, got really hoggers and we had to put him to bed here.

The Army news is really good; the Huns are on the run from Mareth. Very bad visibility prevented some planned shows but 145's Poles and 601 got three Ju88s and a 109 around Sfax 'drome.

It was believed that Sails was shot down by JG77's Heinz Bär, who dived right through 92 in a lone attack, so typical of this top German ace who at this stage had well over 100 kills and would end the war with 220. However, another possibility was Oberleutnant Siegfried Freytag CO of II/JG77 who also claimed a Spitfire for his 90th victory. Or even Oberleutnant Dudeck of JG77 who gained his 4th victory with a Spitfire although he was himself shot down and baled out. Nobody appears to have claimed him.

Reference to the Poles in 145 Squadron concerns the Flight of Polish fighter pilots attached to the Squadron. Led by Stanislaw Skalski, they were called the 'Polish Fighting Team' and scored a number of successes while so attached.

Monday, 29 March 1943

Army news still good. Gabes is ours and types are pushing on for Sfax. Led a Flight Scramble this morning and intercepted some six 109s up the coast well north of Gabes. We were about 1,000 feet up-sun of them and were not seen until we attacked. I closed behind a 109G with a couple of cannons under his wings—fired a few bursts and saw strikes on his wing root and fuselage. He rolled over and straight down and I saw an aircraft exploding on the ground near a Hun Red Cross hospital. F/O T 'Doc' Savage also got a 109 and the pilot baled out.

Led a Suicide Four to Sfax to delouse for bombers with the rest of the Squadron. Weather right down and raining so had to turn back.

Combat Report for 29 March
Time: 1200 hrs, 25 miles north of Gabes

I was leading six aircraft on a patrol of the Gabes to Sfax road at 20,000 feet, when I observed six plus Me109s below, going south. I dived on one 109G and closed to about 300 yards astern. I fired six bursts and enemy aircraft took no evasive action although I observed strikes after nearly every burst on wing root and fuselage. The enemy aircraft eventually turned over and crashed on the ground near the coast road.

The enemy aircraft had blackish-green camouflage and two cannons under wings.

Claim: 1 Me109G Destroyed.

No.244 Wing recorded this as Neville's 20th victory.

Tuesday, 30 March 1943

Dawn stand-by and led a Flight Scramble after 3+ near El Hamma but no see. Patrolled up towards Mahares along the coast but no fun at 20,000 ft.

Suicide Four to Squadron in the afternoon and they ran into some Me210s and 109s near Cekira where we were escorting some Kittys to. I was at 25,000 and chased odd 109s, and because my R/T was not working I did not get into the mêlée below, not knowing it was going on! Peeved, but Hunk got a 210 damaged and Ted Sly a 109 probable.

Wednesday, 31 March 1943

Another Suicide Four job when the Squadron went to Sfax to delouse for Mitchells bombing El Maou aerodrome just outside Sfax itself. Nothing seen. A couple of Warhawks of the USAAF had a shot at one of our Spitfire IXs but missed it!

Only one trip for me today. Must get about 40 hours next month then I can bind to get home, although at times I wonder if I really do want to go home. Strange, but true.

Friday, 2 April 1943

Led Flight on patrol of El Noual and Mahares area at 19,000 ft but nothing seen except 601 who we finally intercepted after considerable vectoring about the sky.

Squadron on cover patrol in El Noual area for Kittys. Flew Spit IX on a Suicide Four cover patrol but nothing seen. Followed home when short of petrol by some 109s. Three of which the Poles intercepted and shot down.

In fact these 109s—from I/JG77—had been after Warhawks of the 87th US Squadron, whom the Poles were escorting. Skalski, Flight Lieutenant Eugeniusz Horbaczewski and Flight Sergeant Machowiak shot down three, Flying Officer Bohdan Arct damaging another. The 109s shot down one Warhawk and the Americans claimed one in return.

The Luftwaffe and Regia Aeronautica, who had been pretty aggressive of late, were now well and truly on the defensive as the RAF and USAAF units increased. The area of operations was now dwindling for the Axis forces. The next drive was about to begin, known as the advance on the Wadi Akarit Line.

Tuesday, 6 April 1943

The battle for the Tebaga mountains started in the early hours of this morning, and by breakfast time the 51st Division had reached its objective. Although the 50th Division and the Indian Division were having some trouble, all their objectives were taken during the day. The battle continues.

A standing patrol over our troops all morning but it brought forth no fun, although two 109s passed through the CO's formation. A Sweep in the Cekira area in the afternoon covering Kittys; jumped the odd Kitty, but no enemy aircraft. Another Sweep of same area in a Spit IX later in the afternoon covering light bombers and Kittys but still no EA although the WingCo leading our Spit Vs was accosted by some 109s when short of petrol.

Wednesday, 7 April 1943

Dawn trip when we covered a Walrus between Gabes and the Isle of Kneisse looking for bods in the sea. Some Huns about but they did not bother us luckily.

Two more trips for me during the day brought forth no action, although in the evening patrol with six Spit Vs at 8,000 ft or so, a Macchi 202 came whistling down past us with glycol pouring out. An offering from a fight going on above.

Kittys strafing and Mitchells and Bostons coming all day into the Cekira-Mahares area.

Thursday, 8 April 1943

Two patrols today, one in the morning in the Sfax-Mahares area—Kittys still strafing and Mitchells still bombing. Late evening patrol of the IXs during which sixteen squadrons of Kittys(!) were busy strafing—landed back at dusk. Sgt Ives was wounded this morning, Hunk's patrol being jumped by 9+ out of the sun.

Friday, 9 April 1943

Bad weather today. Luck to lead a show in the morning to Sfax when Kittys were to bomb a ship in the harbour. Patrolled Sfax town and saw Kittys attempt to bomb an 8 to 10,000 ton ship off the harbour. Bombs fell nowhere near! The town looks very deserted. Our army types are doing a good job and should be in Sfax any time now.

In fact the ground forces went past Sfax the next day. The recent Kittyhawk ground attacks had mainly been upon concentrations of German troops in the Fondouk Pass area. The Welsh Guards attacked Djebel Rohrab on the 9th, but the brigade suffered heavy casualties in the Pass before clearing it. Once through the Pass, the Allied forces moved forward on to the northern plains, but left 39 destroyed tanks in the process.

While all this was going on, German transport aircraft were continuing to deliver fuel, arms and ammunition on the northern coast, around Cap Bon, then evacuating the wounded, despite enormous losses to roaming Allied fighters.

Sunday, 11 April 1943

Probably moving off today to [La] Fauconnerie, west of Sfax. Wing Commander Gleed came to lunch and I heard the first talk of going home when he asked me what I wanted to do after this campaign. Said I should like to go home for a spell and he said that was what he thought and that he would put it up, with every chance of success. Home by July?

Squadron moved off late afternoon for Fauconnerie and found the place after some trouble—a railway line which we attempted to follow on the map, being in reality non-existent! This is an ex-Hun 'drome with a few pranged 190s and 109s around.

Monday, 12 April 1943
Dawn Readiness and later stand-by, which nearly killed half of us, it was so hot in the cockpit. Took my faithful 'R' up for a look around Sfax and the Isle of Kenkeune in the afternoon. Our troops now past Sousse and looks very easy now to 'squeeze the pus from North Africa'.

Tuesday, 13 April 1943
Lazy day—up late and over to attend a conference at Wing. The gen is to re-equip this Wing [totally] with Spitfire IXs for the next European campaign. The Wing will go back to Bu Grara to rest for a month, types having leave and then on to the next theatre of war.

More confirmation of my going home by the WingCo! This may be over now in less than two months. Spend my leave in Kent!! Probably moving again today, up near Sousse.

Wednesday, 14 April 1943
Good trip to the other side today when I took two types—Baker and Sly—to collect three Spit IXs from Montesquieu, south of Bone. A Hudson picked us up and we had this all to ourselves. Very low cloud and bad vis around Montesquieu. Very tense trip when we started wandering about amongst the mountains in cloud. Had to land at Bone to wait for weather to lift. Had a chat with 242 Squadron types who were there. They seem to do themselves pretty well on that side. 40 bottles of whisky and 18 of gin is their issue ration for a month!

Beautiful country around Montesquieu, where we eventually arrived and picked up our Spitfires. Nice place but how disorganised they are.

Thursday, 15 April 1943
Moved to another 'drome 15 miles south of Sousse this morning [Bou Goubrine Main]. Green grass, flowers, birds—

wizard country here after the desert. Two 'dromes, almost joining. We share one with 145; 601, 1 SAAF and 417 share the other.

Friday, 16 April 1943

Readiness this morning after breakfast and our Spit Vs got off on a flip but I was left on the ground in the IXs. Lot of chaps off to Sousse to see the form.

Big stuff this afternoon and the biggest fright of my life. Wing Commander Gleed led some Spit Vs of 145 and three Spit IXs of 145 with myself with three Spit IXs as top cover, to Cap Bon to clobber a Hun standing patrol.

When we were over the Cape, I saw a large number of transport aircraft low down and I called the WingCo and went down. They were Savoia 82s, large three-engined jobs—about 18 of them. The first one I attacked I was going so fast I couldn't get more than a short burst in. I attacked another after throttling right back and let him have everything, and closing right up, just skimmed over the top of him having seen my shells explode on him. He flew into the sea with a terrific splash and I had a fleeting vision of pieces of cowling etc., flying up with a sheet of spray.

I attacked another, scoring hits from astern and he also went into the sea but more or less made a landing on the water. As I was about to attack a third, I was attacked from astern by a FW190 and had to turn and dodge him. He was joined by several more 190s and 109s and I really thought this was it, as I chased above the deck, twisting and turning as they attacked. I finally got away by a terrific climb.

A flight sergeant of 145 Squadron was shot down and baled out OK. Sad to say, Wing Commander Gleed has not returned—probably had my experience, of a lot of Huns round him—last heard calling for help.

Combat Report for 16 April
Time: 1430 hrs, Tunis, Square K.66

I was leading Black Section at 20,000 feet covering 145 Squadron on a Sweep of Cap Bon area. I observed many large aircraft flying low just crossing the coast in Square K.66, heading for Tunis.

I dived down with Section and attacked aircraft from astern, but owing to high speed only fired a short burst before overshooting target. I closed behind another and having passed several aircraft by this time, identified them as SM82s. I fired a very long burst and saw strikes in the fuselage and front engine. This aircraft hit the sea at flying speed and as I passed over saw the machine breaking up and cowlings etc., flying off.

I attacked another SM 82 from dead astern, again firing very long burst. I observed cannon shells explode in the port wing root and the aircraft, which was flying very low, struck the sea. As I was about to attack another SM 82, I was attacked by a mixed formation of FW190s and Me109s, which I evaded by climbing away after a long chase at ground level. I was able to evade the FW190s' attacks by turns which the 190s would not follow me in.

The 190s had outboard cannons fitted. Some considerable return fire from SM82s. I observed at least five or six SM82s down in the sea. Saw a Spitfire shot down and pilot bale out early in the engagement. My first SM82 went down in Square K.57, the second in Square K.47.

Claim: 2 SM82s Destroyed.

The formation—in fact 13 SM82s—were en route from Sciacca to Tunis. In all four crashed into the sea and three others ditched, their crews being picked up by an Italian motor torpedo boat. The escort consisted of four Macchi 202s, and 15 fighters of JG77 on a freelance patrol of the area.

In addition to Neville's two kills, 145's Flying Officer Laing-Meason claimed one, Flight Sergeant Anderson another; Neville's wingmen, Flying Officer Doc Savage and Pilot Officer G Wilson got two and one respectively.

When Neville first spotted the transports and reported them to Gleed, the WingCo was unable to see them himself, and so ordered Duke to lead the attack. With the others then following, it left the Wing Commander exposed to attack from above, and they were indeed bounced by German fighters.

Leutnant Ernst-Wilhelm Reinert of II Gruppe claimed to have shot down a Spitfire at 1544 hours, and Leutnant Heinz-Edgar Berres of I Gruppe, a second at 1548. Heinz Bär also claimed a Spitfire although there is no time recorded. It seems pretty certain that Gleed and his wingman—Sergeant J K Rostant—were shot down by the former two, Reinert noting his victim as a Mustang. As Gleed was flying a clipped-wing Spitfire Vb, this may well have confused the attacking German.

Neville saw Rostant bale out. Exactly what happened to Gleed is not certain. Some time later his Spitfire was found on the Tunisian coast, some 50 yards from the sea. It had seemingly bellied in, suggesting Gleed—probably wounded—had at least got down in some sort of order. What happened next is not known. There was a torn piece of

RAF serge a short distance away but that was all. Was he found dead or dying by Germans or locals? We shall probably never know.

Recalling this action some time later, Neville wondered if in fact it had been Gleed who had called for help. Neville himself called for assistance when pressed closely by the Focke Wulfs, seeing other Spitfires withdrawing from the general area, but does not now remember hearing any similar calls.

Squadron Leader Pete Olver DFC took over 244 Wing.

Saturday, 17 April 1943

Taking the day off today and getting over yesterday's fright. Went out again yesterday evening on the same job but saw nothing; I was rather glad.

Sunday, 18 April 1943

Up at dawn and Squadron on stand-by. Later took off, myself in the Spit IXs, as cover to Kittys of 7 SAAF Wing going on another Ju52 Sweep in the Cap Bon area. Kittys turned up late and kept us circling for ten minutes and then went on the Sweep at about 180 mph, which left us hanging on hooks up at 18,000 ft, the IXs doing about 160 to 170 indicated!

Then went out between the Cape and Pantellaria, then down to Tunis which I thought was nothing hair-raising. Didn't see anything and only a couple of bursts of AA directed at us, although we flew well near Tunis itself.

Enormous do in the evening when I led the Squadron as cover to four US Kitty squadrons on a Cap Bon Sweep. They engaged large numbers of Ju52s near Cap Bon and claim to have destroyed 58 and 14 Me109s!!

It was one of the most amazing sights I have seen in this war; 48 Kittys attacking this enormous gaggle of transports right on the deck. A 52 would start to glow then become a ball of fire and, still a mass of flame, would continue a little further across the sea trying to make land and then crash or blow up. This happened a dozen times, in the last light of dusk—these burning aircraft showing up for miles. Some make the coast and crash-land but not many. Poor devils. 73 Squadron went out at night and strafed some on the beach.

Initially the Americans claimed over 110 aircraft destroyed with another 11 probables and more than 50 damaged—including several enemy aircraft types that were not even involved! However, there were many duplications of claims and it was later reduced to 59 sure kills over transports and 14 fighters—109s and Mc202s, plus a couple of Me110s.

TRIPOLITANIA—S. TUNISIA

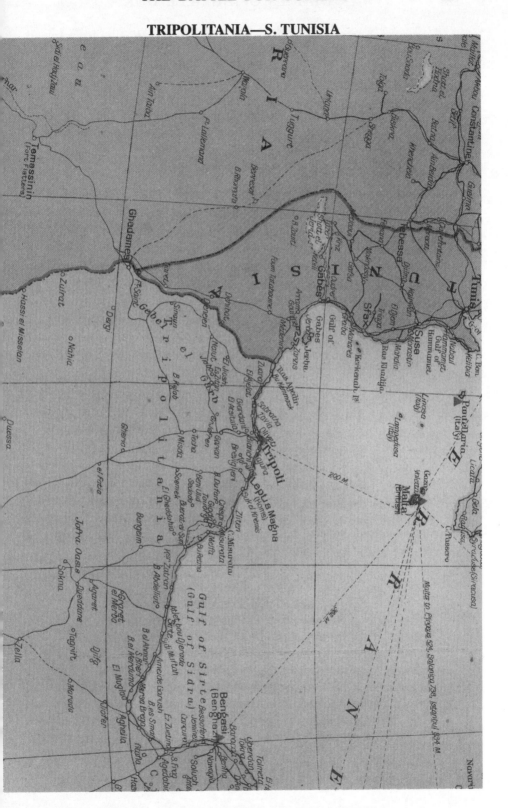

Monday, 19 April 1943

Same job again covering the Kittys in Cap Bon area. Led cover to 7 SAAF Wing but no joy. This morning 7 SAAF Wing shot down 15 out of 15 Ju52s! They lost one pilot. Last night the Yanks lost six pilots—I saw two go into the sea.

Our Wing has also had [recent] losses: W/C Gleed, 145 have lost two or three, the Poles one, 601 two or three, 1 SAAF lost one. We have, so far, lost nobody. 417 this afternoon lost five pilots when jumped by 24 Huns.

Tuesday, 20 April 1943

Led the Squadron on early morning escort to 7 SAAF Kitty Wing in the Cap Bon area. Uneventful until Kittys chased a Hun along the sea and I think got him. I then saw two large white three-engined seaplanes (Cants?) and went down to mix it, only to find they were hospital aircraft. The top cover of Spit IXs then jumped three Macchi 202s and Ted Sly shot one down and Sgt Askey another.

The push to Tunis starts again. The army is only advancing a short distance this time I understand.

Wing Sweep Cap Bon-Pantellaria with four Spit squadrons. 12+ Mc202s appeared. The Poles jumped them and our Spit IXs got stuck in as well. The Poles got six. I climbed with three of 'em up to 19,000 ft from 8,000 and followed one down in a 440+ mph dive, but couldn't catch it. Very brassed.

The seaplanes were Cant Z506Bs with Red Cross markings, escorted by six Macchis, in the Korba area. Later they were engaged by some P40s and landed on the water, but took off again—with a reduced escort—when the fight above them ended.

Thursday, 22 April 1943

Another big transport day. Having received prior warning of transports coming across from Sicily this morning early— some type with a transmitter?—the whole Wing was up at 7-minute intervals and each squadron escorted three Kitty squadrons. 1 SAAF Squadron got amongst some Me323 powered glider jobs and destroyed six of them and some 109s. The Poles got some 109s and 7 SAAF Kitty Wing got about 23 Me323s. Big time. We didn't see a thing!

Friday, 23 April 1943
(Good Friday)

Day dawned hot and clear in the sky. Squadron covering Baltimores bombing the other side of Enfidaville—uneventful. Escorted bombers and Kittys back and then returned and swept up to Tunis. Late evening show with three Kitty squadrons on a Cap Bon expedition but nothing came of it.

Gubby Allen returned from Cairo with a truck load of grog and goodies—the relief of Goubrine. An official war artist type came along after dinner to 'draw' me.

Saturday, 24 April 1943

Only flew once on a Scramble. Hunk and self were at Wing Ops when Group 'phoned through for a pair of Spit IXs to go off on a shufti kite interception. We Scrambled! Patrolled around Sousse at 19,000 feet but no see.

Paid a visit to Monastir in the afternoon where we bartered tea. The idea is we buy tea at ten shillings per pound and the wogs pay at least £4 per pound!!

Pissy in the Mess in the evening when Jerry Westenra came over. Finished up by types throwing lemons around and odd fights going on. My head was nearly pulled off. Fried eggs and sausages in Ted's tent afterwards.

Sunday, 25 April 1943

Escort to some Kittys on another Cap Bon expedition but saw nothing. P/O Probert was hit by flak as we crossed the Cape and turned back and had to bale out off the coast at Korba. After lunch we escorted a Walrus out to pick him up and found him OK about six miles off the Hun coast.

R H Probert, in a Spitfire IX (EN458), was hit by flak from the Rass-El-Fortass area and he took to his parachute ten miles east of Korba, being seen safe and sound in his dinghy. He spent the next two and a quarter hours paddling around until a Walrus of 294 Squadron picked him up. His main complaint was centred around the fact that he had lost one of his shoes, a pair he had purchased only the previous day.

Monday, 26 April 1943

Took off by myself on a shipping and weather recco in the Tunis area. Would not take other types as the weather was very bad at dawn. Vis only a few yards on the ground—my first instrument take-off since FTS.

Tuesday, 27 April 1943

Pretty cloudy so only did one show. Led four IXs on a patrol round Soliman area. Split into pairs and rushed around in between ack-ack bursts. We had four machines hit by flak today; this flak is not funny at all.

Thursday, 29 April 1943

Covered some Kittys in morning bombing four lighters in the Gulf of Tunis. No hits. Later in the day the boys ran into some 109s and Macchis. Topsy Turvey got a 109 and Sachs damaged one.

Friday, 30 April 1943

Two shows today, leading the IXs on a delouse in Cap Bon to the Gulf of Tunis area, covering Kittys bombing a destroyer. Nothing doing but later on in the day, types ran into some Macchi 202s and diced around in the cloud which has been about the last few days. They got two damaged— Brad Smith and Sachs.

Received Major General Lam and Major Kwang of the Chinese Air Force this afternoon. I showed them the Spit IX—gave them all the secrets! I have been invited to China!!

Saturday, 1 May 1943

Had an early delouse sweep in the Gulf of Tunis covering Kittys bombing landing jetties. Another delouse in afternoon but nothing doing. Sgt Inchcombe on another patrol, developed a glycol leak and apparently tried to bale out over our lines but his 'chute failed to open.

Learn today the 1st Army is having trouble so 8th Army is reinforcing them. Looks as tho' this will continue for some time. Several people are trying to persuade me to bung in my hand and get out of this. I don't want it thought I am running off but I could do with a spell in England.

Wednesday, 5 May 1943

Final push postponed until tomorrow. Big news—looks like I am on my way home! Hunk is now S/L and taking over 92, vice S/L Harper, and Ted Sly is taking his Flight. My marching orders are liable to appear any time and they are trying to ground me. But they won't!

Thursday, 6 May 1943

Another dawn weather recco in the Tunis-Mateur area over

the plain, down which the 1st Army is driving for Tunis as from this morning. Big artillery barrage from Mateur area.

Moving to Hergla today. Our dispersal is very near the sea and I had a great swim in the afternoon.

Friday, 7 May 1943

Readiness until 9.30 when we went off to cover numerous squadrons of Kittys up to the Gulf and Cap Bon. I led the IXs and rushed around in the cloud but didn't see anything. 1st and 8th Armies are doing a wizard job. They have broken thro' the plain and are now only 6 to 8 miles from Tunis itself.

Another show with nine Mitchells but cloud very bad. Lost bombers and swept Cap Bon with the four IXs. Chased a Macchi into cloud and shot at a 109 which came whistling out of cloud head-on.

Saturday, 8 May 1943

Tunis and Bizerta are ours at last. Army doing wonders and street fighting was taking place in Tunis yesterday. Lots of Huns cut off in Bizerta region.

The aerodrome at Hergla bogged by rain last night. CO flew off back to Goubrine to operate from there. Led the IXs on a bomber raid on Pantellaria in which 120 or so medium bombers took part.

Sun bathed in the afternoon and then led the IXs again on a Sweep in the Gulf-Cap Bon area. Did a roll over Tunis! Lots of Kittys and Mitchells from 1st and 8th Armies bombing the Cape area. Getting quite a few flying hours in, considering I am now 'grounded' as OTE. [tour expired]

Sunday, 9 May 1943

Weather and shipping recco off Cap Bon-Pantellaria area. A ship was blazing off Cap Bon and saw several destroyers in the Gulf and between Pantellaria and the Cape. The Hun must be feeling a bit brassed but one must admire the 109 boys who are operating from Korba on the Cape. Their's is a tough job considering there are almost constant [Allied] sweeps of 40 to 50 aircraft nearly all day.

Tuesday, 11 May 1943

It's nearly the end now. Bizerta is ours, Tunis is ours, our armoured columns have taken Soliman and Grombalia and this morning troops entered Hammamet and Korba, thus cutting off the Cape and isolating the 20,000 Hun and Eyetie troops in the Enfidaville area. From here, only nine miles away, we hear the continual pitiful thunder of their guns as they still fight on—they must realise they are trapped.

Somehow I feel sorry it is over. It's been a long and pretty hard drive but full of changes and excitement. From Tunis comes the news that already there are over 50,000 prisoners from the Bizerta area and they still pour in. I am proud to have stayed on until the end and seen this final great victory for us. Eighteen months almost to the day when I arrived out here and then the weeks and months of desert fighting followed by defeat and retreat to Egypt. A period of rest in the Delta and then joining in the push for Tripoli and finally this drive for Tunis and so the whole of North Africa.

I shall probably be going home now but the memory of these days will be in my mind for all time. I shall remember the combats, the sand, people who have died, people still going on—I'll remember it all.

This morning we escorted 12 Kittyhawks up to Menzel Tmimi to bomb the road. Two of our MTBs were engaging two German E-boats or some such, off Kelibia. It presented quite a spectacle; the German vessels were boarded.

This afternoon, on the last show around Cap Bon that the Spits were to do in this campaign, I got my 200 [operational] hours in my second Ops Tour and am now grounded as far as flying operationally is concerned. It was after the Kittys had bombed near Cap Bon that the controller called up on the R/T recalling all aircraft and saying 'Return to base—the show's over.' Stirring words. Cap Bon is ours and now the whole of North Africa. But in spite of this the enemy is still gallantly holding the hills north of us, although he is completely cut off and shelled continuously. He can't last long. Prisoners to date are more than 118,000.

Thursday, 13 May 1943
This morning all armed resistance ended when the German 90th Light and the Italian Young Fascists hoisted the white flag in unconditional surrender on the Enfidaville front. What do we do now?

Ted Sly off to Tunis in a lorry to collect loot. Hunk off to Malta with Group Captain Darwen. I spend all day on the beach and am burned red.

Saturday, 15 May 1943
S/L Harper left us today to go to Middle East HQ. Suppose

I shall be next to go. Went over to 145 Squadron to see Lance Wade and his team this evening along with Hunk, Ted Sly and Ken Simpson.[1]

Our looting parties did quite well: we have two saloon cars and a Fiat runabout, several motorbikes and odd guns etc., but no Lugers.

Thursday, 20 May 1943

My papers came thro' this morning, recommended by the AOC to return to the UK! Only remains to get by the stooges at MEHQ.

---

[1] Squadron Leader Lance Wade DFC and Bar, an American from Texas commanding 145 Squadron, having earlier fought with 33 Squadron in the Western Desert in 1941-2. He had around 20 victories by this time and was the highest scoring US pilot to serve wholly with the RAF in WW2. He was killed in a flying accident in January 1944 having received the DSO.

CHAPTER X

CHIEF FLYING INSTRUCTOR

With the war in Tunisia and North Africa now ended, Neville was even more hopeful of getting back to England. And why not? First, however, he had the wrench of leaving 92 Squadron and the twin task of getting back to Cairo and finally to get someone to agree to him going home.

For several days, he swam and sun bathed, and had the occasional drink with friends in other units. He managed to fix up a flight in a Lockheed from Castel Benito for 1 June, so during the final days of May, he pottered about, had the odd flight to keep his hand in, and continued the life of leisure. Then he found that all Cairo flights were booked by senior personnel, being refused to fly a Spitfire there and almost daily had to check if there were any spare seats in almost any available aeroplane.

The first day of June was his last day with 92. He was virtually the last survivor from the old days, Ted Sly having already gone on leave to Alexandria and Hunk was on a course in Cairo.

Tuesday, 1 June 1943

Left 92 Squadron this afternoon along with Doc Woolgrove. [Doc was 92 Squadron's medical officer and had been since Biggin/Digby days.] Extremely sorry to leave—92 meant a lot to me and I half wish I was staying behind as CO, but this is my one chance to go home with the excellent recommendation from Broadhurst, the WingCo, and S/L Harper—everybody says I am as good as there. Even the C-in-C Middle East, Sholto Douglas, said I would most likely go home when I taxed him with it the other day.

Unable to get aboard an RAF aircraft, so went along to the Americans and can probably get a lift down on a Douglas tomorrow morning.

Wednesday, 2 June 1943

Got a lift down all right on a freight plane with two aero engines inside with me. Landed at Benina on the way. Arrived in Cairo about tea-time and took over the room which Hunk had booked for me in Shepherd's. Cleaned up and tore along to Middle East HQ with my papers but they couldn't tell me anything this evening; will hear tomorrow.

Thursday, 3 June 1943

Rushed around to MEHQ this morning and was sent along to W/C Ayst. His first words were that nobody was going home. I explained I thought this a mistake and after a bit of binding he said he would see Sholto Douglas and I was to come back this evening. I went away knowing that this evening I should know I was on my way to England. I went out to Ghezira where I swam and had lunch with Ted Sly and Hunk, plus several other types. [Anyone with any knowledge of the top brass, of promises, not to mention the true drama of a good story will not be surprised to learn that when Neville returned to MEHQ . . .] Arriving back at MEHQ again, I was informed I was NOT returning to England. Imagine my horror and disappointment after months of waiting and fighting. It was the thought of going home at the end of my tour which made me fight harder. To hear in a few words all my hopes smashed. The C-in-C had recommended me for a staff job as Squadron Leader. How could I sit at a desk all day? I argued and argued to no effect, except to get off the staff job. Then Ballah was suggested to me—God above!

Neville was understandably upset and bitter. Here he was, the top scoring fighter pilot of the desert air war, with the DSO, DFC and Bar, having been promised a home posting after 19 months in the Middle East being messed about, with not even a clear idea of what he was to do; even the 'brass' did not know—or would not say. All they told him was that he wasn't being allowed home. Understandably too, the next few days of his diary are blank!

Finally, on 9 June came a posting to No.73 Operational Training Unit at Abu Sueir, situated about ten miles due west of Ismailia. This is just on 60 miles to the north-east of Cairo, and ten miles north of the Great Bitter Lake, while to the north runs the Suez Canal, up to Port Said. With such landmarks it was difficult for the students to get themselves too lost!

Resigned to his inglorious fate, Neville packed his bags.

Friday, 11 June 1943

Caught the 11 o'clock train for Abu Sueir, arriving about 2 without incident. Quite a nice station I must admit. Very nice Mess and good living quarters; shower and baths, good food and drink. Met a lot of people who were up in the desert before. Most of them are binding to leave now. All very sympathetic and can't understand why I have not gone home. Who can?

Saturday, 12 June 1943

Interview with W/C Hudson, the WingCo Flying. To my horror I am taking over a Tomahawk Flight. Hell—what have I done to deserve this? I understand, however, that I shall probably go over to Spits when a relief comes, in about a fortnight. May even become Squadron Leader CFI, in place of S/L Woods who should be leaving.

Flew a Spit around this morning and looked over Ballah, etc! Terrific party at Ismailia RAF Station tonight—a really good binge. Drove over to 106 Hospital with 'Windy' Smith, ex-army liaison officer of the Spitfire Wing, who I share a room with, and collected numerous nurses. Met lots of types at Ish, including Sammy Samouelle, ex-92, Biggin Hill. Ended up by taking a nurse home in the back of the Group Captain's car at 3 am.

The form at Abu Sueir was that nobody worked on Sundays, and during the week, flying occurred between 5.30 am and 1 pm, when the rest of the day was free. By 16 June, Neville had been told by the Station Commander, Group Captain W A J Satchell DSO, that if he coped alright, he would indeed be made Chief Flying Instructor of the Spitfire section, and in any event was to take over A Flight (Spitfires) from this date, which was something. Satchell had been in the Battle of Britain, and in 1941, Wing Commander and Station Commander at Takali, Malta, having seen much action despite his 35 years.

Life became a little more tolerable, for with the Great Bitter Lake and Lake Timsah nearby, sailing and swimming took up much of Neville's spare time. Sailing, in fact, has remained a much-loved sport with him ever since. There were a number of pals about too, to sail, swim and drink with: Timber Woods DFC, who'd also been on Malta, and Geoff Garton DFC, who had been in France and the Battle of Britain before serving with 250 and 112 Squadrons in the desert. Alan Boyle was another, along with Mike Le Bas, both having been on Malta with 601 Squadron.

Tuesday, 29 June 1943

Rushing along on a cross-country to Almaza and Zifta—
foxed the pupil by cutting the throttle a couple of times! I am
to take over the job of CFI next week when Timber Woods
is away. I shall be more or less on trial to see whether I should
have the job when Timber goes back on Ops.

Neville began to get into a routine; so routine in fact that he once more
began to neglect his diary, unless something of extra interest occurred,
such as . . .

Saturday, 3 July 1943

Usual day—afraid I neglect this diary nowadays as there is
very little to write about—nothing to shoot down. Quite a
good night tonight when we gave a drinking dance and got
lots of popsies from the hospitals. I brought six nurses along
and distributed them around. Had to take 'em back too, at
2.30 am! A goodly night.

Neville acquired a new friend in the shape of a half-dead kitten he found
in a wood pile; he named it 'Quoise', and soon had it taking milk, then
milk and bread, then milk and fishcakes! Quoise was the RAF form of
Arabic, said or understood to mean nice or lovely (eg: 'shifti quoise
bint' ie: 'look at that lovely piece of crumpet!' or 'mish quoise'—'no
bloody good!').[1]
   In mid-July came the news that Brian Kingcome had become Group
Captain with 244 Fighter Wing. Neville cursed again at not staying on
at the sharp end.

Wednesday, 28 July 1943

My days seem quite full now. Getting up early and lots of
flights and I usually go swimming at Ferry Point or the US
Club, or else I stay in my room and read and sleep. Wander
over to the Mess about 7 pm when its cool and drink under
the trees outside.
   Two fatal accidents this past week, and dozens of minor
prangs, mostly Tommys ground-looping. Sgt Clarke spun in
in a Spit and crashed near the hangars into the church. He
went up in flames. Sgt Randell spun in from 10,000 feet in a
Kitty during a dog-fight with a Spit.
   Timber Woods left today, leaving me to take over as CFI.

---

[1] The correct Arabic spelling is kwayyis for good/lovely, and 'mish kwayyis' for the
other.

Several training courses passed through 73 OTU during Neville's spell there. It was his job to test the trainees on Harvards before letting them loose on either the Kittyhawk or Spifire. In July came the news that 239 Kittyhawk Wing was to be re-equipped with clipped-wing Spitfire fighter-bombers, so that 73 OTU would soon go over totally to Spitfires. Meantime, spare time was spent swimming and sailing, with the occasional bit of news or rumour of old pals.

Monday, 2 August 1943

Rumours coming to the fore again. W/C Olver has been shot down by an 88. F/L Doc Savage also shot down by an 88 on same show. Doc is buried in Sicily. F/L Taylor, 601, shot down by Ju87. Force-landed in Sicily. They say the Eyeties killed him then set fire to him in his aircraft.

Peter Olver DFC and bar, who had seen action in the UK and in the Western Desert, was operating with 244 Wing, often flying with 92 Squadron when flying as Wing Leader. He became a prisoner. Doc Savage had been in 92 with Nev. John Taylor DFC and Bar, had flown with 145 Squadron in 1942-43, then commanded 601 Squadron. Flying from Malta during the invasion of Sicily he had just shot down a Stuka but was then hit by ground fire and crashed as he tried to glide down for a landing.

A few days later, Wing Commander Grant from 203 Group visited the OTU and showed surprise that the CFI was not wearing squadron leader's stripes. Apparently Neville had been promoted to this rank from 26 July. Despite this nice bit of news, Neville was starting to get itchy feet again, starting to get brassed off with everything, and wishing he could be back on Ops. However, he knew perfectly well from experience that it was difficult to make the change until he had done his six month stint. As he confided to his diary...

Thursday, 5 August 1943

Still brassed with everybody. Don't like the atmosphere here much. About the only place I am meant for is a fighter squadron on Ops and that's about the only place I want to be, so there!

Days and weeks passed.

Saturday, 21 August 1943

We have three Spit Flights now and only two Kitty Flights, so I shall be pretty busy in future. I heard from Hunk last night—a good letter. Tony Bruce is back with them, a good show I think. They are not doing much now the show is over in Sicily.

Squadron Leader Taylor was shot down and had to force land. He hit some telephone wires and got burnt. The commandos had to shoot him. A new Course of pupils came in today.

Monday, 30 August 1943

A fatal accident today. Capt S----, one of our pupils, collided with a Hurricane in a dog-fight. The Hurricane chappie baled out but poor S. went down with his aircraft, although it looks as though he did try to get out but left it too late. The Harvard caught fire when it hit the ground and they saw him hanging out of the cockpit burning, minus his head and his stomach all over the place. Nasty business. He was very experienced with 2,000 hours.

Friday, 3 September 1943

Grand news today—our troops, British and Canadian, have landed on the Italian mainland. The boys will be busy again.

Tested a new Spitfire [Vc] today, one we brought up from Helwan. Pretty nice and I am making it my own! Must get a white spinner and white wingtips painted on as usual!! Thrashing the air with pupils again on the dreaded CFI's test.

Saw Bill and Ronnie off to the Union [South Africa] at lunch time with the odd drink. These SAAF types get me a bit. They do 150 hours on Ops and then off to the Union; as far as they are concerned they have done their bit and the war's over.

Played squash with Geoff Garton this afternoon. Drank a little in the evening. Been here three months now.

Thursday, 9 September 1943

Big news last night—Italy has packed in; shame of it. It makes me curse myself all the more for leaving the Squadron. Think what times they'll have now! I suppose next thing will be Burma. I hope not. I am going to sit here quietly for the next three months and watch developments. Events in the next few months should be interesting—very.

If Neville or any of the others thought that Italy's surrender meant an end in the Middle East, they did not reckon on the Germans. They and some Fascist units continued to fight strongly against the Allied armies struggling up the Italian 'boot', and would do so for the rest of the war. A slight bit of irony came along on a trip to Cairo.

Sunday, 12 September 1943

Went along to Canada House with Gerry Wright to see Jowsey and Probert, just down from 92, but they had left for Alex. There is no room for them in this country at OTUs so they are going to England!!

Milton Jowsey DFC, from Ottawa, was RCAF and was posted to the UK to join 234 Squadron in 1942, then came out to the Middle East and to 33 Squadron. Gaining his DFC and becoming tour expired he went back to the UK and in 1944 joined 442 RCAF Squadron, which he later commanded, adding a Bar to his DFC. He was shot down in February 1945 and ended the war as a prisoner. Rex Probert RCAF, of course, had been in 92 with Neville and had featured in the Air Sea Rescue drama of 25 April 1943, Neville leading the Sweep in which he was brought down by ground fire. He later received the DFC too.

Monday, 13 September 1943

Usual panic this morning getting the new Course sorted out. It looks as though Group Captain Satchell will be posted any moment now. They have found a relief for him. The next G/C will probably not be so 'operationally minded' as old Satch.[1] Did a spot of night flying in brilliant moonlight; so clear you can hardly call it night flying.

Tuesday, 14 September 1943

'Bound' the new Course again before breakfast. Told them how lucky they were and how not to mind at being here for six weeks—I'm here for six months, I says!

Tested another pupil—a bone-headed South African—in the heat of the day and nearly went nuts. Round and round the circuit we went to no good purpose. Oh dear. Kept me banging things about in the back cockpit for an hour.

Another Kitty lost today, later found on its belly south-west of Ismailia in the sand. Same chap did same thing t'other day! One of the Spit [Flight] Harvards went over onto its back this morning, landing and using too much brake. Nobody hurt apart from cuts.

---

[1] In fact it was Group Captain John Grandy DSO, later Marshal of the RAF Sir John and a future Chief of the Air Staff.

Wednesday, 15 September 1943

A binding parade this morning after breakfast. Didn't go off too well, S/L Garton was leading the pupils and I was trailing along. Garton wheeled left and the pupils went marching straight on! Panic.

Binding with the WingCo. Brought up my desire to go on an Empire CFS Course, which by coincidence, is held in England! Am putting my application in tomorrow.

I either want to go on this Course, which is the goods and would be the cat's whiskers after the war, or else I want to get back to 244 Wing. I don't want them to think from my application that I have 'had' Ops, far from it. I've asked for it to be stopped if this is going to be the case. The Groupers is enquiring.

Tuesday, 21 September 1943

Flew down to Bilbeis [half-way between Ismailia and Cairo] early this morning to try and get some news of 2/Lt S---. Saw the MO there who had been out and found the body. He appears to have jumped too late. I searched for the spot where the aircraft was supposed to be but no see. It is apparently almost out of sight and in little pieces under water. Brought back his parachute. Seems he was trying to force land. He was streaming white smoke—glycol—and his flaps were down when he jumped at about 300 feet. Suppose he got it on fire and couldn't put it down in time.

Some shadow firing with Geoff Garton—good practice and some goodly shooting. A spot of formation in and around the clouds—then dog-fighting. Did some more work on my photo album this afternoon and then a game of squash with Geoff.

Friday, 1 October 1943

What a beginning to the month. Led a low-level attack on Suez this morning. My No.2 went into the sea at some considerable speed! He bounced and when he finally went in was able, by the grace of God, to get out of the Spit. I sent the rest of the formation back to base and stayed circling him. A boat put out from the shore and I led it to him and saw it pick him up OK. I landed at Suez, Egyptian Air Force base, and only just got down in one piece. Got a car and chased down to pick him up; finally laid hands on him none the worse for wear.

Wednesday, 13 October 1943

Good news—my application for an Empire CFS Course has

been recommended by HQ Middle East and has gone to Air
Ministry. If they accept it I shall go to England—what a fine
thing. I was very surprised to hear Middle East had recommended me: very few manage to get on this Course and I
don't think I am exactly in HQME's good books since the
strife I started when I came down from the Squadron.

Thursday, 14 October 1943

Beating up the Pongos and their guns on LG 208 after breakfast. Really did them over—nobody was hurt! Spits and Kittys
were screaming along the deck in all directions—so
dangerous!

Monday, 18 October 1943

Flew Geoff Garton to Helio this morning for his Junior
Commander's Course. Went into Cairo to meet Brian
Kingcome at the Continental as arranged. Very pleased to
see him; he doesn't appear to have changed much except by
way of rank—now Groupers. He was a bit battered having
been in a car crash with Dudley Honor in Sicily, and was cut
and bruised; still had a patch on his lip. A wicked looking
specimen.

He has asked for me and was trying to get me to take 92 in
Hunk's place. A fine thing, but 203 Group, I believe, won't
let me go until my six months is up. If my Empire CFS thing
falls flat, as it probably will, I'd give anything to take over 92.
I don't want to boob by leaving here too soon and going to
Italy and then my England thing comes through too late.

[Later.] Met Brian again at the RAF Club at Helio, along
with Johnny Kent and a couple of WAAFs, and drank to the
small hours. Terry took my Harvard back to Abu Sueir with
instructions to pick me up in the morning and bring back some
spirit for Brian to take to Italy.

As mentioned earlier, Dudley Honor had flown Battles in France in
1940 and then Hurricanes in the Battle of Britain. Moving out to the
desert he was a flight commander in 274 Squadron. Operating over
Crete he was shot down by a 109 but swam ashore and was fortunate
to be flown out by Sunderland just before the island surrendered.
Johnny Kent DFC and Bar, of course, had previously commanded 92
Squadron in England just prior to Neville's posting to it. He had been
commanding 17 Sector at Benghazi, now taken over by Honor, and his
present job at Air HQ was in planning the invasion of the Aegean
islands of Kos and Leros.

Friday, 22 October 1943

Another death this morning. P/O Gray in a Spitfire was hit by a Kitty taking off. Gray was taxying up to the end of the runway after landing and would never have known what hit him. The wheel of the Kitty caught his cockpit, smashing it in. The Spit still had throttle on and was going round and round in circles, quite fast. I was first there and swanned onto the wing and pulled the throttle off. He looked OK and not badly hurt, a bit of blood but not much. I undid his straps and tried to heave him out but he was too heavy for me. Some erks rolled up and we pulled him out, but he was dead.

Monday, 1 November 1943

November—things should happen this month, my sixth month here. This month will, or should, decide whether I go back on Ops or back home!

Took my Spit up after breakfast after chasing the Flight and trying to get them all to start flying on time. Weaved around the sky but didn't find anybody to dog-fight. Have got a terrible stiff neck—not used to weaving so much these days.

Tuesday, 2 November 1943

Usual thrash around in a Spit, keeping my hand, and eye, in. King Peter of Yugoslavia arrived here this afternoon in a Liberator, after a hair-raising attempt to get the thing onto the ground—flown by a Yugoslav crew!

Met him in the evening at the Grouper's house where we indulged in alcohol on the Air Ministry. Seems not a bad type; keen on flying so must be all right. Enormous dinner, then along to the cinema where drinks were supplied during the show. I fell over a couple of times!

Wednesday, 3 November 1943

More tearing about in a Spit but not feeling so very active after last night. A lunchtime session with the royal party and the AOC. Bad thing. Tried to lecture in the afternoon too!

Sunday, 14 November 1943

[Cairo] . . . had a few noggins at Shepherd's and the Continental, where we (Geoff, Ted, Adj, Biddy (a WAAF)) met Denny (another WAAF). Big panic outside Shepherd's when the clutch packed up and amidst terrific screeching and grinding of gears we had to get out and push right in the heat of Cairo. Never laughed so much.

Met Babe Whitamore and Bruce Ingram, both over from Italy with their Squadrons—81 and 152. [Off to] India?! So secret.

Squadron Leaders W M Whitamore DFC (who'd been at Biggin with Neville) and New Zealander M R Bruce Ingram DFC, who had been operational in the UK, Malta, Sicily and Italy, were indeed off to India. Their squadrons were equipped with Spitfire VIIIs, and it was planned for the Spitfire Vs used in Burma to be gradually replaced with the Mark VIII, and be reinforced with these two Spit VIII units. Babe Whitamore led a Flight of his Squadron into 'Broadway'—a stepping off airstrip used by Chindit forces in March 1944, but they were severely mauled by Japanese fighters—they had virtually no radar to help warn of approaching aircraft—and Babe was killed on the 17th. Bruce Ingram was injured in a crash at Imphal early in 1944 and, in hospital with a smashed nose, contracted tetanus and malaria, and died within a few days.

North Africa was no picnic, but Burma . . . ! At least the Germans might take you prisoner; the Japanese often gave prisoners a hair-cut—starting at the shoulders!

Tuesday, 23 November 1943
Led a co-operation exercise with torpedo Beaufighters and Wimpeys [Wellingtons] from the Coastal Command Training School at Shallufa. They were to attack an Italian cruiser in the Bay of Suez, steaming at 23 knots with AOCs, Admirals, and Groupers on board! We were the defence and took nine instructors. Quite a success and everybody seemed pleased— 'shot down' lots of Beaus and Wimpeys.

Saturday, 27 November 1943
News at last from Air Ministry about my application for Empire CFS Course. I've had it as they are now only taking people with CFS Courses which I don't propose to take and become an FST instructor for the rest of the war. At least now I know where I stand and can bind to go back on Ops.

For the next two weeks, Neville was in Cairo, on a Junior Commander's Course. Then, on 12 December, he talked with the AOA (Air Officer Admin), Air Vice-Marshal E B C Betts DSC DFC, a former RNAS type, then had an interview with the C-in-C, who suggested it was time Neville returned to Ops. Neville wasn't arguing! First, however, he had to return to 73 OTU. Then he had to get past the Wing Commander, whose view was that with two tours behind him, he would be far more useful as an instructor, and suggested a short CFS Course at Upavon, England!

Then just before Christmas, Geoff Garton was given command of 232 Squadron and rumours abounded that Neville too would soon be posted. After a liquid Christmas, Garton left on the 28th. Neville was a bit apprehensive, as Geoff Garton had already done two tours and was, according to Neville, no longer a youngster—he was 28! In mid-1944 he would command 87 Squadron and end up with a DSO.

Early in January, Wing Commander Grant confided that Desert Air Force had asked for Neville. Meantime, the daily round continued. It had long been the custom for the instructors and pupils to 'beat-up' the army types—pongos—especially at the end of each Course. On 8 January, some army type obviously got a bit ticked off with this, for on the Spitfires return, they found a bullet hole in the propellor of Nev's No.2! As Neville noted in his diary, '. . . if they want to play at that, we can join in too with pleasure!'

His birthday came round again on the 11th—'Getting so very old'— was his diary comment. He was now 22. Then a pilot from 92 visited him and Nev got him to take a letter back to Brian Kingcome, urging haste in a posting to his Wing.

In February his relief arrived, which put his posting a bit closer. The sad news was that his kitten 'Quoise' had been savaged by a dog and had to be put down by the Doc. Finally, on 26 February, he was posted back to the Desert Air Force. There was a sudden bout of goodbyes and packing, then he caught a Dakota to El Adem. Across to Malta on the 29th (leap year), then onwards to Catania, Sicily on 1 March; refuelled, then took off for Naples. He had finally got back to the war.

CHAPTER XI

THIRD TOUR—ITALY

At the time Neville was joining the Wing in Italy, the Allies were struggling to hold the Anzio bridgehead, where troops had landed back on 21 January 1944. With a deadlock occurring further south, the Allies had decided to land forces on the west coast of Italy, south of Rome but north of the German's defensive positions (known as the Gustav Line). This threatened an advance on Rome as well as putting troops behind the German front line, and the Germans reacted vigorously with powerful counter-attacks. The Anzio-Nettuno area became a hot bed of flak fire and occasional forays by Luftwaffe aircraft. While the latter were few and far between, the DAF had to keep aircraft on almost constant alert and patrols in case of air assaults. This was the situation as Neville Duke returned to the war front—in a DC3.

Wednesday, 1 March 1944
Took off from Malta after brekker and flew to Catania, Sicily, landing there to pick up passengers. Good-looking country. Took off for Naples but returned with ropey engine. Got off later and reached Naples through poor weather. Rain and low cloud.

Went to BPD and there met Mackie, CO of 92! Thought I had arrived in time but apparently someone else has taken the Squadron. Shame. Phoned up Brian Kingcome; he is sending transport for me tomorrow.

Squadron Leader E D 'Rosie' Mackie DFC and Bar was a New Zealander. He had served with 485 Squadron in the UK, then 243 Squadron in 1943 over North Africa. He had assumed command of 92 Squadron in December and was on his way back to the UK when Neville met him, having handed 92 over to Squadron Leader G J Cox DFC.

Graham Cox was a Battle of Britain pilot, who had then come to the Mediterranean to join 43 Squadron in May 1943. He had then been with 229 Squadron, and after a brief stay with 72 Squadron, had been given command of 92 in February 1944.

Thursday, 2 March 1944

Left BPD this morning in a truck for 244 Wing sent down by Brian Kingcome, then went along to see 92 Squadron. Good to see all the types again. Old Joe still there and most of the ground crews remain the same. Flew one of their Spit VIIIs and very nice too.

Dinner with them and later went into Naples with their CO, Squadron Leader Cox, and Nicholls, one of the flight commanders. Visited the Officer's Club and drank a little.

Flight Lieutenant John H Nicholls DFC had earlier been with 601 Squadron in the Western Desert.

Friday, 3 March 1944

I assume command of No.145 Squadron at Marcianise, near Naples. A good squadron with an excellent record. They were formed at the outbreak of war, at Croydon, and served thoughout the Battle of Britain. The first Spitfire squadron in the Middle East, it has a score of 196 which will doubtless increase considerably.

The pilots seem a good crowd although I haven't got to know them yet. We are in 244 Wing along with old 92, 601 and 417. Brian Kingcome is the Group Captain, Stan Turner the WingCo Flying. Groupie Kingcome took me around to see the other squadrons.

Neville's predecessor as CO had been Squadron Leader O C Kallio DFC, who had previously served in 33 Squadron. On 20 February, he was landing back from a sortie but was caught in a cross-wind. After a bounce, he decided to go round again but then realised he would not be able to clear some trees, tried to get down again, crashed and suffered a broken leg.

Wing Commander P S Turner DFC and Bar—a Canadian, although he'd been born in Devon prior to his family emigrating had flown in the Battle of Britain with Douglas Bader's 242 Squadron. Later, in fact, he had commanded 145 Squadron. Going out to Malta he had commanded 249 Squadron in 1942, and then 417 RCAF Squadron, but had then been made Wing Leader of 244 Wing.

Saturday, 4 March 1944

Went on my first show this afternoon. Led the top section so as to have a look around the countryside a bit. Cover patrol of the Anzio bridgehead at 15,000 feet. Didn't see anything and cloud prevented much of a look-see at the ground. Very strange after being off for so long. Weather here bad. Raining on and off every day and cloud low. Mud up to your ankles everywhere.

Sunday, 5 March 1944

Led a formation of eight on another bridgehead patrol below cloud at 4,000 feet. Nothing about but some flak and some shelling on the ground. Led another show in the afternoon with four aircraft on the same job. Cloud low and patrolled again at 4,000 feet. Was hit in the starboard wing by flak, making a pretty fair-sized hole just out-board of the cannon ammunition. Hole was big enough to put your head thro'! Shrapnel peppered radiator cover and a bit on the port leading edge.

Monday, 6 March 1944

Led a patrol of eight (two returned u/s) over Anzio area in the morning. Chased odd Mustangs about the sky but no joy. Little flak from Cisterna. Weather better, vis very good.

Led another cover patrol over Anzio area with eight a/c at 4,000 feet. Weather poor again and raining. Lots of Kittys and Spits in the area. Such a small area gets overcrowded and it gets unhealthy crossing the bombline low down! Eddie Edwards of 92 has been posted to command 274, so there was a party at 92's this evening. Finished up at 417 Squadron's Mess.

Squadron Leader J F Edwards DFC DFM, from Battleford, Canada, had flown all his operational life in the Middle East, starting with 216 Squadron at the beginning of 1942, but managed to get to fighters with 94 Squadron and then moved to 260 Squadron. He also served with 417 before taking a flight commander post with 92, and now had taken command of his old 417 Squadron. Indications are that it was Edwards who shot down Neville's old 'friend' Otto Schulz, of JG27, on 17 June 1942. He had only claimed one probable, but had in fact destroyed two 109s.

Tuesday, 7 March 1944

Led an eight aircraft patrol over Anzio at 7,000 feet early

this morning. Patrol long and uneventful as far as we were concerned but 601 who were patrolling same area higher up, were engaged by ten or so 109s or 190s. They got four but one of their flight commanders, 'Hindoo' Henderson, is missing. Lunch with G/C Kingcome at Wing Mess.

A new aircraft arrived for me this morning, a Spit VIII. Am having the letter 'J' put on—hope it's lucky! [JG241].

Saturday, 11 March 1944

Wizard show this morning when the boys up on a dawn Anzio show engaged some dozen 190s and 109s. F/L Radcliffe got one in flames and Sgt Sutherland got a 190 after a long chase. [Flight Lieutenant A J Radcliffe RAAF and Flight Sergeant A Sutherland] The German pilot baled out. The Huns were keen to play and dog-fought a lot. Probably from the new aggressive Gruppe just out from Europe, known to us as the eager beavers! 601 got one too. It makes our score 199! I must get the final one.

Led an eight on patrol at 19,000 in Anzio area. Patrolled off the coast between Anzio and the Tiber River to Rome. Rome looked very nice in the afternoon sun and so close too. P/O Evans was hit by AA in this morning's flight when he was chasing a Hun—crash landed at Anzio. Yanks flew him to Largo in a Piper Cub and I flew over at dusk in our 'pisser' (Saimen 202) and brought him back in the dark. Shaky do!

Monday, 13 March 1944

Up early and patrolling the Anzio area. Nothing seen at all. Went to a conference at the 64th [US] Fighter Wing, representing the G/C, and bound about bomber escorts with the Yanks. Got nobody nowhere. A good lunch with them and a visit to their Ops Room.

Flew in the afternoon on another cover patrol and again nothing doing but lovely flying weather. Hunk came over so a party started at 92 and finished up pretty hoggers at 417. Got to stop!

Wednesday, 15 March 1944

Led a patrol over the Cassino area covering bombing by everything our bomber force has got in Italy. All day long bombers—Forts, Libs, B25s, B26s, Lightnings, Kittys—have been bombing the area for the attack at 1200 hrs today. The weather closed down to 6,000 feet on our patrol so sat over Cassino and watched the terrific artillery barrage and the

Kittys bombing. Saw my first E/A on this tour, two Me109s, but they ducked into cloud. Cassino is one mass of bomb craters and shell holes and covered in smoke.

Sunday, 19 March 1944

Up before dawn and patrolling Cassino area at 15,000 feet— no fun. Some doubt now as to whether Cassino and Monastry Hill are in our hands. Weather has changed and it's very pleasant now—things are drying up and the mud is going away at last.

Lunch time patrol of Anzio with two sections of four; one at 8,000 and one at 16,000 feet. On way out was sent to chase two bogeys coming in towards Naples. Intercepted and found a P38. Then was sent to chase two bogeys at 26,000 ft over Cassino area. Chased around and found another P38. In fact, I think we chased ourselves quite a lot.

Led another Anzio patrol in the evening and after take-off heard of Huns over Cassino so altered course in that direction, arriving too late however, only seeing one 109 being shot at by about six Spits, and encountered some flak! On our way back from Anzio, flying down the Cassino valley, doing a recce of the road, my engine cut; it picked up but sounded very rough. Didn't know whether it was best to make inland for the hills and bale out or to glide towards Cassino. Made home OK, tho' after some twitching.

Friday, 24 March 1944

A big day. Led a patrol over Cassino after breakfast and engaged 30+ Me109s and FW190s, who were on a Sweep of Cassino at about 16,000 feet. Fired at one who rolled over and went down vertically—chased him but no luck. The rest of the types got three.

Led another patrol over Cassino in the afternoon and again engaged 109s and 190s. The Huns going pretty fast but the types shot down another two. Not a bad day's work. Squadron now up and past the 200. Big party in the Mess, including all the ground crews, Squadron COs, etc., came along and one couldn't move much.

The other 'types' were: Flight Lieutenant W A R MacDonald, 'B' Flight Commander, Flight Lieutenant B J Blackburn and Flying Officer J C Minto. In the afternoon combat, the victors were Lieutenant H E Wells SAAF, Flight Sergeant Sutherland and Flight Sergeant J J Thomson, sharing one FW190 destroyed, with Flight Sergeant J C Stirling claiming a Me109.

The Public Relations people put out a press release to impress the civilians and embarrass the pilots:

MAAF HANDOUT

Pilots of a Spitfire Squadron operating on the Fifth Army front shot down five enemy aircraft during two patrols over the Cassino area—two FW190s and one Me109 on the first patrol and a FW190 and a Me109 on the second—taking the Squadron's total of enemy aircraft destroyed over the 200 mark.

A formation of more than 30 FW190s and Me109s encountered over Cassino turned and fled when they saw our fighters. The Spitfires followed them north-west.

Fifteen FWs were chased over the Cassino-Arce road by F/O J C Minto, of Paignton, Devon. He closed in on one, opened fire and saw it spin to the ground east of Frosinone.

A bunch of Me109s chased by F/Lt W A R MacDonald, of 41 Kingsway, Livingstone, Northern Rhodesia, split up into three formations of four each. He got on the tail of one box and shot down an Me near Aquina.

Twenty Me109s and FW190s were dived on by F/Lt B J Blackburn, of Streatham, London, SW16, and one FW190 was shot down near Arce.

Minto had previously destroyed one enemy aircraft and both Blackburn and MacDonald had one destroyed and a half share in another. The Squadron's second bag of two victims on a later patrol was almost entirely a Scottish occasion, three of the four pilots concerned being Scots.

Again over Cassino, the Squadron sighted between 20 and 30 FW190s and Me109s. One Me was chased from Cassino to Anzio by F/Sgt J C Stirling of Rothesay, Scotland, who saw it dive down and hit the ground. Three pilots attacked an FW190—F/Sgt J J Thomson of Kirn, Argyllshire; F/Sgt Alastair Sutherland, of Aberdeen; and Lt H E Wells, of 45 Greenway St, Greenwood Extension, Johannesburg—the concentrated fire blew the FW190 to pieces, the pilot baling out before his aircraft disintegrated.

Leading the Squadron on these successful patrols was its Commanding Officer, S/Ldr Neville Duke DSO DFC and Bar, of Tonbridge, who has himself destroyed 22 enemy aircraft—one for each year of his age. A former CO of the Squadron was the American ace, Squadron Leader Lance Wade DSO DFC and two Bars, who was killed recently. [Lance Wade was killed in a flying accident, in an Auster aircraft on 12 January 1944, shortly after becoming tour expired.]

Saturday, 25 March 1944

Led early morning patrol of Cassino but cloud lowering and nothing doing. Just as well after last night. Some party. Lunch in Naples with Wing Commander Morris, Jock Wooler and Steve Woods. To the opera in the afternoon and good too—terrific opera house. On to the Orange Grove for food and drink, then an extraordinary impromptu party with S/L Cox and Co at a RAF transit camp with some RAF nurses. Drink and dance—grand fun. Got back with 12 glasses from the Orange Grove, a coffee pot, mat and a chair from the transit camp.

Sunday, 26 March 1944

Feel a bit funny this morning, but slowly recovering! The chaps got another 190 over Anzio—good show. Of course, I wasn't on the show. MacDonald and W/O Martyn shared it and it went down near the Tiber. Quite a mess apparently when it went in. Drove over to 324 Wing at Lago with Cox and Co in the afternoon. Intended coming home in daylight but as usual got mixed up in a pissy, so stayed overnight, sleeping in the Mess.

Monday, 27 March 1944

Back from 324 Wing and feeling strange! Led a patrol of Anzio at lunch time, with W/C Morris as my No.2. Chased about after a couple of Huns but no see. Lovely weather, warm and clear. Evening patrol of Cassino but saw nothing. Could hear 93 and 72 chasing Huns from Anzio to north of Rome on the deck—most unwise I'd say. They lost three pilots. Flak most likely. Saw some cine-gun films of the other days do. Some are very good. Mine came out quite well.

Wing Commander E J 'Teddy' Morris DSO was a South African who had joined the RAF pre-war and had seen action in the Battle of Britain. Moving to the Western Desert with 238 Squadron in 1941, he later took command of 260 Squadron, when Neville was in 112. He was about to take command of No.251 Spitfire Wing.

Tuesday, 28 March 1944

Led a patrol of Anzio in the morning and poached on the

Cassino sector and followed some 109s down from Frosinine to Cassino way above us all the time, but a couple of chaps chased seven to Rome area at 33,000, when the 109s turned on them and beat hell out of 'em at that height. They got back OK. Another Anzio patrol in the afternoon but saw nothing.

Intended a quiet evening but found myself over at 417 with W/C Morris and then 601! Nuff said. The WingCo got pretty hoggers.

Wednesday, 19 March 1944
Led patrol of Anzio in the morning. Went via Cassino as Huns reported in that area, but saw nothing. Got chased out by flak from Gaeta Point, and accurate too! One flak position that is not plotted on the map! Quiet afternoon, then led special patrol off Terracina late afternoon to catch reccos that come in every evening. Cloudy and they never came. Very early to bed for a change.

Thursday, 30 March 1944
Up at 4.30 this morning to take off at 5.30. Got off early at 5.15 and lucky too as we arrived at Anzio before our time and caught some 190 recco aircraft. W/O McCully and F/O Harrington got a flamer and Harrington a probable plus a damaged, all below cloud about 3,000 feet. I was, as usual, in the wrong section although I came down to look-see. [Warrant Officer G P McCully and Flying Officer B T Harrington.]

Saturday, 1 April 1944
Up early and led an Anzio patrol but nothing seen. Weather bad over 'drome and terrific milling in the circuit area with Beaus and Spits trying to land. Led a lunchtime Anzio patrol and again nothing seen. Very good visibility in the area, crystal clear.

Old 'J' is on an inspection so can't fly on last show this evening. 67 hours up last month. Will soon finish this tour at this rate.

Monday, 3 April 1944
Led Anzio patrol this morning—still nothing doing, but lots of flak pumped up around. Have had strips torn off by the Groupy and WingCo Flying, for flying too much! I am now limited to 40 hours a month. What a life!

Neville failed to record another kill for the Squadron on this day, Flight Sergeant J J Thomson bagging a FW190. And Flight Lieutenant Basil Blackburn left to go to 72 Squadron as a flight commander. The latter was replaced on the 9th by Flight Lieutenant F S Banner DFC, from 73 OTU. Banner had gained several victories flying with 243 Squadron on his first tour. Another experienced pilot, who would join on the 13th, was Flying Officer J S Ekbury, whose first tour had been spent with 232 Squadron.

Friday, 7 April 1944
Anzio patrol produced nothing. 417 Squadron getting their Spit IXs with bomb racks which they are rapidly removing. 601 will next be replaced with IXs and we should be the remaining VIII squadron besides 92.

Monday, 10 April 1944
A bomber escort to Orvieto marshalling yards this morning. Taxied out for stand-by, waiting for the Mitchells to arrive and went into a soft spot, breaking my prop! Big panic whilst I rushed around and found another aircraft. Took off and waited for the B25s which turned up over the 'drome at 8,000 feet. Escorted 27 of 'em without incident. Excellent bombing in the target area each time. They bombed in two boxes of 12 or so.

One of my pilots, Sgt Newman, baled out on a patrol of Terracina. He was picked up OK, by a Walrus which burst a float on take-off and had to be towed back.

Flight Sergeant A G Newman, a New Zealander, went into the sea 12 miles south-east of San Fellice point due to engine trouble. A Walrus of 293 Squadron fished him out and they did indeed have to taxi back, the Walrus gunner and Newman having to stand out on the lower wing to help keep the damaged float out of the water. All three men were eventually taken off by a rescue launch, having to abandon the Walrus in a six foot swell. It later sank.

Neville was now having to curb his sorties, because of the restriction in hours imposed by his bosses, but he managed to get in two bomber escorts before flying south to Malta for a vital operation!

Thursday, 13 April 1944
Off to Malta for a day or so this afternoon, with Cox of 92. Flew via Stromboli, Messina, down coast of Sicily past Catania, thence to Malta, landing at Luqa. Weather was poor

on way but improved near Malta. Contacted Cox's friends—
Lancashire Fusiliers. Major Lister took us around all the pubs
in Valetta with the usual result.

Friday, 14 April 1944

Our visit here to Malta is primarily to buy beer and gin, but
this day ends with no alcohol bought but lots consumed at
various pubs in Malta. Finished tonight at a troop dance
where everybody was tight and drinks were in abundance. No
doubt but they drink far too much in Malta.

Saturday, 15 April 1944

Determined to be away today but only just made it. A farewell lunch time session in the Fusilier's Mess lasted till about
4 o'clock when we at last persuaded someone to buy some
crates of beer for us. Got three crates OK. Set off for Luqa
where we bought two cases of gin then bustled off to our
Spitfires and loaded up like fiends in the fading light. Took
off at last in the setting sun and flashed over Sicily making
Naples just at dusk. Hell, what a place to go to is Malta!

Sunday, 16 April 1944

Don't feel too bright this morning but bucked up and went
on a bomber escort with 601, covering 26 Mitchells to bomb
the railway near Orvieto. Some flak from the area, which
smartened things up a bit, otherwise uneventful, except that
the bombers took us nearly to the other side of Italy.

A horrible lunchtime session in which nearly all the beer I
brought back from Malta was consumed in one ugly rush.
Even WAAFs from 92 turned up! 92 is almost known as the
Waafery now.

Wednesday, 19 April 1944

Doing nothing all day. 'A' Party moved off to Venafro this
morning—early. Squadron at 30-minutes during the morning
and released in the afternoon. A lot of our pilots left for BPD
at Naples, having finished their tours: Francis, Minto,
Romain, Powell, McCully and Thomson.

Lunch over at Wing with G/Cs Kingcome, Duncan-Smith
and W/Cs Stan Turner and Searle. Flew up to Venafro in the
afternoon to look see. Seems quite a good place but is surrounded by enormous hills.

Sunday, 23 April 1944

Wing moves to Venafro aerodrome not far from Cassino. Very pretty scenery and good to have a change. Very strong wind blowing, but luckily down the one runway. Our camp site is some distance from the 'drome but better than most.

Escorted some 24 Boston bombers near Velletri from 11,000 ft, bombing some tented areas. A little flak on the way back from target; 92 Squadron intercepted some 12 109s and 190s this evening and got three.

Wednesday/Thursday, 26/27 April 1944

Simply pouring with rain and, of course, the 'drome completely u/s and the whole camp area is a sea of mud. Squadrons released. The boys started drinking at 9.30; I got up at 12 o'clock!

After lunch off in S/L Cox's car for Naples; two-hour drive. Bath at Circeula and picked up two WAAFs, Madge and Anne, and took them to the Orange Grove. Car broke down coming back. Rad leak; it took until 5 o'clock to get the girls back to work—five hours late. Phoned up for transport from the Squadron then sat in car at dawn, dozing and waiting. That's life.

Having spent a sleepless night in the back of Cox's car, was met by our MT corporal with transport at 8 o'clock, so left him with the car and buzzed off for a wash and shave at Circeula Palace, feeling like death. Got back to the Squadron about midday and had first food in days it seems.

Some of the chaps climbed one of the hills back of Venafro and found several decomposed Hun bodies, etc.

Friday, 28 April 1944

Stopped raining at last and day breaks clear and dry, with a high wind that should dry the 'drome up quickly. After lunch, set off for Lago aerodrome for a party with 43 and 93 Squadrons of 324 Wing. Went in a truck along with Cox and Johnny Gasson of 92. Arrived to find the G/C and friends pissed. Not a bad party; stayed the night with Hunk Humphreys and 111 Squadron.

Sunday, 30 April 1944

The WingCo led the Squadron on a bomber show to the north-east of Rome. Bostons nipped under cloud and turned and Jock lost 'em; Black! They bombed the target though. I led a dusk Anzio patrol and we intercepted the usual two Hun

Top left: Squadron Leader R E Bary, El Ballah, June 1942.

Top right: Ex-Turkish Air Force Spitfire at Ballah (HK856), summer 1942.

Middle left: NFD on another ex-Turk (HK854) El Ballah.

Middle right: Ballah, the Middle East Fighter School, Refresher and Conversion Unit, 1942

(l to r) S/L Pike, NFD, S/L Bary, Sgt Chubb, – unknown Canadian.

Bottom: The B24 Liberator *Hail Columbia*, a flying visitor at Castel Benito. This Lib later led the 9th AF strike on Ploesti on 1 August 1943, piloted by Col. John Kane. He crash-landed on Cyprus after the raid and received the Medal of Honor.

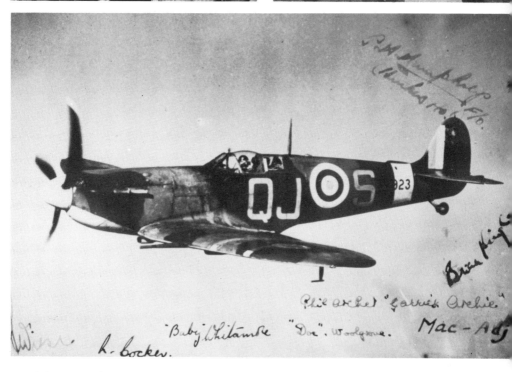

Top left: Wing Commander A G 'Sailor' Malan DSO DFC, Biggin Hill's Wing Leader in 1941. NFD flew as his wingman on occasion.

Top right: Pilot Officer N F Duke, 92 Squadron, Biggin Hill, 1941.

Middle left: 92's dispersal 1941: (l to r) NFD, Gordon Brettell, ?, Geoff Wellum (standing), F/S H Bowen-Morris, Brian Kingcome and Roy Mottram.

Middle right: At Wimpy Wade's wedding: Jami Rankin, Phil Archer, NFD. Note all three have the top button of their jackets undone, a sign o the fighter pilot.

Bottom: Signed photo of 92 Squadron Spitfire Allan Wright flying.

Top left: Neville's CO in 112 Squadron, Squadron Leader Tony Morello.
Top right: From brick Mess to tent; Western Desert home to Neville and Hunk November 1941.
Middle right: NFD's Tomahawk GA-F, on all-threes . . .
Bottom right: . . . . on all belly—shot down 30 November 1941, by Otto Schulz.
Bottom left: NFD and Hunk Humphreys, 112 Squadron 1941.

Top left: Line shoot for the press boys, March 1943.

Top right: Still posing!

Middle left: Me109 of JG77 in NFD's camera gun, over Mareth, 3 March 1943.

Middle right: Neville's victim (Muller) of 4 March 1943 came to visit.

Bottom: He asked to see a Spitfire and gave Neville his flying badge.

Top left: Another 109 pilot visits 92 Squadron, at Hassiet.

Top right: Spitfire IX of 92 Squadron, at Goubrine, near Sousse, Tunisia.

Middle: Wing Commander Ian Gleed DSO DFC, Wing Leader 244 Wing, but killed in action 16 April 1943.

Above left: 92 Squadron Spitfire landing, Tunisia, April 1943.

Right: Neville's private Spitfire Vc (LZ978 Trop), CFI Abu Sueir, Egypt.

Top left: Hunk Humphreys, J F Soden and Nev Bowker, 112 Squadron – on the bottle!

Top right: NFD, Jerry Westenra, and 'Blue' Leu, 112 Squadron.

Middle left: Jack Bartle in P40 cockpit – note the name 'Nan' and the kangaroo with boxing gloves motif on the fuselage.

Bottom left: Flying Officer 'Butch' Jefferies, killed in action 12 December 1941.

Above right: Ofhr Waskott, I/JG27, brought down by NFD near Sidi Rezegh, 22 November 1941.

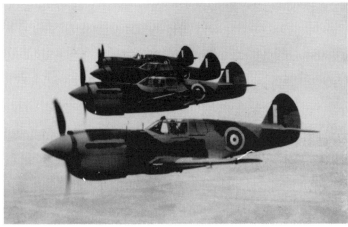

Top left: In the mud at Antelat, January 1942 – just before German tanks appeared over the horizon, with the Squadron bogged down.

Top right: The Kittyhawks arrive – 112's first P40Es January 1942.

Middle left: Neville's Kittyhawk GA-V (AK578).

Middle right: 112 Squadron: (l to r) Leu, NFD, Humphreys, Sabourin, Bowker, Soden, S/L Morello, Ambrose, Dickinson, Burney, Carson, Westenra and Bartle.

Bottom: 112's new CO from 6 January was Clive Caldwell DFC and Bar.

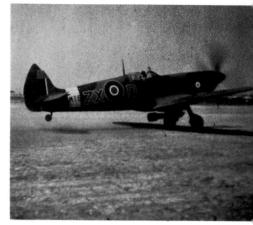

Top left: Graham Cox, Wg Cdr Hugh Dundas DSO DFC, NFD, Foligno, 1944.

Top right: Spitfire VIII fighter bomber, 145 Squadron, taking off from Fano, Italy, September 1944.

Middle left: NFD in 'J' (MT775) Fano, September 1944.

Middle right: Flying Officer J E Hamer, NFD's No.2 on 3 September 1944. Killed just after the war in a collision.

Bottom left: End of the road. With Neville tour expired, Squadron Leader S W Daniel DFC (right) arrives to take command of 145. Neville looks elated!

Bottom right: Squadron Leader Neville Duke, with Gwen, outside Buckingham Palace, 1945. Home is the Hunter.

dusk recco machines but was about six miles behind and slightly below them. Flew full bore for hours (!) but unable to catch 'em. Anzio AA opened up making things warm for us at 21,000 feet. Some of the Squadron landed short of fuel at Nettuno. I got back OK with my No.2 just at dusk.

Thursday, 4 May 1944

Early morning escort to some 24 Baltimores to Orte again, but as we were late joining them they bombed bridge and railway over the bomb line on the east coast. Carried out some upside-down flying coming back and engine cut, causing some panic and frantic pumping and priming to get it going again. Cloud covered our 'drome and the hills causing me to lead the boys up the wrong valley at 5,000 feet and got lots of accurate flak. Panic again!

Drove up to Piedmont, way up in the hills with Cox in the afternoon. On way back called in on 40 SAAF Squadron for tea and left at midnight after a pretty good party. Cox tried to cross the Volturno River by the tank crossing and got stuck half-way, in three feet of cold, fast running water. Waded about and got pulled out by some Poles. Never a dull moment sitting in the cold water at 1 o'clock in the morning.

Thursday, 11 May 1944

Two new pilots arrived yesterday, SAAFs, Beisiegel and Milborrow, ex pupils of 73 OTU when I was there. Led an Anzio patrol in the late afternoon but nothing doing. Went down and recced the small rivers near the Tiber for reported assault craft. No see.

Meeting of all pilots in the Wing at 417 Squadron this evening when we were given the griff on the battle, or rather campaign, for the rest of Italy. Terrific barrage of 2,000 guns started at 11 o'clock tonight on the Cassino front. Alamein had 400 guns. The noise and flashes in the sky were tremendous.

Friday, 12 May 1944

Guns quiet this morning. Barrage was to lift at 1 am when the Poles are storming the Monastry. The Indians and British, under a creeping barrage at 11.45 last night—a tough job. French troops are to storm the heights south of the Liri valley and the 'goons' are to be turned loose on ear collecting sorties! The Yanks will advance along the coast.

The Cassino front is the Gustav Line—next up the Liri

valley is the Hitler Line, as yet not manned. Two months is
given to reach a line north of Rome and casualties are sure
to be heavy. Scores of heavy and medium bombers have been
going out since dawn while our Spits cover the area.

The German Gustav Line had been subjected to continual bombard-
ment throughout the winter and spring, especially its key point, Monte
Cassino and the surrounding mountains, which protected the
approaches to Rome. Having contained the Allied assault at Anzio,
deadlock had continued over the whole front, despite innumerable
fights, skirmishes and minor battles, fought over difficult terrain.

Finally, on 11/12 May 1944, the British Eighth and American 5th
Armies, together with other Allied forces, opened what was hoped to
be the final assault on the Gustav Line. If all went to plan, the forces
in the Anzio bridgehead would attempt a break-out in about ten days.
It would be over this area that 145 Squadron were to have several 'field-
days'.

CHAPTER XII

OVER THE GUSTAV LINE

Saturday, 13 May 1944

Great things at last! This afternoon, 92 Squadron ran into 22 FW190s which bombed the French troops on the Cassino front. 92 passed over them once without recognising them. Finally engaged and shot down three. I led a Fighter Sweep to the Perugia area in the evening.

E/A reported around Cassino and we met up with six Me109s over Arezzo, the other side of Perugia (near Florence). There were six of us and we had a good dice. I got a burst at one and saw strikes under its belly before he rolled down and off. Stayed up and dodged and turned for a bit, finally fixing on to one up above whom I climbed and turned with, easily climbing and out-turning him. I could see him flicking on the stall—he throttled back and straightened out, kicking his tail and skidding violently. Observed strikes in fuselage and forward, around the engine cowl. Pieces started coming off as E/A went down in wide spiral. Lost sight of E/A near the ground but saw explosion where it had disappeared.

Returned and landed at Anzio for the night. Out of the six Me109s engaged, we destroyed three and damaged the other three. MacDonald and Lorimer each destroyed one; Parbury and Greene damaged one each.

In point of fact, as the Squadron Diary noted, this was the deepest Sweep by any Spitfire squadron in the Wing to date, west of Arezzo, to the north of Rome. 244 Wing recorded Neville's 23rd kill.

Sortie Report for 13 May—RAF Form 441A

Six Spitfire F.VIIIs flying south at A.17, just west of Arezzo, saw six

Me109s flying north below them at A.16½. Spitfires half rolled and attacked with following results.

S/Ldr N F Duke DSO DFC + Bar, 1 Me109 Destroyed, 1 Me109 Damaged: F/Lt W A R MacDonald 1 Me109 Destroyed; F/Sgt D H Lorimer 1 Me109 Destroyed: F/Lt C R Parbury 1 Me109 Damaged; Lt S M Greene 1 Me109 Damaged.

Spitfires jettisoned long-range tanks before attack. One tank (JF959) would not jettison. E/A carried no bombs or overload tanks. Blue circles were seen round the black crosses on E/A.

The only pilot not to score was Lieutenant F M Du Toit SAAF, the unfortunate pilot flying JF959, whose long-range tank would not detach itself.

Combat Report for 13 May
Time: 1915 hours, Arezzo

I was leading six a/c on a Fighter Sweep at 17,000 ft in the Perugia area. When flying south near Arezzo, six Me109s passed below us flying north at 16,500 ft. I gave turnabout and chased E/A. When closing astern, E/A turned to port. I engaged one Me109 in a turn and it dived after I fired a burst from 300 yards without observing results. Following it down I fired a further burst from 300 yards observing strikes under fuselage to rear of the mainplane, causing small pieces to fly off. E/A continued in its dive and I pulled up to engage some Me109s which were above.

I claim 1 Me109 Damaged.

On climbing up, I saw one Me109 circling above me. I started climbing and turning with him and easily climbed with and out-turned him. At 14,000 ft when I was about to fire, E/A throttled back and skidded and slipped into a stalled position. I fired several bursts into E/A from 100-150 yards, saw many strikes [and] large pieces flying off, apparently from engine cowling. E/A slowly dropped away in a wide spiral, more pieces blowing off. I lost sight of E/A when just near the ground but observed a burst of fire where it disappeared, approx five miles south-west of Arezzo.

I claim 1 Me109 Destroyed.

I fired, in all, 800 x .303 and 130 x 20 mm.

Also on this day, Flight Sergeant J C Stirling ran into 12 Me109s, attacked and shot down one, probably a second, and damaged a third. Before the month was out, Stirling was commissioned and received the DFC.

Sunday, 14 May 1944

Still great doings. Took off at dawn from Anzio, crossed coast
north of Tiber and swept in and around Rome area and
Perugia. Nothing seen until on our way home, between
Frosinone and Cassino. At Cassino we turned back towards
Frosinone and met eight Me109s with bombs on, at 15,000
feet. I pulled around behind one E/A, all of whom let go their
bombs on their own troops. Picked on one and followed it
down in a dive. Easily held and gained on E/A, firing several
bursts. A large piece came off, perhaps the hood, followed by
smaller pieces from around the cockpit. Observed a fire start
in cockpit and e/a crashed in the valley. Newman and a new
chap on his first Op—Beisiegel—each destroyed one;
McKernan, Greene and Lorimer a damaged.

Last night, Stirling got one destroyed, one probable and
one damaged over Cassino. Squadron total 7 destroyed, 1
probable and 7 damaged.

Sortie Report for 14 May—RAF Form 441A

Eight Spitfire F.VIIIs were returning to base at Venafro along high
ground via Frosinone and were approaching Cassino when bogeys
were reported flying south-east at A.15 behind Spitfires. Squadron
turned about and met 8 Me109s at 200 ft above them. E/A split up
and jettisoned their bombs over their own territory diving away.
Spitfires gave chase, making the following claims:

S/Ldr N F Duke 1 Me109 Destroyed
Lt D J Beisiegel 1 Me109 Destroyed
F/Sgt D H Lorimer 1 Me109 Damaged
F/Sgt R W McKernan 1 Me109 Damaged
Lt S M Greene 1 Me109 Damaged

F/Sgt A G Newman, after chasing an Me109 until he lost it in
haze, saw 2 a/c flying north-east at 7,000 ft at high speed. He
identified one as a FW190 and destroyed it.

Combat Report for 14 May
Time: 0635 hours, Cassino

I was leading a Fighter Sweep of eight a/c returning from the Rome
area. When approaching Cassino at 15,000 ft, from Frosinone,
control reported bandits at Frosinone heading for Cassino. I called
a turnabout and when near Aquino, came head on and slightly
below to four Me109s with 4 more top cover. I pulled around and on
top of E/A which jettisoned bombs. I closed astern on one Me109

which started a fairly shallow diving turn to the south-west—easily held and closed on E/A. After firing two bursts, opening at 300 yards, closing to 200 yards, the hood and parts of the fuselage came away and fire broke out in the cockpit (Witnessed by F/Sgt A G Newman). The E/A crashed in the foothills south-west of Aquino (area G.6520). I fired 320 x .303, 60 × 20 mm.

I claim 1 Me109 Destroyed.

No.244 Wing somehow failed to note this as Neville's 24th victory; see also later comment for 21 May.

According to the Squadron diary, when Newman was closing in on one of the two enemy aircraft, and about to open fire, the pilot baled out. A Spitfire IX had been seen near it just beforehand, but whether this fighter had done any damage to the 190, or the pilot simply baled out when he saw Newman closing in, was not determined. Flight Sergeant Stirling's escapade made the press releases:

HEADQUARTERS
MEDITERRANEAN ALLIED AIR FORCES
Public Relations Section

At dusk today twenty-two year old Flight Sergeant Colin (Jock) Stirling, from Rothesay, Scotland, climbed out of his Spitfire on an advanced airfield in Italy and reported that, single-handed, he had taken on four Me109s over the battle area, destroying one, probably destroying a second and damaging a third.

Stirling went out with his Squadron of the Desert Air Force Spitfire Wing on a Fighter Sweep late in the afternoon, and when one of his fellow pilots developed engine trouble and had to turn back, Stirling was ordered to escort the lame duck, as they were then a long way from base. Only two minutes after leaving the main party, Stirling sighted an enemy formation of about 15 FW190s and Me109s at 15,000 feet.

Being assured by the lame duck that he could manage back to base all right, the young Scot decided to have a crack at the enemy single handed, and climbed up to mix it with four Me109s which were acting as top cover for the Focke Wulfs. The enemy fighters had been flying in line abreast, and when they spotted the lone Spitfire they formed up in line astern, but neither then nor at any other stage in the unequal contest did they show any fight.

Stirling singled out one, scored strikes on the radiator, and the enemy fighter broke away. Later the Scot saw this machine going down with black smoke pouring from it, and what looked like flames coming from one wing. This is claimed as destroyed. He had gone for a second opponent immediately the first aircraft broke away, and this time fired from point blank range. Enemy aircraft No.2 went down in a very steep vertical dive, with smoke pouring from the engine, and is claimed as a probable.

With very little ammunition left, Stirling, nevertheless, chased after a third Messerschmitt, and succeeded in scoring strikes before the enemy fighter made good its escape into the clouds. The fourth 109 also decided on discretion before valour, and took to the clouds.

Stirling now has a score of three confirmed successes. He shot down a high-flying Ju88 on the east side of Italy in January, and destroyed a Me109 over Anzio beach-head in March. END.

These periodic PR press releases could be quite interesting then as well as now. At this time, there was a release covering the squadrons in 244 Wing, which is worth recording here:

14th May 1944

MAAF HANDOUT

A Spitfire Wing of the Desert Air Force, formed in July 1942, yesterday topped the 400 mark in enemy aircraft destroyed. Starting the day requiring three more for the fourth century, the Wing got four. War is funny that way. Weeks go by sometimes without our fighter pilots seeing an enemy aircraft, and then suddenly their luck turns, and they get the chance they have been waiting for. This particular Wing has done a great job of work all through the desert campaign, with its victorious finale in Tunisia, through the Sicilian campaign and now in Italy it is still going strong.

There are stations in the United Kingdom which have many more enemy aircraft destroyed to their credit than this Spitfire Wing of the Desert Air Force, but whereas there is constant coming and going of squadrons on home stations, there has been only one change of squadron in this particular Wing. The change took place when the City of Windsor Squadron of the Royal Canadian Air Force took over from a South African unit towards the close of the Tunisian campaign. The other squadrons are original members.

They include the East India Squadron, which got three of the four successes today, bringing its total for the war up to 311, and only require six more to establish a new squadron record for the Royal Air Force.

The East India Squadron arrived in the Middle East in April 1942, with a score of 193 enemy aircraft destroyed, having played a distinguished role in the Battle of Britain, when it operated from Biggin Hill, Kent.

The present Commanding Officer is S/Ldr Graham Cox DFC[1], who comes from Birmingham, England, and who brought his total of confirmed successes up to eight today by shooting down a FW190. He also damaged another Focke Wulf in the same engagement. Among the pilots are South Africans, Australians and New Zealanders, as well as pilots from the UK.

Another of the squadrons is the County of London Auxiliary, which has to its credit 213 confirmed successes. Once known as 'The Millionaire Squadron', because it had five among its personnel, including Lord Beaverbrook's son, the Hon. Max Aitken, the late Sir Philip Sassoon and Air Commodore Whitney Straight, it also won a great reputation in the Battle of Britain, in which on a single day the County of London pilots shot down more than thirty enemy aircraft.

In the spring of 1942 the County of London Squadron took part in the heroic defence of Malta for two months, and then moved on to the Middle East. This was the first squadron to fly clipped-wing Spitfires in the desert. It was also the first Spitfire squadron outside the UK to be used for ground strafing, and it built up a formidable reputation as 'train-busters' in Italy last winter. In November last, this Squadron destroyed a train carrying over one hundred thousand gallons of petrol to the enemy's front line troops, and it was shortly after this success that the Squadron scored its two hundredth victory in the air. A number of the ground personnel have been members of the Squadron for upwards of ten years. It was formed in 1925.

A third squadron of this Wing has a total score of 205 enemy aircraft destroyed. The late Wing Commander Lance Wade DSO DFC and two Bars commanded this Squadron for over a year, and the present CO is S/Ldr Neville Duke DSO DFC and Bar, who is top scorer among fighter pilots in this theatre, with 23 enemy aircraft destroyed. At one time in the Tunisian campaign, this Squadron included a Polish combat team, which did very valuable work and destroyed 25 enemy aircraft.

The City of Windsor Canadian Squadron has 27 victories in the air to its credit, almost all of these having been scored in Italy. For months bad luck dogged this Squadron, in that they never even saw an enemy aircraft, and actually went right through the Sicilian campaign without any of its pilots firing his guns in anger. It was

---

[1] Cox, a Battle of Britain veteran, also fought over Tunisia and Sicily. After the war he was killed in the northern territories of Canada, the Cessna in which he was flying icing up in bad weather.

still the same for a time in Italy, but the Canadian pilots 'struck oil' during the Sangro River battle, when the Luftwaffe put up its biggest effort for a long time, and since then they have had their fair share of what has been going.

Commanding Officer of the Wing is Group Captain Brian Kingcome DSO DFC and Bar, Battle of Britain pilot.

Monday, 15 May 1944

An early patrol in the Cassino area covering the advance across the River Rapido. Nothing about at all except Tac/R people and the Kittys on their standing patrols looking for bombing targets. Another patrol in the evening covering the Gaeta area when boxes of Baltimores were bombing troop positions. Chased after two smoke trails up to 27,000 feet but after chasing them around a cloud, found nothing on the end of them! Battle of Cassino going strong—our casualties 4,000 so far but progress good.

Reference to Tac/R people and the Kittyhawks on patrol, refer, in the first instance, to fighter aircraft, usually Spitfires, of such units as 208, 225, 318 or 40 SAAF Squadrons. Their main function over a fluid battle area was to locate and pin-point where Allied and German troops were positioned or moving to. By necessity they generally flew at low level, therefore coming under ground fire from both sides. Often, the first they knew they were flying over enemy positions was the sound of bullets striking their aircraft! It meant they had found them!

The fighter-bombers had now honed their skills into an art form, and in fact took on a task made successful by the Stuka dive-bombers in the early days of WW2. Bombed up, they would patrol behind the battle area, ready at a moment's notice to attack any strong-point or any armoured vehicles, tanks, etc, spotted by either the Tac/R boys, or by advancing troops (in Normandy, after the invasion, it was known as 'Cab Rank'). These troops would have an RAF liaison officer with them, equipped with a radio set to the aircraft's frequency, and could call the aircraft down to an attack. In Italy, this was given the code-name of 'Pineapple'.

Wednesday, 17 May 1944

The battle continues and with some success; the French still doing very well. Sound of shellfire all day and night long. Thank God I'm not on the ground fighting.

Air tested the mighty 'J' this morning after new ailerons had been fitted—very good. Jumped the boys patrolling

Cassino! Still no Huns about—they come at a rush sometimes. A Baltimore crash-landed here this morning after one
engine was shot up by flak. Overshot on one engine so pulled
wheels up and nicely belly-landed.

Led an area cover patrol of the Cassino area but nothing
doing. Told to get off the ground quickly as the Hun was
airborne but he never came our way, worse luck.

Friday, 19 May 1944

Up at dawn on stand-by. A patrol before brekkers and still
nothing doing. On stand-by again before lunch and
Scrambled. Some 109s and 190s bombed Venefro of all
places, shook the types here but didn't hit the 'drome. We
raced out towards Avezzano and then Viterbo but only
contacted Huns over their own 'drome. F/O Ekbury got one
and Mackenzie and Anderson chased one until he put his
wheels down in the circuit. Bags of flak for them at 500 feet!!
I only saw three which I chased and who went into cloud.
Raining again now; hope it doesn't hinder the pongos who are
going like bombs at the moment.

Saturday, 20 May 1944

Panic this morning. Suddenly ordered to pack and move off to
Lago to operate with 324 Wing for a while as two Tac/R
squadrons are to come here and 324 Wing have sent 43
Squadron to operate from Anzio. It's stopped raining thank
goodness and we hear the pongos are well on their way to
Rome.

Sunday, 21 May 1944

Great day! Squadron moved to Lago and eight a/c spent day
at Anzio. Leading an area cover from Anzio in the Velletri
area in the evening [second patrol of the day], we suddenly
found ourselves confronted by 20 or more FW190s and
Me109s slightly on our starboard, and in sections of approx
six in line abreast and stepped up. Turned in behind them and
got amongst it. Picked on the second from the end in the first
row and fired at close range. Everything blew off and he
crashed in flames north-east of Velletri. Second one in the
line was hit as he rolled over; pilot baled out but did not see
'chute open. Squadron got eight destroyed, one probable and
one damaged.

F/L Somer is missing but he should have got one as he
followed me in. F/O Ekbury got two and a probable; Lt

Milborrow, a new boy, got one and a damaged. F/L Wooler got one; Lt Anderson got one; and F/Sgt Stirling one. Great thing. Party thrown by 72 and 111 Squadrons tonight. Lots of women and wine, and lots of congrats.

A great deal of paper was generated over this action, and it is worth recording it all in some detail, being of the greatest victories over enemy fighters in Italy. First 244 Wing's Diary: '21 May: S/L Duke closed in on a 190 from 150 yards, raked it until it crashed. He followed another, and got in bursts as the 190 turned on its back and dived. The pilot baled out from 14,000 feet but the 'chute was not seen to open. Turning south, the CO saw our bombers coming in and gave them a lone escort without let or hindrance. It was his 24th destroyed, a record for the DAF and Mediterranean War. None of our other patrols could match up to these impressive results.'

As mentioned earlier, the Wing noted this as Neville's 24th victory, because they had forgotten to note his victory of 14 May. In point of fact, however, his score was now 26!

MISSION REPORT
DATE: 21 May 1944

ORGANISATION: 244 WING (145 SQUADRON)
A/O #8
NO. OF PLANES: 8 Spits
TIME UP: 1820 hrs, NETTUNO TIME DOWN: 1930
MISSION: AREA COVER FOR 24 A-30s BOMBING VELLETRI.

ENEMY AIR:
Just airborne and orbiting for rendezvous when at 1830 hours, 20+ E/A reported east of Rome coming south. After two minutes, saw 10+ FW190s at 15,000 ft, 10 at 17,000 ft line abreast, 4 Me109s at 20,000 ft. Our planes between 15-17,000 ft. Bombers had not arrived so engaged the FW190s head on. Chased to north. Most of FW190s jettisoned their bombs. Lt J M G Anderson chased a 190 in shallow dive to north, fired from 250 yds astern, strikes on tail. Another burst from 150-200 yds followed by white flash from engine. The 190 was at deck level when pilot pulled up and turned; saw E/A hit a hill at F-9999 and blow up.

F/L J S Ekbury chased a lagging 190, at 3,000 ft, fired from 200 yds, hitting fuselage and port wing. Black smoke came from 190 and it went down like a falling leaf. Last seen going down at 2,000 ft near

G-0647. Claims a probable. He then turned into another 190 and fired from 200 yds. With hits on fuselage and wing. Hood jettisoned and pilot baled out at G-0162. Saw another 190 east of Rome, overtook 500 yds, 2 bursts from 200 yds, bits flew off. E/A went in at F-9159. Claims two FW190s Destroyed.

F/S J C Stirling chased a 190 north of Rome and at deck level fired from 100 yds astern. Bits flew off, cockpit in flames. E/A tried to pull up, went in flames at F-7596. Stirling fired at others, but no results seen. Claim 1 FW190 Dest. S/L N F Duke fired on 190 from 150 yds. Saw flashes and strikes on rear starboard side of fuselage, raked it again and E/A went in at G-0961. Chased another 190 and fired from 250 yds, and while E/A turned on back going down, got hits with long burst. Pilot baled from 14,000 ft at G-0765 but 'chute did not open. S/L Duke turned south and saw bombers and escorted by himself to target where lot of heavy AA, and out. Claims 2 FW190s Destroyed.

F/L J Wooler chased 3 FW190s. 2 stayed together, 1 dived away which Wooler followed and plane blew up after hits. Claims 1 FW190 Destroyed. Lt G E Milborrow chased a 190 north of Rome. Fired from 200 yds, hits around cockpit. Spit was then attacked and lost the E/A. Claims 1 FW190 Damaged. Going south he saw 2 190s going north at 400 ft. Dove and fired from 50 yds. Pilot baled. The 190 blew up at G-8595. Claims 1 FW190 Destroyed.

F/L Somer was last seen at 15,000 ft east of Velletri going north. Has not yet returned.

CLAIMS—8 FW190s Destroyed
           1 FW190 Probably Destroyed
           1 FW190 Damaged

LOSSES—1 Spit Missing

Sortie Report for 21 May—RAF Form 441A

Spitfire FVIII No's JG241, JG110, JG244, JG246, JG179, JG249, JG952, JF962

S/Ldr N F Duke DSO DFC + Bar, F/Lt A F S Somer, F/Lt J Wooler, F/Sgt J C Stirling, F/O R MacKenzie, F/O J S Ekbury, Lt J M G Anderson, Lt G E Milborrow.

Time up: 1820
Time down: 1930

Duty: Area cover to 24 Baltimores bombing Velletri area.

Eight Spitfire FVIIIs were flying NW up Highway 6 just SE of

Valmontone, 4a/c at A.15 and 4 at A.17, in box formation when Grubstake reported 20+bandits just E of Rome flying SE. At 1833 hrs, Spitfires ran head on into 19 FW190s stepped up from A.15 to A.17 in three layers of 6 a/c flying line abreast. E/A were bombed up. Above at A.20 a top cover of Me109s were flying in line abreast. Me109s numbered 4 a/c and were not involved in combat. The FW190s however, turned about and dived away N some of them jettisoning their bombs. Spitfires gave chase and the following claims are made:

S/Ldr N F Duke DSO DFC 2 FW190 Destroyed
F/Lt J Wooler 1 FW190 Destroyed
F/Sgt J C Stirling 1 FW190 Destroyed
Lt J M G Anderson 1 FW190 Destroyed
F/O J S Ekbury 2 FW190 Destroyed,
1 FW190 Damaged
Lt G E Milborrow 1 FW190 Destroyed,
1 FW190 Damaged

After combat, bombers arrived in area and leader escorted them to target and back to our lines. 1 Spitfire FVIII (JG110) was lost and the pilot, F/Lt A F S Somer has not yet returned to unit.

Combat Report for 21 May
Time: 1830 hours, Valmontone

I was leading 8 a/c on area cover NE of Velletri. When at 15-16,000 ft flying NW, approx 10 miles NE of Velletri, we were confronted by 20+ FW190s with a top cover of a few Me109s. E/A were flying SE down Highway 6 towards Frosinone in close line abreast formation in 3 layers of 6 a/c. The bottom layer was slightly below and to starboard of us. E/A were carrying one large bomb slung under the fuselage. As they came abreast and to starboard of us, I turned in behind them and selected No.2 in the bottom layer of six, firing from 100-150 yards from starboard quarter astern. I saw the E/A heavily hit by cannon and many pieces flew off and it finally went down and exploded on the ground at G-0961.

I then closed on the next in line and after firing one burst it started to barrel roll onto its back. I followed it round, firing from 150 yards, and saw the hood fly off and the pilot left the cockpit. (F/Lt J Wooler later saw this FW burst into flames, area G-0765.) I then continued after the other E/A which had broken up and were diving home and when at low level I was engaged by HAA, I broke away.

The first E/A I engaged was a FW190 with the BMW 801 engine, but the second had the DB 603. Both had green and brown camouflage with dark blue underside.

I claim 2 FW190s Destroyed.
I fired 600 × .303, 160 × 20mm.

A press release, typical of the period, was rapidly produced for the media. It is presented here in its entirety:

SPITFIRES GET ANOTHER EIGHT

Pilots of a Spitfire squadron yesterday intercepted about 20 bomb-carrying FW190s north of Anzio. During a chase which took them north of Rome, they shot down eight, with one probably destroyed and another damaged.

The successful pilots were S/Ldr Neville Duke, of Tonbridge, Kent, the squadron commander and top-scoring fighter pilot in the Mediterranean, who got two; F/O J S Ekbury, 51 Irving Place, Blackburn, Lancs, two and one probable; F/Sgt Colin Stirling, of Craigmore Hotel, Rothesay, Scotland, one; Lt G Milborrow, of 25 Ridge Road, Pietermaritzburg, South Africa, one and one damaged; Lt J M G Anderson, of Windhoek, South Africa, one; and F/Lt J Wooler, of 26 South Street, Greenock, Scotland, one.

As soon as they saw the Spitfires, the FW190s jettisoned their bombs, and they turned in an attempt to reach their own airfields.

This Squadron's bag of enemy aircraft has now reached a total of 222. Of this number, twenty-nine have been destroyed since the beginning of the Anzio beach-head. The Squadron had a notable success last week-end, when it shot down seven of the 12 credited to the Wing in one 24-hour period. S/Ldr Duke then destroyed two, and his personal score is now 26.

In the words of S/Ldr Duke, 'the FWs flashed past us'. They were bombed up and apparently on their way to bomb and strafe our troops in the Cassino area. They came straight by the Spitfires at about 15,000 feet. It developed into a fight on the run, which took the Spitfires to a spot some 40 miles north of Rome.

S/Ldr Duke said, 'I shot my two down over Highway 6, where we were covering the area for the bombers. It was a coincidence that they happened to come right in our path. The pilot of the first one I attacked got out of his cockpit, while the second FW dived straight into the ground.'

'I chased mine for over 30 miles and shot him down east of Rome,' said Lieut Anderson. 'The FW hit a mountain and burst into flames.' This was Anderson's first victory.

'I saw three FWs in front of me,' said F/O Ekbury. 'The first one I hit went down, but I had no time to watch him, so it must rank as a

probable. After I fired at the second one, I saw the pilot thrown out
of the machine. The third went straight into a field.' F/O Ekbury's
total is now six. END.

Apparently the Squadron had intercepted aircraft of SG4, which
reported the loss of seven pilot killed (plus one assumes, at least one
more aircraft from which the pilots baled out). Those lost were: Oberleutnant Robert Reiprich and Hauptmann Rolf Strossner of I/SG4,
both east of Rome; Leutnant Herbert Bertram, Oberfeldwebel Hans
Schmidt and Unteroffizier Rolf Manske at Fabrica di Roma, and Unteroffizier Gerhard Assmann and Leutnant Kulpa, at Viterbo, all from II/
SG4.

Monday, 22 May 1944

A headache this morning but worth it. W/C Turner got a DSO
yesterday—good show, he deserves one. Led an area cover in
the Velletri-Avezzano area at 15 to 16,000 feet but bags of
cloud about and I don't think the bombers turned up. Hunk
was up at the same time leading 111 Squadron. Hunk and S/L
Cloete of 93 Squadron came to dinner and lots of 93 and 72
Squadron came along in the evening for several drinks.

Squadron Leader J H Cloete commanded 93 Squadron between
February and September 1944, following on from Jerry Westenra,
who'd commanded it from the previous September.

Tuesday, 23 May 1944

Led a Cassino patrol this morning without incident. Trying
hard to impress 324 Wing with quick take-offs and landings
in smooth formation! Anzio push starts too this day. Army
pushing from Cassino to Littoria via Terrachina, Cassino to
Frosinone, Cassino to Avezzano. Anzio people are pushing
to Littoria and the Albano hills.
    Led another Cassino patrol but 601 were doing the job so
carried out a Sweep from Anzio to north of Rome and
home—nothing seen. 111 Squadron got four this evening.

Wednesday, 24 May 1944

Air tested old 'J' after 160-hour inspection. Flew up to Anzio
as I heard 20 Huns reported near Valletri but got there too
late. Recco'd around Frosinone etc, watching the battle.
Anzio and Cassino lines join up at last.

Thursday, 25 May 1944

Early morning patrol of the Liri Valley and again nothing doing. Watched some Kittys strafing and setting trucks on fire. Flew to Venafro to see WingCo about a new flight commander now MacDonald tour expired. Can't get Monty now as Captain Gasson also tour-ex'd and Cox wants Monty for the job.

Chap killed in 92 this morning when his aircraft was hit by another landing behind him. Collected some eggs and gin from 92. Another party in the Mess. G/C Duncan-Smith, W/C Barrie Heath and numerous 111 types.

Friday, 26 May 1944

Feel awful this morning. Must have been the gin. Hundreds of Forts and Libs going out this morning—probably to Northern Italy. Also scores and scores of medium bombers bombing around Rome. Bomb line now 15 to 18 miles from Rome itself. S/L Kallio came along to see us.

Banner is going to 72 Squadron; pity as I had great hopes of him. He is brassed off. Am worried about the lack of experienced pilots. Orlebar came back from Cairo last night and thank goodness he brought some desert boots back—I was nearly going about barefoot.

Flew over to Venafro this evening to see Kingcome re cancelling Banner's posting as I said Banner was shaken to the core. He stays. W/C Turner is posted; don't know who is taking his place.

Tuesday, 30 May 1944

Feel worse this morning after going to bed early last night. Area cover and escort to more Bostons in Frescati area; lots of flak. One Boston force-landed at our 'drome in an awful hurry. Swam in the afternoon at last—a bit cold. Stirling's DFC came through this evening so a pissy tonight.

Neville had a change of flight commanders now. With MacDonald tour-expired, B Flight was taken over by Flight Lieutenant J A O'Brien, in from 417 Squadron. Later in June, with Jock Wooler also tour-expired, A Flight was taken over by Flight Lieutenant R F Starnes DFC, from 72 Squadron.

With the changes and the job in hand still tremendously important, everyone was going to have their work cut out for them over the next few weeks.

CHAPTER XIII

FIGHTER BOMBERS

The new Wing Commander Flying arrived at the end of May to replace Stan Turner. This was Hugh Dundas DSO DFC, a veteran of the Battle of Britain and of Bader's Tangmere Wing in 1941. He arrived just in time for the party to celebrate Turner's departure, which was held in an abandoned farm house. No less than five drinks bars were set up, each looked after by a squadron. Each unit vied to out-do the others in the potency of its drinks, rivalry which soon began to sort out the men from the boys! The other news was that 145 Squadron was also due to move back to its old base at the foot of the western slopes of the Appennines.

Saturday, 3 June 1944
All set to move to Venafro today. Took off from Lago and did an area cover of Frescati to 24 Bostons. Nothing about, no flak, no nothing.

Landed back at Venafro and was greeted by the Groupie with news of a second Bar to the DFC!! Surprise—pleasant one. Will please the folks no end. The rest of our party arriving tomorrow morning. Big party tomorrow night!

Sunday, 4 June 1944
Our forward troops enter Rome. Standing by for a press propaganda show over Rome with our Spits in close formation over the city. To be filmed from a Hudson. Cancelled first thing in the morning as apparently there is still some flak there! They wanted us at 3,000 feet too!

Big party tonight. Intended to give it myself but the boys insisted on giving the party for me. Lots of people and drinks.

Tuesday, 6 June 1944
[D-Day in Europe]
W/C Dundas led the Squadron on another area cover, again

without event. Over 200 mediums operating. Second Front starts in Europe with landings in the Le Havre area—at last.

There is little doubt that Neville liked swimming, a pastime generally enjoyed by most people who had served in the desert, for obvious reasons. Italy too is hot in the summer, so again, any opportunity to swim was taken. However, wanting to swim and being forced to, are two different things as we shall see.

Wednesday, 7 June 1944

Went strafing with the most amazing results! Shot up a couple of trucks in the Rieti area and set one on fire. Must have flown into some of my own shots bouncing off the ground or enemy flak and was hit in the radiator.

Flames started issuing from the exhaust stubs and the engine vibrated excessively. I set course for our lines and, although losing height, kept going slowly by opening the throttle and closing it quickly when flames appeared. Finally smoke became excessive in the cockpit. On breaking through a hole in the cloud, found myself at between 2 to 3,000 feet over Lake Bracciano (nine miles across!). Straps and oxygen were already released, so I rolled the aircraft onto its back at about 150 mph and dropped out of the cockpit, my 'chute jamming in the hood which I had not jettisoned.

The nose of the Spitfire started to drop and I could see the ground coming up, through the smoke and flame from the engine, at an alarming speed. Finally kicked myself free, my helmet blew off, and my new goggles. It was a few seconds before I thought to pull the rip-cord as the sensation of just hanging there in the air was so nice. On pulling the rip-cord the 'chute quickly opened and I was turning over and over; it opened with a strong tug and one of the shoulder straps came away—either coming out of the release box or it had snapped. I half fell out of the harness but pulled myself back and hung onto the cords—clutching my parachute D-ring at the same time, as they cost 4/6d [22½p]! [Pilots who failed to bring this item back were often charged with the cost of replacement. Luckily they were never asked to pay for the aeroplane!]

The 'chute was swinging quite a bit but the sensation of detachment from the world was grand. I saw the aircraft going down in flames and hit the water—poor faithful old 'J'. I saw I was drifting towards the northern shore, where the Huns were supposed to be. I seemed to fall very slowly until near the water when it came up with a rush. I did not take long to come down as the thing must have opened about 1,000 feet. As I hit the water I banged the release box—all straps came away except one leg strap. I was dragged across the water at high speed by the parachute and swallowed a quantity of water. The 'chute finally settled and started sinking fast and by the time I had freed my leg, the 'chute had sunk and was pulling me down. I was forced to slip the dinghy and rely on my Mae West.

The rest of my section—Mackenzie, Milborrow and Anderson—had watched me bale out and circled me as I came down and swam in the water. After swimming for about 20 minutes a boat appeared with two Italian boys who picked me up. On reaching shore I was met by several Italians of the peasant or farmer type, who rushed me up a hill and took my clothes off. One Italian gave me his trousers, another a shirt and another his coat and hat. The trousers came nearly up to my knees and the coat came half way up my arms, while the hat sat on top of my head!

They were dead scared of Huns coming along and made me hide for a while. In actual fact the Huns had withdrawn about two hours before. A little later we crept along the lake side and to a house where I had wine, tea, cheese and bread. I was treated exceptionally well and half the population came along to look at me. After I had been fed they put me to bed and about midday some advanced recce units—American— arrived and found me. When we entered the nearby town there was a terrific reception, with flowers, wine—the lot. I was transported eventually back to Rome where I spent the night. A wizard town, and the women ...!

Next morning I got a lift in a Taylor Cub to Aquino and to Venafro in a Fairchild. The chaps were pleased to see me back. Spent the next couple of days swimming in the Volturno with Squadron Leader Cox. My only injuries were bruises on the right thigh when the 'chute opened, and cramp from wandering about in wet shoes and socks.

What might really have upset Neville, however, was to learn when he returned, that he had missed a great party on the 7th. It impressed No.244 Wing who noted in their War Diary: '7 June: The officers threw a party to all other ranks to celebrate the 400th Hun destroyed. "Demon Vino", doorstep sandwiches, a piano, and slightly unsteady bon hommie, made up an excellent evening.'

Monday, 12 June 1944

Have spent last few days quietly swimming in the Volturno. Squadron moved up to Littorio aerodrome on the outskirts of Rome. Took off this morning, but when over Littorio was told to buzz off as 'drome u/s. However, finally flew up and landed. Three prangs—CO of 417 Squadron ran into one of my aircraft when landing and completely wrote both off. One of 92 Squadron ran into the remains. A pretty ropey aerodrome—fairly small and very rough.

Tuesday, 13 June 1944

Very hot here—stinking! A quiet morning getting settled in. Two armed recces but no strafing. Led an armed recce in the afternoon in Foligno area; strafed a couple of trucks but did not observe results although sure they were hit. One truck ran into a ditch and the types baled out of same.

Wednesday, 14 June 1944

Loitering about doing nothing. Into town in the afternoon and a thrash started at the Grand on Spumante and carried on until midnight. A short break for food!!

Friday, 16 June 1944

Into Rome again in the morning for lunch, a drink and a look around the city. Into town again in the evening for a final fling before moving. Visited the 'Florio', 'Savoia' and the 'Regina'. Rest of the Squadron went in and had a terrific party at the 'Grand'. Stirling fell out of a second floor window but only sprained his ankle and cut his hand.

Saturday, 17 June 1944

Left Littorio and the fleshpots of Rome for the country once more. Squadron to Fabrica, near Lake Vico, which is north of 'Duke's Folly'—Lake Bracciano. Lovely country and cooler than Rome area but aerodrome very dusty. Only staying a few days anyway.

Swarmed up a cherry tree and had lunch on cherries. Flew around in the afternoon to see the countryside and looked up my friends at Lake Bracciano. Snaffled a new machine which turned up in our dispersal. The old 'G' in which I was hit by flak over the beach-head.

However, Neville did not fly this machine again, taking over instead JG953 'J', which he air-tested on the 26th, and which he continued to fly until early July. After then he had MT775 as his regular machine.

Sunday, 18 June 1944

Raining like hell. News of bomb racks on the way and two squadrons to be fitted right away. Curses. During the last few days the Wing has lost three pilots and about seven or eight aircraft on this fool strafing business.

Flight Lieutenant Jock Wooler, one of Neville's flight commanders became tour expired on the 19th. His place was taken by Flight Lieutenant R F Starnes DFC, posted in from 72 Squadron.

Wednesday, 21 June 1944

Aerodrome still pretty u/s although the weather is better today. We are now, after all, getting bombs! Ourselves and 417 will deal shrewd blows to the Hun!

Captain Johl of 7 SAAF Wing, ex-73 OTU pupil, came over to give us all the griff on bombing. Not over-excited at the idea, but what's to be . . .

Friday, 23 June 1944

Still pottering about amongst bombs and things. Boys out again and had a shot at a train. Led a wizard strafe of stationary railway trucks, supposed 200 plus on the Fano-Pesaro line. Went out low via Ancona and along the coast to Fano. Went in on the train and did four strafing runs. Squadron got several flamers and no losses. 92 followed us but lost Lieutenant Steenkamp in the sea.

Monday, 26 June 1944

Start practice bombing. Each Spitfire with one 500 lb bomb under the belly. Starting dives at 8 to 9,000 feet and dropping at 4,000. Results not bad but mostly dropped short. They make a nice splash and bang when dropping them on a florescent target on the sea.

Wednesday, 28 June 1944

Led the first bombing show of the Squadron on an armed recce in the Leghorn-Florence area. Weather bad—rain and cloud at 8,000 feet. Bombed a road junction and to my surprise hit same direct just behind a staff car.

Led a Squadron show to bomb and strafe a train near Rimini. Had to go out to sea and up the coast from Ancona due to cloud and rain at 6,000 feet. Found the target and bombed from 6 to 7,000 feet. More surprise when I got another direct hit on the trucks; strafed them on the way down. Squadron scored four hits on the train, and one hit on the railway; started fires. This trip seemed to take hours around low clouds and hills. However, Operations were pleased with the results.

Thursday, 29 June 1944

A dawn armed recce with bombs in the Rimini area again. Just as I was about to start my bomb dive onto yesterday's target, which was still there, I looked around and there were two Me109s hairing along parallel with us. Jettisoned my bombs at 1,000 feet and turned after them. They jettisoned their long-range tanks and dived. Lost them as they were going like the clappers. Our bombs fell into the town and onto a main road—can't go wrong! Pity we couldn't get the 109s but good show to know they're around.

This was the problem for fighter pilots in Italy at this stage of the war; the Luftwaffe were keeping a very low profile and their aircraft were few and far between. The Luftwaffe, of course, knew the Allied pilots had air superiority in Italy and had no desire to throw aircraft away. They were more likely to engage Allied bombers rather than fly about the front line areas which swarmed with all manner of British, American and South African fighter pilots, all eager to get into a scrap with anything that had black crosses on it. This was one reason why so many RAF squadrons were turning to the dangerous activity of dive-bombing and ground strafing. Some COs actually requested adding this type of sortie to their repertoire; others were not over-keen. German ground gunners had had years of experience of shooting at aircraft, which made it an especially dangerous pastime.

Saturday, 1 July 1944

Dawn bombing show to cut the railway lines between Rimini and Ancona. Direct hit on the lines by both sections. I seem to be extremely lucky with my bombing—slap on again!

Had a shower under a waterfall up in the hills before brekker; cold but quoise [service Arabic for nice/lovely].

A tricky show in the evening to bomb two tiny little road junctions near Florence. Found 'em after a struggle and bombed. Mine overshot and Mackenzie's hit the road nicely. Bags of flak about but not much at us.

Sunday, 2 July 1944

Took off early and led the Squadron to Fermo on the east coast, to stand-by for bomber escort. A show to Pesaro in the morning covering 12 Marauders but bombing fell mostly in the town. One B26 was hit by flak and crash-landed at Fermo, going through fields, hedges and ditches before it stopped. Most of the crew were injured but so lucky.

Sat on the beach in the afternoon and sunbathed until another long range show to Lugo in the afternoon came up, covering 12 Baltimores. Excellent bombing. Ground parties left for Perugia today.

Monday, 3 July 1944

Led an area cover to Kittys bombing Rimini area. Swept the Rimini-Bologna locality without incident. Another area cover show in the evening and we swept the Ravenna-Ferrara-Bologna regions without incident, except for some slight heavy flak. Landed at our new base at Perugia—seems like a good 'drome.

The Squadron's new base, Perugia, was situated almost dead centre of Italy, in the province of Umbria. The ground troops were rapidly advancing up 'the boot', making for some rapid movements and changes of airfields for the Desert Air Force squadrons.

Leghorn, on the Tuscany coast just south of Pisa, had fallen to the Allied troops in the west, and Ancona on the east coast. However, the Germans were making a stand at every opportunity, and the next major target, the ancient city of Florence, seemed no nearer capture, with Kesselring making the Allies fight for every yard.

Until now the Desert Air Force had fought alongside the MATAF—Mediterranean Allied Tactical Air Force but this would soon depart for Corsica for the forthcoming invasion of Southern France, Operation Anvil. Until that happened, in mid-July, operations over Western Italy came from Corsica, leaving the DAF alone to provide close support and air cover for the British 5th and 8th Armies. Once Southern France was invaded—15 August—DAF took on the bulk of operations over Italy. Once the units had departed for Operation Anvil, DAF had to step-up its sortie rate in order to conceal the deficiency in aircraft numbers.

The new German Gothic Line would be the next defensive position to assault in August, but for the moment, that was some way off for the pilots of 145 Squadron.

Tuesday, 4 July 1944

Cover to 12 Marauders bombing Faenza. Cloud a bit fickle

and we got down to the bombers' level over the target—8,000 feet. No flak till we were on the way home.

We were clamped down for the rest of the day so I went into Perugia with Squadron Leader Cox. Bought some things at the officer's shop then beetled along to the hotel for wine and food, and a good evening. Whole of 145 sat down at one table for dinner!

Wednesday, 5 July 1944
Still clampers and no flying. Got up late and had tea at 92. What a headache after last night. Read a little in the afternoon, then dinner at 92 with more beer to follow. We now have two Fleet Air Arm types with us to learn the trade.

Friday, 7 July 1944
A dawn show with four aircraft to bomb railway between Ravenna and Rimini. Very pleasant trip with one hit on the line. Later an escort to 12 Baltimores to bomb the jetty at Rimini. Uneventful, and bombing poor.

A brand new aircraft arrived in from Corsica. Got my hooks on it and gave it a run around. A beautiful aircraft— new 'J'—built in May this year.

Led a late evening show to bomb bridge over canal near Pesaro. Difficult to find the target and eventually bombed and got lots of flak from everywhere. Nobody hit.

Saturday, 8 July 1944
Lieutenant DuToit was killed when landing with a bomb hung-up on his aircraft. Bomb fell off and exploded as he landed, killing him instantly and completely destroying his Spitfire. Bad luck—a good type.[1] Two of 601 shot down strafing Rimini 'drome—one safe. One of 417 also killed strafing—a bad day.

Messing about with safety devices for the bombs, trying a string jettison device! Works. Also took an aircraft up and attempted to jettison bomb and bomb rack which is said to be a bad thing to do; didn't work anyway.

Big pissy at Wing re. Groupie having held his office for one year. Lots of drunks—AOC well away!

Sunday, 9 July 1944
Weather bad, thank God, as hangover pretty terrific. Hunk

---

[1] Lieutenant F M 'Butch' DuToit SAAF.

came down for yesterday's party and stayed overnight. Lunch with him and Cox at Assisi, plus a gin bottle. Into Assisi again in the evening for wine and food. Lots of doubtful Italian popsies there, thundering around a dance floor.

Thursday, 13 July 1944
Quite a day—first a shot-up Marauder force-landing; hit one of my Spits in its dispersal area after bursting a tyre. Both aircraft went up in flames. All the crew of the Marauder got out except the co-pilot who was burnt to death. Two other members of the crew were badly burned and one later died. Two other Marauders of this formation received direct hits by flak near Florence. A Baltimore crash landed on the 'drome after two of the crew baled out—another force-landed. An aircraft of 417 made an extraordinary landing and wrote two Spits off when it went into its own dispersal.

Saturday, 15 July 1944
Up at dawn and off to bomb a road junction at Sestino, but my blasted bomb didn't go off! Getting a lot of bombs hanging up today, so WingCo Dundas and self flew over to see 7 SAAF Wing to get some griff, but only the ground party of the Wing had moved up and as they were still under shellfire we didn't stay. Landed at 239 Wing and got inveigled into a big thrash—stayed the night.

Sunday, 16 July 1944
Up early and flew back. Wizzo hangover but a nice day. Bombing show in the evening to cut roads north of Arezzo where the Hun is retreating—Arezzo fell this morning. We're getting lots of hang-ups on the bombs. Most depressing after flying out and belting through flak only to find the bomb won't come off. Dropping some 6-hour delayed action bombs which are pretty nasty things.

Tuesday, 18 July 1944
Feel pretty fit this morning considering the amount of beer we consumed last night. Gave escort in the afternoon to 12 Marauders bombing Faenza marshalling yards. Not bad bombing, slight flak from Ravenna area. Bombers rendez-voused in different area to original idea and took us miles out to sea on our way out and back. Jeff Milborrow, my No.4, ran short of fuel, or may just have had engine trouble, and force-landed only two minutes away from base.

Drinking gin at Cox's place with WingCo Dundas, and then over here drinking stout with the boys, Sandy Kallio and Topsy Turvey.

Wednesday, 19 July 1944
Up at dawn on an armed recce with bombs. Bombed target south-west of Rimini—and the flak! Heavy 88 mm stuff chased us for what seemed hours. Followed us in dives, climbs and turns—extremely accurate. Worst experience on this tour and most persistent.

Weather clamped, cloud and rain started coming down in buckets; aerodrome u/s. Lunch time session in my trailer with Cox, Banner, WingCos Dundas and Wootten.

Friday, 21 July 1944
Up at the crack of dawn and off to bomb a road near Lucca, north of Pisa. Pottered up between Pisa and Florence but no flak until after bombing. Hit a house by the road.

92 Squadron produced immediate results and shot down a recce Ju188 this morning on their first trip—the dogs!

No. 92 Squadron had sent up a detached flight to the west coast on the 19th, in order to counter German reconnaissance flights, and much to Neville's annoyance, they got lucky at the first attempt. The next day 145 were released so Neville flew up to visit 92's flight and had a swim on the coast. He had to get back though, for it was Cocky Dundas's birthday, so there was a party that night, with much 'potent grog'.

Monday, 24 July 1944
Big flap on today, people rushing around organising this and that. Paraded at two o'clock after lunch at Wing. The King landed in a DC3 with Spitfire escort, and drove around the 'drome from squadron to squadron. We cheered as he passed —but he didn't hang about much. Our Spits polished up no end.

Entertained half a dozen Yanks plus Cox and WingCo Dundas in the trailer afterwards with gin. Drove into Assisi in the evening with a bottle of Scotch!

Saturday, 29 July 1944
Led a bombing show to bomb railway bridge over the canal near Portomaggiore. Weather pretty u/s—raining and low cloud at 7,000 feet over the target. Bombed from 6 to 2,000 feet. Hit on road but missed the bridge. No flak!

Flying Officer Mackenzie posted to 601 as flight commander, and Flying Officer McKay posted to take his place. A quiet evening. WingCo Dundas away, so I'm acting OC the Wing. Cancelled shows in evening due to weather!

Flight Lieutenant G R S McKay became OC B Flight on 4 August. He later commanded 87 Squadron, winning the DFC. His brother was Donald A S McKay DFM and Bar, who had fought in France, the Battle of Britain and in the Middle East.

Thursday, 1 August 1944
Lieutenant Anderson was lost today when hit by light 20 mm flak while bombing a railway bridge, which was already pranged, north-west of Bologna. He caught fire but said he was baling out OK, but was not seen as flak was pretty intense against rest of formation.[1]

Wednesday, 2 August 1944
Quite a day. Early show bombing a level crossing north of Bologna. No hits on rail crossing but a lucky bomb hit on ammo train hidden in trees near target—set the thing going wizardly. Took the chaps out again to bomb same crossing. Again no hits but trucks still burning and more of 'em north of target. Again took chaps out, eight aircraft, self to bomb crossing and then strafe trucks south of target. Banner to bomb trucks north of target and then cover me. Cloud messed things up a bit; my bomb failed to drop in bomb dive but, after strafing, fell off when I was taking evasive action between trees, and exploded under me, throwing my aircraft about. Thought I was clobbered by flak! OK though, except for a 20 mm hole thro' the wing. Luckily it didn't hit the main spar. Strafing didn't seem to make much effect on trucks either!

Friday, 4 August 1944
Stayed at Assisi last night, wizzo cold shower and bath before brekker. Not much doing today, weather poor. Party over at 601 tonight on account of Nicholls is leaving and Paddy Turkington, ex-241, is taking over. Good party on 'Vat 69' but walked into a wire when I swerved out of the Mess; it was nicely placed at eye level!

---

[1] Lieutenant J M G Anderson SAAF did indeed bale out, although Neville did not become aware that he had survived until told by Jeff Milborrow in 1985.

Squadron Leader John H Nicholls DFC joined 601 Squadron in the Western Desert in late 1942, winning the DFC the following year. He had then commanded a Flight in 92 Squadron before returning to command 601 in March 1944. Squadron Leader Robert W Turkington joined 124 Squadron in 1941, later serving with 611 Squadron, then 43 Squadron. Moving with the latter unit to North Africa during the Torch landings he received the DFC in late 1943. After a rest he commanded 241 Squadron prior to being given 601. He would go on to command, briefly, 1 SAAF Squadron and be awarded the DSO in January 1945.

Tuesday, 8 August 1944

Squadron released today—thick mist in the morning but it cleared later. Sunny Italy! Visited dentist then flew over to Falconara in the famous 'J' job to see Sergeant Garth who force-landed there after being hit by flak; his aircraft is completely u/s. Lunched with Mike LeBas of 241.[1]

Flew on to Fermo and swam and sunned all afternoon. Into Assisi in the evening and had an enormous dinner in some odd place with Group Captains Kingcome, Duncan-Smith, WingCos Dundas, Morris etc. Bed 0130.

Wednesday, 9 August 1944

Escorted 18 Marauders to Rovigo, south-west of Venice. Venice looks nice. No incident re. Huns but one of 92, giving top cover, had his engine cut and appears to have entangled with his aircraft when baling out—no sign of him. Very hot and close today—feel shagged.

Friday, 11 August 1944

Up early and off to bomb a train seen by Flight Sergeant Melville on a dawn weather recce—the fool! Train was in Ferrara station by the time we got there and flak persuaded us not to bomb. Attacked a railway bridge south of Ferrara—two very near misses. The other section led by Major Venter, bombed and strafed a train successfully. Rained like hell in

---

[1] Squadron Leader M LeBas came from the Argentine. After operations from England he had flown with 601 Squadron on Malta and in the Western Desert. An instructor at 73 OTU in 1943 he was then a flight commander in 242 Squadron in Sicily prior to taking command of 241 Squadron. He would be awarded the DSO in late 1944. He became an Air Vice-Marshal in the post-war RAF.

the afternoon—it poured and poured.[1]

Sunday, 13 August 1944

Flew over to Rosignano for secret conference re. invasion of Southern France. Had the whole plan explained to us—most interesting and looks easy. Time will tell.

Swam in the afternoon on Cox's beach with Group Captain Kingcome and WingCo Dundas. Back to Perugia for a pissy in the evening—good one too!

Monday, 14 August 1944

After lunch the Squadron flew over to Rosignano on detachment from the Wing for a few days to operate in the invasion of Southern France, which is taking place tomorrow. 92 and 145 are to do the job—must say they pick the right squadrons.

Tuesday, 15 August 1944

Early morning patrol of the south coast on the Franco-Italian border to beat off any fighters from Milan and Turin who attempt to attack the 300+ glider train going to the beachhead. Completely uneventful but marvellous scenery. The Alps looked wizzo in the early morning light.

Another similar patrol in the Savona-Genoa area later in the evening also uneventful but somewhat long—nearly three hours. Landed very short of fuel; two aircraft force-landed on the 'drome. Invasion going extremely well.

Wednesday, 16 August 1944

Up early at dawn and on another patrol of the Alps area. Patrolled up as far as Alessandria, between Genoa and Milan. Nothing seen but we got the first flak since being on the job. Pretty accurate but not much of it. Have got a very sore backside after these long patrols—over two hours. Moving back to Perugia today—only told us at the last minute. Geoff Garton has arrived in the Wing and is taking over 87 Squadron.

Monday, 21 August 1944

Flew over to Corsica and landed at St Catherine aerodrome where 251 Wing are situated. Saw WingCo Morris and

---

[1] Major P W Venter SAAF was a supernumerary on 145 from 3 August, prior to taking command of 92 Squadron later that month.

'Windy' Smith. Had lunch during which time Cox rolled up.
Set off after lunch for the South of France beach-head to see
324 Wing. Arrived OK amidst lots of shipping and balloons;
awful dusty 'drome and crowded. Chaps doing lots of flying,
standing patrols like over Anzio, and seeing nothing.
Pottered around with Hunk, Groupie and WingCo Heath.[1]
The 'drome is right on the coast but no swimming allowed on
account of the mines.

Tuesday, 22 August 1944

Flew with 111 Squadron this morning, as No.2 to Wing
Commander Heath on a sweep of Valence-Lyons area, after
some reputed 109s, who are said to turn up at 8 am everyday.
They didn't appear this morning.

Hunk drove self and Cox along the French Riviera towards
Cannes in the morning—wizzo country it is too. Invasion here
going well; hundreds of Yanks about and still landing. Flew
back in the afternoon to Perugia—so ends the visit to the
South of France.

This actual sortie was flown by Group Captain Duncan-Smith, Wing
Commander Heath, Hunk Humphreys, 'Chips' Carpenter, Graham
Cox and Nev, a very experienced bunch.

Thursday, 24 August 1944

Flew over to Falconara for bomber escort but weather poor so
waited about all day. Swam and read until the evening when a
show turned up to escort Baltimores to bomb Ravenna wharf.
Terrible bombing—Balts all over the sky. Good flak. Other
half of Squadron on an Air Sea Rescue mission, covering a
Walrus taxying home! And a launch with bods from a
Liberator on board.

Major Venter takes over from S/L Cox to command 92
Squadron. Sorry indeed old Cox is going. A wizard type to
have around, full of good cheer.

Friday, 25 August 1944

Over to Falconara again to escort Marauders in the morning,
bombing Forli marshalling yards. Poor bombing; no flak, no

---

[1] Wing Commander Barrie Heath DFC had been a Battle of Britain pilot with 611
Squadron and then commanded 64 Squadron in 1941. Came out to the Middle East in
late 1942 and was WingCo Flying of 324 Wing DAF in Italy in 1944, commanded by
Duncan-Smith.

nothing. Another show in the evening with Marauders to bomb the road south-west of Faenza—bombing not good. Lots of accurate flak and one B26 from other formation was hit but landed wheels-up OK.

Squadron landed at Loreto, south of Ancona, our new base for the coming battle. Much secrecy attached to the move. Seems a good place, grass runway near the sea. Good camp site by the 'drome, but the whole place is a bit crowded with six squadrons.

CHAPTER XIV

THE GOTHIC LINE

The ancient city of Florence had been entered, but not occupied, on the 5th of August. The Germans had now established their Gothic Line across the mountainous region of northern Italy and everyone knew it was not going to be easy to dislodge them.

To the north of Florence, the Appennine mountains turn to the north-west eventually to join the Alps, and this virtually sealed off the western coastal plain. To the east, however, there was sufficient low ground along the coast to allow an armoured assault, which if successful would allow a breakthrough to the Po Valley.

Initially the idea had been to attack the central mountain area but at the last moment a switch to the east was chosen; the main strength of the British 8th Army was sent to this area. Meanwhile, preparations for the Desert Air Force to support this battle had been made. It would provide cover for the 8th Army as well as the 5th, who would still make an advance in the west. It was for this battle that 244 Wing had moved to Loretto.

The offensive began on the evening of the 25th, with the usual massive artillery barrage. Early the next morning Polish and Canadian troops spearheaded the attack.

Saturday, 26 August 1944

Two shows this morning, bombing gun positions near Pesaro; second show produced good results with hits. The battle started at 11 pm last night for the rest of Italy. By great secret methods, the Army has crept back to the east coast without the Huns knowing it—they hope. We have about 11 divisions agin' his one or so, so the pongos should break thro'. Once the Gothic Line falls, it seems it won't be long now—where then?

A prang this morning; one of 87 Squadron turned over on

take-off and caught fire. Pilot OK but burned. A new pilot arrived yesterday, F/L Sarll—on his second tour.

Sunday, 27 August 1944

Led four aircraft to bomb reported 30+ MT near Pesaro. Flew around the area at 8,000 feet but only saw 2 MT which we bombed and strafed without effect. A 36 aircraft show in the evening on Borgo Maria village. 145 first on to target and bombed from 8,000 feet; went down strafing. Some direct hits on the road and bods hit by strafing. A good show—nice to be able to lead the Squadron on a full 12-aircraft show instead of the usual fours and sixes.

Monday, 28 August 1944

No fly today. Bad news this morning that 'Monty' in 92 has been killed trying to force-land short of fuel, on the 'drome over at Rosignano. Shame; Montgomery was one of the better types in life.

Tuesday, 29 August 1944

An abortive bomber escort in the afternoon. We were to escort B26s to the north of Venice. Bombers did not let us get airborne before setting off and we couldn't catch them or find them. Dinner with Geoff Garton over at 87 and drinks to follow; some rough scotch vino!

Wednesday, 30 August 1944

Another bomber show this morning, only bombers didn't turn up this time—Yanks from Sardinia. However, we swept the Rovigo area near Venice which was their target. Led some of 92 and 185. Later we dive-bombed AA guns.

Awful hot today; looks like a storm. Battle still going slow but sure—only a matter of time. Chaps lapping up close support work. Chasing odd Huns with cannon and machine gun—killing a lot too.

Thursday, 31 August 1944

Didn't fly today. Pretty rugged party at 417 last night—pretty u/s this morning. Lost Lieutenant Field today unfortunately. He was hit when strafing after bombing on close support work. Pulled up to about 4,000 feet, spun down to 500 then suddenly burst into flames and went in. Cinema show at Wing in the evening, watched from a jeep and sucked Vermouth. Later went along to 601 Squadron.

Friday, 1 September 1944

Spoke to the Wing Commander about staying on here until this thing is over. Says I shall probably be thrown off at the end of this month at the most. Hope to stay though.

On an anti-recce patrol in the evening but saw nothing except suspected vapour trail which I clambered up to 26,000 feet after. My No.2, F/O J Hamer, had his engine cut and he had to force land OK at Falconara.

Saturday, 2 September 1944

No fly today, busy holding a Court of Inquiry into death of F/O Cross, killed in an accident at Falconara. Hot as hell— swam in the evening.

Sunday, 3 September 1944

[fifth anniversary of the war]

Up before dawn and pre-dawn take-off which produced excellent results. Patrolled the battle area between Pesaro and Rimini but as it was still pretty dark, whistled off after a while so as not to be shot down by the pongos. After some time, control reported two bogeys coming my way up the coast from Ancona. Vectored after same but missed them. However, picked them up about five miles ahead, making for the coast between Rimini and Ravenna.

Closed in, after a long chase with F/O Hamer, my No.2, with three Me109s going like bombs at 10,000 feet. Took the left hand chap and fired at long range and got a strike in the first burst, behind the cockpit. Closed, firing another burst and hood and pilot baled out.

Asked my No.2 to check on the pilot baling out. Chased after other two 109s who started climbing, closing in with leader easily, after the blower came in. Fired and after a couple of bursts got hits in fuselage and he caught fire. Later the pilot baled out. The other 109 dived and as my fuel was very low I broke off and headed back home. Pity about that third chap.

Combat Report, for 3 September
Time: 0645 hours, Rimini-Ravenna

I was leading 2 a/c on patrol over the Battle area. Control reported 2 bogeys at 13,000 ft going NW along the coast from the Pesaro area. Section climbed from 10 to 12,000 ft SE of Rimini, near the coast. Control gave positions of bogeys which must have passed in cloud or haze as they were next reported going away NW of us. I turned NW and saw three a/c crossing the coast N of Rimini about 5 miles ahead going NW. Gave chase and, although seen by these a/c, which opened up and poured black smoke, I closed slowly on them and identified them as Me109s in line abreast formation with the port E/A lagging slightly behind the others. E/A were in slight dive.

I engaged the port E/A from astern at 10,000 ft, fired a short burst at very long range (6-800 yards) in an attempt to slow it down, and observed a bright flash in the fuselage from cannon strikes. I rapidly closed and fired another burst, observing the hood fly off and what appeared to be the pilot leaving the a/c. E/A was seen going down and catch fire by F/O Hamer, my No.2, in area M.5820.

I then continued after the other two E/A still going NW at approximately 10,000 ft. E/A started diving and then went into a steep climb up to about 14-15,000 ft. I quickly caught E/A in the climb as my supercharger came in and closed with the leader as he levelled off. After firing a burst at fairly long range (3-400 yards) and observing no strikes I closed to about 200 yards and scored strikes behind the cockpit, presumably in the rear petrol tank, as E/A started to burn in the fuselage. The pilot baled out and his 'chute opened. A/C crashed in area M.3636. I lost sight of third E/A which had turned and dived as leader pulled up to the left. He was reported by my No.2 but fuel was short and we broke off and returned to base.

E/A were a blackish brown colour. They took no evasive action except some slipping and skidding and took no advantage of cloud cover which was available at all time. I fired 800 × .303 and 240 × 20 mm.

Claim 2 Me109s F or G Destroyed.

Action Report

Two Spitfires LFVIII were patrolling 30 miles N of Ancona at A.10 when at 0645 hours. Highfield reported 2 bogeys at A.13 flying NW up coast of Pesaro. Spitfires searched area and sighted 3 a/c crossing the coast in Cesenatico area, flying NW. Identified as Me109s. Spitfires closed in. Claims:- S/Ldr N F Duke DSO DFC— 2 Me109s F or G Destroyed.

F/O J Hamer fired 2 bursts at the third Me making off NW at ground level but observed no strikes. A/c returned to base without further chase for petrol reasons. E/A carried no bombs and no long-range tanks.

Excerpt from 244 Wing Review, dated 3 September 1944:

By destroying two Me109s shortly after dawn this morning, S/Ldr Duke brought his record up to 28 destroyed.

It is not proposed to turn the limelight on this remarkable achievement for even by the glow of a match it would appear as good, but with our passion for understatement we feel that in the words of higher formations, 'Superior Show', about meets the case.

The double leap was achieved when S/Ldr Duke and F/O Hamer intercepted three 109s homeward bound across the coast near Cesenatico. Cloud condition was ideal for evasion but the Huns took little advantage of it. This was much to their detriment, as opening fire from 800 yards, the CO got strikes on one from which the pilot soon baled out. Fire quickly burst from the second he attacked and there was another quick bale out. The third, at which F/O Hamer got in a burst, scurried away diving for the deck, when Hamer had to break away owing to shortage of petrol.

It is believed these 109s may have come from Villafranca, 8½ miles south-west of Verona, where fifty fighters, now minus two, are stationed.

Wing HQ had finally got Neville's score right!

Monday, 4 September 1944
Squadron A-parties moved off early this morning for Fano aerodrome. Squadron flew a couple of close support shows until the evening when I flew a close support show with W/C Dundas and landed back at Fano. We bombed guns which were shelling poor old Cox in his job as Rover Jimmy.[1] Lots of intense light flak and P/O Dixon was hit in the cockpit and slightly wounded in the neck. 241 Squadron shot down a 109 this evening.

Tuesday, 5 September 1944
Rest of the party arrived this morning. Led an evening show on a Rover Jimmy to bomb some 88 mm guns. Led four a/c of 92 and Cox was controlling. Searched the area and eventually bombed and strafed some guns; not very exciting but hope we did some harm.

Over to 601 for a drink. Mike LeBas turned up—nuff said!

---

[1]This refers to a Forward Air Controller, usually a pilot either on rest, or 'volunteered'. He would be with the army and could call up aircraft to attack with any targets the army wanted dealing with. Graham Cox was doing this job after leaving 92 Squadron.

Wednesday, 6 September 1944

Led an armed recce in the morning but weather u/s so asked
Rover Jimmy (Cox) if he had anything for us. Found us some
guns which we swapped bombs for shells with for a while!
Made the old gunners work a bit anyway. My tail wheel went
u/s so had to land poor old 'J' with tail-wheel up. No damage
apart from the rudder. Air Commodore 'Bing' Cross arrived
at the Squadron to see me—nice of him.

Thursday, 7 September 1944

Weather u/s again and 'drome waterlogged after rains yesterday. Feel like death this morning after a slight session last
night on Eyetie grog which Banner brought back from Vasto.

Visited 92 and had coffee which helped a bit; also lunched
there. Rained like hell again in the afternoon. Tried to spend
a quiet evening but an awful pissy started at our Mess.

Sunday, 10 September 1944

Flying at last today. Cox had paid us a visit and buzzed off this
morning back to the front. Led eight aircraft on a bombing
show to gun positions west of Rimini. We got hits in target
area and then strafed. Stirred up some flak and Lt Milborrow
was hit and slightly wounded in the leg. OK, tho' his aircraft
has had it.

Monday, 11 September 1944

Woken up awful early this morning and asked to examine the
runway. Pretty parky in the mornings now too. Flew 'J'
around and did a couple of landings—didn't go on my back so
runway must be serviceable! Tested some 'screamer whistles'
which have been fixed to my wing tips—will put fear into the
heart of the Hun!

Planned last night to do a dawn patrol but couldn't as
'drome was u/s—two 109s appeared on a recce, needless to
say!? Led six a/c to bomb rail bridge near Lugo. Went out via
the Rimini battle area to look see; artillery duels still going
on. Our bombing was a bit u/s as only my bomb fell OK and
went off! Jacobs insisted on seeing trucks to strafe as we
recce'd the area. Dusk anti-109 patrol—no results.

Captain Lawton of 92 baled out off Rimini and seen going
down OK and one of 92 landed with bomb hung-up; dropped
off and exploded but clear of aircraft. Put runway u/s tho'!

We had to land at 241 for the night.[1]

Tuesday, 12 September 1944

A good night at 241. Drank all Mike LeBas's cognac while he is on leave and I slept in his feather bed! Up at dawn on anti-109 patrol again, with F/O Pierson—no joy.

Led a close support bomber show controlled by old Cox disguised as Rover Paddy. Given target 500 yards in front of our troops, which was indicated by green smoke shells fired by the pongos. The six of us got five bombs in the target area and one about 200 yards wide—not bad. Bombed from 8,000 to 500 feet and strafed on the way down. A good trip.

Wednesday, 13 September 1944

Intense Ops; weather perfect, a real September morning, fresh breeze from the sea, crisp and clear. Led a Rover Paddy and again we did close support bombing and strafing within 500 yards of our troops. Circled target at 8,000 feet with my No.2, area given by Paddy as a strong point. Pongos shelled the target to make sure of identification and then we bombed from 8,000 down to the deck. Two direct hits on a house which was the target and strikes in the whole area from cannon and machine gun fire.

On Readiness in the evening and of all things got two Scrambles which is odd these days. The panic that ensued! On the first Scramble, two 109s were reported inland going home on the deck—no contact. Second Scramble was against 6+ at 20,000 feet, but false alarm. Carried out search for Marauder which went into the sea near Rimini—no sign. Carried out patrol for the usual 109 reccos until dusk and although vectored after bogeys, nothing seen.

Thursday, 14 September 1944

A dawn patrol looking for cursed elusive 109 recces but again no see. We can reach Austria from here. A quick strafe of the Hun country? Led an armed recce of the Ravenna-Ferrara-Octiglia area, finding numerous railway trucks near Ferrara so bombed them, getting two direct hits with six aircraft. Strafed same several times but could start no fires. On the way back strafed a couple of trucks. Flew on the deck amongst some Eyetie farmers causing panic!

---

[1]Captain M D Lawton SAAF was picked up by a Walrus ASR amphibian, but when taxying back was mistakenly attacked by two Navy MTBs and sunk. Lawton and his two rescuers were then picked up by one of the boats.

Led a close support Rover David sortie in the afternoon and, after a lot of looking, found the target—a gun position and strong point. I got a direct hit! Must record same! Strafed the area well. Lots of shelling and bombing going on in the whole Rimini battle area.

Friday, 15 September 1944

Another dawn recce patrol with McKay, at 500 feet over the sea off coast between Pesaro and the Po Estuary; completely uneventful. Saw a rowing boat complete with oars in the middle of the Adriatic, also a German hospital ship—mit lights on.

Led a close support show after breakfast. Bombed and strafed odd transport and troops in battle area. Cut road with direct hit and clobbered several MT and things. Pottered about in the afternoon, then led Frankie Banner on the dusk anti-recce patrol. Uneventful patrol over the sea between Ancona and Yugoslav coast. At dusk two Huns came down to Rimini at 20,000 feet but not a hope of getting them.

Group Captain and Wing Commander both u/s celebrating Battle of Britain anniversary.

Brian Kingcome and Hugh 'Cocky' Dundas had both been in the Battle, Kingcome with 92 Squadron, Dundas with 611. Dundas' brother John had also fought in the Battle, with 609 Squadron, winning the DFC and Bar, but he'd been killed in November. In his now famous last action, John Dundas had just shot down a 109 flown by the German ace Helmut Wick, who had over 50 victories, but was then shot down in turn by the German's wingman.

Saturday, 16 September 1944

Dawn anti-recce patrol but although vectored and chased after bogeys they all turned out to be friendly. Pottered about all day until the evening when again on anti-recce patrol with Banner. Patrolled Rimini at low altitude until almost last light, then clambered quickly to 19,000 feet as last two evenings Huns have appeared at last light at 20,000 there. No joy—and darkish landing.

Party at 601 as MacKenzie is off to Aussie. Sgt Britten shot up fairly well by 20 mm and had to belly-land in the morning. On the evening show, P/O Dixon was hit while strafing, by 20 mm, and after pulling up to 4,000 feet pouring smoke, went straight in on fire.

Sunday, 17 September 1944

Dawn anti-shuftie patrol off Rimini again. Still no go, damn Huns. Was informed by G/C a couple of days ago that AOC rules that I go off at the end of this month and that I fly, at most, once a day! Says he would like to keep me on but if anything happened he would have it on his conscience! Offered a job as wing commander of training flight but don't go on that much. Beer at 92 and then party at 417.

Monday, 18 September 1944

Quiet morning recovering from the 417 party. Air and cannon test on 'J' in the afternoon—port cannon jammed. Had a look at the battle around Rimini—still going hammer and tongs but Huns refuse to budge.

Dusk anti-recce patrol. Started patrol at 8,000 feet over battle area but so many aircraft bombing we had to go to 11,000 feet to get clear of the crowd! Stooged around until dusk when two bogeys were reported north of Rimini at 12,000 feet. Dashed up there but they went away north.

Wednesday, 20 September 1944

Dawn anti-recce patrol again; still nothing doing. We rushed about off Rimini amongst the clouds and chased a Wellington. Led a Rover Paddy in the afternoon and bombed and strafed an area where tanks were reported to be. Some good bombing—four out of six on the target. Raining this evening —aerodrome very u/s.

Thursday, 21 September 1944

Drove down to Ancona with Pete Venter, Bob Sarll and Frankie Banner. Pottered about the town all day seeing the sights. Awful news this evening that I am to hand over to Squadron Leader Daniel tomorrow.[1] Doesn't sound as though I shall be going home either. Looks like Training Flight. Greatly disappointed but it's not the first time.

---

[1] Squadron Leader Stephen Walter Daniel DFC and Bar came from Scotland and had flown with 72 Squadron in 1942, operating over Northern France. Moved to Tunisia where he became a flight commander, and saw action over Sicily. He then took command of 72, one of those few men to have risen from junior pilot to CO of the same unit. After a rest he was given command of 145 Squadron. At the end of the war he would receive the DSO and later served in Korea, flying with the Americans. He retired from the RAF in 1963. Died in 1982.

ITALY

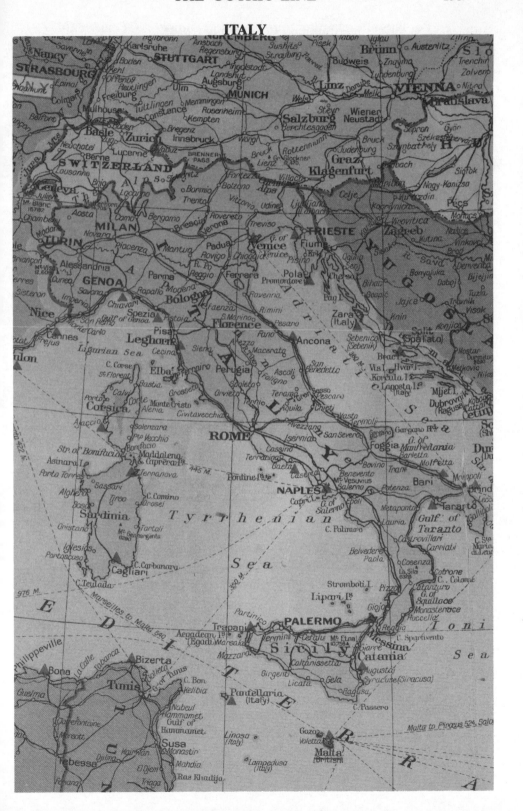

Perhaps after another tour I might get home! AOC suddenly realised I had more hours than he thought, so ordered me off.

Friday, 22 September 1944

Dismal day. Will be very sorry indeed to leave the Squadron. Frankie Banner OTE [tour-expired] and Brown-Gaylord takes over A Flight—a good lad. Think I can get Banner home but not myself!!

[Later.] Saw the Groupie and he said OK for UK? Seems pretty well certain—wizzo. Drinking at 92, then 417 in the evening. Pongos driving on hard past Rimini.

Saturday, 23 September 1944

Handing over to S/L Daniel today. 'Drome still u/s but no more rain—yet. Said a couple of words to the pilots but a prepared speech went by the board when the time came so I just said 'thanks'. Drinking at our place and then 92 again. Cox turned up from the front looking shagged. Chaps passing out right and left!

Sunday, 24 September 1944

Feel a bit hang-dog this morning. Drove up to DAF HQ with the G/C in the afternoon as the AOC, Air Vice-Marshal Dickson, wanted to see me. The old boy said lots of nice things etc., and that he was recommending me for the UK.

Monday, 25 September 1944

Flew this morning on air test of old 'J'. Flew around the Rimini battle area and shuftied scene of recent fighting. No flak!

Tuesday, 26 September 1944

Quiet morning and afternoon but what a night. Threw a party and had all the Wing types over—an excellent party; finished up in the Sergeant's Mess playing cock fights. Many bruises but nothing broken.

Wednesday, 27 September 1944

Got up for lunch. Most ginormous party started spontaneously in the trailer when ten bottles of beer and five bottles of whisky consumed by five of us! Continued over at 92 where more boozing went on. ENSA people arrived in force. Big game of cock fighting where I believe I broke a shoulder and elbow but Banner and self cleared the floor.

Thursday, 28 September 1944

Drinking at lunch time at Pete Venter's place. Beer continued in G/C's trailer where ENSA popsies were visiting! G/C took up the Fairchild and pranged the thing landing or taxying—laugh!

Sergeant's Mess threw a farewell party for me this evening. Nuff said! Presented me with a lot of whisky. Cox turned up.

Friday, 29 September 1944

Feel like nothing on earth this morning. Managed to get up for lunch but I was off noggin this afternoon to bring things around.

For Neville now it became the same old story, pottering about hoping, and wondering what was going to happen to him. Having finally been taken off operations, he was longing to get back to England, but until he was actually on his way . . .

Monday, 2 October 1944

Still loitering. Drove up to DAF in the afternoon with Daniel and Cox. Pouring with rain and soaked to the skin. Saw W/C Turner and reminded him of my UK things! They are trying to get Frankie Banner on Rover Jimmy job in the front line but he as good as refuses to do it. Cox is off Rover Jimmy and thinks he may get home. He's only just come out, more or less, so I hardly think he has much of a chance.

Graham Cox had been in the Battle of Britain and had come out to the Mediterranean in May 1943. Neville had been out since the end of 1941 which is why he thought Cox had little chance of a UK posting just yet!

Tuesday, 3 October 1944

And yet still pottering. Bad day for 145. Sgt Piercy, on his first operational trip, had to bale out after being hit by flak, out to sea from Cervia. No news of him yet but believe a Walrus picked him up OK. On the same sortie, F/L Gaylord was badly hit by heavy flak and he was extremely lucky to make Rimini where he crash-landed at 180 mph without straps—unhurt! Sgt Garth also hit by AA, aircraft Cat.2, and had to land with tail wheel up. Three aircraft lost and nought to show for it. Drove up to Rimini with the Adj to pick up Gaylord but passed him on his way back. Visited Pete Venter in hospital—seems cheerful but badly bashed about. Back broken in three places and head injuries.

Friday, 6 October 1944
Papers back from AOC with good recommendation for UK.

Sunday, 8 October 1944
I am leaving on the 11th by air for Naples—perhaps. BBC and press types around to get me to broadcast. Bind.

Monday, 9 October 1944
Did a broadcast about nothing. Flew over to Florence with Cox, Daniel and the Adj in the Fairchild. Stayed at the DAF Hotel—the Majestic. Met Hunk and all of 324 Wing who are just back from France. Looking so shagged too, and not surprising by their stories.

Tuesday, 10 October 1944
145 Squadron's 5th birthday so had to make an effort and try and fly back from Florence, which we did in some rugged weather. We had to cross the bomb-line to get through! Twitch!! Terrific thrash, 92 and 145 having parties. All the types turned up including Pat Burke—surprise. She stayed the night.

Wednesday, 11 October 1944
Feel most peculiar today, but what a party. Covered in mud and stuff last night but think I'll live. No air transport to Naples today.

Thursday, 12 October, 1944
Fixed up for air transport to Naples tomorrow. Drove up to DAF to arrange same and visited 'haunted' castle near Cattolica. Went round to all the squadrons and Wing to say farewell. Made it too.

Friday, 13 October 1944
Left the Squadron this morning along with Cox and Frankie Banner. All the pilots turned out early to see us off. Needless to say am very sorry to go and I don't think I am wrong when I say the chaps were sorry to see us leave.

Drove to Rimini at break-neck speed and flew down to Capidachino in an Anson. A good day for flying—Italy looked at its best as we flew over the hills. No transport or anything to take us to the BPD for hours, of course, but we eventually arrived OK. Depressing place.

Away from the Squadron and awaiting his next move, Neville neglected his diary for the next ten days or so. He resumed it on the 24th.

Tuesday, 24 October 1944

During stay at BPD, have spent the days whilst waiting for a posting in visits to Naples, to eat at the officer's club and see cinemas and opera. Once I hitch-hiked to Sorrento for a look-see. Spent a lot of time at the Portici officer's club; most outstanding of all I am off the alcohol since coming here. Feel lots better for it too. Cox got a DSO the other day. Banner is posted to UK. Still don't know whether I shall go or not yet.

Wednesday, 25 October 1944

Had lunch with Banner and S/L Parrott who is on his way back to a squadron—ex-73 OTU.[1] Game of billiards after lunch and to the cinema at Portici. Raining again; getting depressed with all this hanging about. Have met dozens of types here who I knew on squadrons. 251 and 322 [Wings] are being disbanded.

Friday, 27 October 1944

Posting to UK!! Came through from MAAF this morning— Hey ho!

Monday, 30 October 1944

Went to bed at 10 o'clock and called at 11 to report to movements with Frankie Banner. Transport by air at dawn tomorrow!

Tuesday, 31 October 1944

Up early and off to Pymigliano airport to board a Dakota for the UK. Three years—but good years. Took off at about 8.30, set course and left Italy via the Anzio beach. Hit Corsica and then on to Southern France via Toulon, Marseille and across to Le Havre, thence to the shores of England. Landed at Lyneham at 5.30 odd. Flew over in 2nd pilot's seat, so had a comfortable trip.

Set course for London. Driven to Swindon in a coach, passed three pubs in as many seconds—Hell! Arrived home at midnight.

---

[1] Squadron Leader P L Parrott DFC and Bar. Peter Parrott had flown in the Battle of Britain with Neville's late Squadron—145. Going out to the Middle East he had served with 72 and 111 Squadrons in Sicily. In September 1943 he took command of 43 Squadron. When Neville met him in October 1944, he was on his way to take command of his old 72 Squadron. He retired from the RAF in 1965 as a Wing Commander AFC.

CHAPTER XV

HOME IS THE HUNTER

Neville had been away for three days short of three years. What he had innocently believed would be just a few weeks had turned into almost 156 weeks. However, in that time he had developed from the novice fighter pilot into the top scoring fighter ace of the Mediterranean Theatre. He had also received the Distinguished Service Order, and Distinguished Flying Cross and Two Bars.

In achieving these accolades, he had flown a total of 486 operational sorties, covering 712 operational flying hours, out of a total flying time of 1,619 hours, 20 minutes. On any terms he was now a vastly experienced pilot. While overseas he had risen from a squadron pilot to a flight commander, been a chief flying instructor, and finally a squadron commander.

A breakdown of statistics can be of interest. Upon leaving the Biggin Hill Wing in late 1941, he had just 350 flying hours recorded in his log book. Posted to 112 Squadron, operating with the P40 Tomahawk and Kittyhawk fighters, his flying hours rose to approximately 500 by April 1942. As an instructor, flying mostly P40s and Spitfires, he had added a further 200 flying hours to this total, before joining 92 Squadron in November. On completing his second tour in May 1943, the total had reached 950.

Following his period as CFI at No.73 OTU, his hours had topped the 1,300 mark, to which he added over 300 while leading 145 Squadron in Italy. The breakdown of his operational hours into his three fighter tours are:

1st Tour	161 sorties	221 op hours	Biggin Hill & Western Desert
2nd Tour	132 sorties	203 op hours	Libya and Tunisia
3rd Tour	193 sorties	288 op hours	Italy
Totals:	**486**	**712**	

Of his 28 or possibly 29 confirmed victories:

1st Tour 8(9) destroyed, 3 probables, 4 damaged
2nd Tour 14 destroyed, 1 damaged
3rd Tour 6 destroyed, 1 damaged

Upon his return to England, there was a period of rest and leave to be taken in the bosom of his family he'd been away from for so long. He had to adjust to being home again. He soon began to visit old friends and old haunts in London. By mid-November he was looking for work, but after three tours of Ops, there seemed little likelihood of him being able to return to operational flying. His diary had become sparse over these days, not un-naturally, but he did record:

Friday, 10 November 1944
Visited Air Ministry re. a job again. Don't seem to have much future; couldn't offer me much. Have put in for testing—may have to wait though. Arrived home after a good lunch with some of the boys at the Brevet Club and some shopping.

Neville had little idea of what the future held, but this thought of testing aeroplanes was in fact the start of his future career and life, in which he would gain as much fame as he had achieved being a fighter pilot. Within a few days, things had started happening.

Saturday, 18 November 1944
Down to Hawkers Ltd, Langley, for an interview with Philip Lucas for test pilot post on the firm. Met all the types including the chief test pilot, Bill Humble, and the rest of the gang.
Interview seemed to go off OK and I am supposed to be going there on 28 December. Chips Carpenter is there whom I knew in Italy. Back in London and a lunch with Humble at some extraordinary place in Greek Street. Met Jamie Rankin and WingCo Turner in the Brevet Club later. Went into a cocktail party of Tony Bartley. Met Moira and Sheila of Biggin fame, then went on to the 'Mitre' after dinner somewhere, and then the 400 Club—ended 6 o'clock next morning!

The scheme, in fact, was that operational pilots on rest were being selected to help production test flying at various aircraft company factories. Neville, afraid of being saddled with a desk job, saw this as a way of continuing to fly.

Philip Lucas had been with Hawkers since May 1931, joining them at Brooklands, when it was known as H G Hawker Engineering Company. Now aged 42, he had served in the RAF between 1926 and 1931, and with Hawkers had been part of the Hawker Hurricane project, which started in 1936 under P W S 'George' Bulman. Lucas had won the George Medal in May 1940, for saving the prototype Hawker Typhoon, rather than baling out, when things went wrong during a test flight. He would become Chief Test Pilot in 1945, following the retirement of Bulman. Bill Humble was the number two test pilot at Hawkers and would later succeed Lucas as CTP, and later become Sales Manager for the company.

Neville's old Squadron Commander and Wing Leader, Jamie Rankin, was now commanding 125 Spitfire Wing, while Stan Turner had recently returned from Italy too, and was about to take a post with 2nd TAF. Tony Bartley, of course, had been with 92 Squadron at Biggin in 1941. He was now a Squadron Leader and was trying to set up an airline for the American Wing with whom he was a liaison officer.

J M V 'Chips' Carpenter DFC and Bar had flown in the Battle of Britain and in the Middle East he'd seen action on Malta, then later with 417 and 92 Squadrons. After a brief stint with 145 Squadron he commanded 72 Squadron, leaving the Wing just after Neville had joined it in Italy. After his period with Hawkers he received a permanent commission in the RAF, retiring in 1959.

A few days later Neville received a telegram from Air Ministry, telling him he would be posted to Hawker's at Langley with effect from 1 January 1945; his period with them would be until 1 January 1946. He would, however, drop from Squadron Leader to Flight Lieutenant, but that was acceptable if he could continue to fly. It had also been suggested that he might be in line for a job as Air Attaché at Chungking, China, as a Wing Commander, but a flying job was preferred.

Now he had to fill in time between November and the New Year. A tour of factories giving lectures and pep-talks scared him to death, so the temporary command of a Comm (Communications) Flight at Inverness was the way to go. The posting came through on 2 December and he left Euston on the 3rd, sleeping on the train all the way north.

Monday, 4 December 1944

Arrived at Inverness about 11 o'clock this morning. Cold! Lunched at the Station Hotel and then went along to Longman [airfield], only a half mile out of the town. Reported to the Comm Flight, consisting of Proctors, Oxfords, Spitfires and a Dominie. We fly odd people about the country and run passengers up to the Orkneys. Only attached here as acting flight commander; real flight commander coming back in a couple of days. Have asked to go home for Christmas.

Wednesday, 6 December 1944

Finding trouble getting up in the mornings—so cold and bleak, even at 8.30. Flashed around in a Spitfire V this morning. A pretty shagged-out Spit but still a Spit. Flew in the afternoon with P/O Patterson in an Oxford on an Air Test and came nearer to death than ever before! Ice on the wings prevented any sort of climb after take off over Inverness town. Weaved between chimneys and church spires—so worried.

Thursday, 7 December 1944

Some Spit flying—local flash around in the morning and did some aerobatics. Flight affiliation in the afternoon with some Coastal Liberators from Tain. Landed at Tain for tea. Have been appointed Station Commander as the CO is on leave!!

Tuesday, 12 December 1944

Thumbed around the sky with W/C Wolfe in the morning in an Oxford. Some solo flying in the Oxford in the afternoon— big twin pilot nowadays.

Wednesday, 13 December 1944

Busy day—bad frost and cold. Took F/Sgt Furnley up in the Dominie to show him the form, also W/O Whittaker after lunch. Can't get away from instructing. Took up Furnley again in the Proctor and frightened myself no end. He's used to heavy aircraft!

Friday, 15 December 1944

The CO of the Station came back today so handed same back to him. Put in for leave for the 20th to 27th. Got same OK'd and can in fact go at anytime, so W/C Wolfe tells me. I shall stay on and get some twin flying. Thumbed a Spit around in the afternoon and did odd aerobatics. Flicks [film show] in the evening. Total war up here!

Saturday, 16 December 1944

Took the Dominie off with four passengers to Skaebrae this morning, via Casteltown. Forced to stay at Casteltown due to high winds up in the Orkneys—gusting up to 70 mph. Lunched there and returned to Inverness in the evening. Visibility bad and wind high at Castletown but returned OK in spite of a bad port engine.

Sunday, 17 December 1944
Wind still holding and most flying stopped. Walked around the aerodrome this morning with Bill Higgins, the aerodrome control officer—got a good deal of fresh air. Air tested the Proctor in the afternoon and looked around the countryside. Went along to the WAAF officer's mess this evening, for what I don't know; some sort of party.

Monday, 18 December 1944
Lovely day in comparison. Flew the Dominie up to the Orkneys to collect turkeys. Wizard trip—could see for miles. Good return trip too with turkeys and passengers.

Tuesday, 19 December 1944
Off back home today. Left for Perth in the Oxford after lunch. Tried to fly over top of the hills straight to Perth but had to turn back and go around the coast. Extreme vibration in the port engine caused some worry and it lost a lot of oil. On inspection we found the prop tip was missing! Didn't low fly or anything. Caught the 8.20 train from Perth—a First Class sleeper was booked for me by Bill Higgins.

Wednesday, 20 December 1944
A good trip down but four hours late due to fog. Caught connection from Charing Cross to Tonbridge, so home. Good to see the folks after only a short stay away this time. Went along to the odd pub in the evening.

This is the final entry in Neville's 1944 diary. That he enjoyed his first Christmas in England since 1940 goes without saying. It had been a long journey.

Neville reported to Langley on 1 January to begin learning as much as he could about the Tempest II and Tempest V fighters. He found that the chief production test pilot was Hubert Broad, a WW1 RNAS fighter pilot, and who had previously been with de Havillands. There were a number of former operational pilots there: 'Chips' Carpenter DFC, of course; Frankie Silk DFC, a Spitfire PR pilot; and Frank Murphy DFC, a former Typhoon pilot with 486 New Zealand Squadron. More importantly, however, he met Gwen, whom he married in March 1947.

Between times Neville attended No.4 Course at the Empire Test Pilot's School at Cranfield, in January 1946, following which he was with the RAF's High Speed Flight in June of that year. This had followed his year with Hawkers and a period with the Aircraft and Armament Experimental Establishment at RAF Boscombe Down in 1947. He received a last wartime decoration, the Czech War Cross in 1946, and then an Air Force Cross in 1948.

Neville had his first taste of test flying at this time, and has rarely been away from it since those days. Now, in 1995, he is still a test pilot, continually passing his flying medical. His only problem is one which affects many long term pilots—his hearing. Having had the constant roar or throb of engines for so long, Neville is now deaf in one ear and the other is not 100%. However, he has a special radio built into his flying helmet, and with many years of listening to ground controllers, knows the jargon off pat, and has not the slightest difficulty. For their part, the air traffic boys know they're dealing with a pro.

He finally resigned his RAF commission in June 1948 to become a full-time test pilot with Hawkers, and three years later became their Chief Test Pilot, a position he held until he relinquished the post in late 1956 due to a fractured back and spinal injuries sustained in a Hunter crash due to engine failure. In between times he held the rank of Squadron Leader in the Royal Auxiliary Air Force when commanding No. 615 (County of Surrey) Squadron RAuxAF at Biggin Hill between 1950-51. He became an Officer of the Order of the British Empire (OBE) in January 1953 and was awarded the Queen's Commendation for Valuable Service in the Air in 1955.

In September 1953 he set the World Air Speed record by flying an all red Hawker Hunter (WB188) 727.63 miles per hour or 1,170.76 km per hour, and also the closed circuit record of 709 mph. The course lay off Littlehampton, along the south coast of England.

The Queen's Commendation came following a sudden bang when flying a Hunter off Littlehampton in August 1955 while carrying out a gun-firing test. The engine stopped but Neville managed a landing at Ford rather than a bale out, thereby saving the aircraft so that the cause could be ascertained—the test pilot's prime job. The engine had had a turbine blade failure.

Two days later, however, taking off with a new engine, he found, at 1,000 feet above Chichester Harbour, the throttle gave him only idling thrust. Trying desperately to get down onto RAF Thorney Island's runway, he lost height but failed to make it. Touching down at 200 mph on some rough grassland, the Hunter went into a series of bounces. Neville rapdily pulled up the wheels, jettisoned the hood, cut the fuel and waited. The Hunter careered into a number of arcs, reached the edge of the airfield, over a ditch and went in nose first into a sea-wall and broke up. Neville came out with only cuts and bruises but a painfully aching back, subsequently found to be fractured.

Back to flying after a period on his back and then in plaster, there was a period of discomfort when flying as he continued with the Hunter development, but a final heavy landing in a P1099 crushed a disc which eventually made it impossible for him to continue high speed flying and testing.

Over the next couple of years Neville kept his hand in on freelance flying and consultancy work with Fairey Aviation and Field Aircraft Services, while 1958-9 was taken up with testing the Garland-Bianchi 'Linnet' light two-seater. Then there followed a period as personal pilot for Sir George Dowty and he then formed Duke Aviation Ltd.

A fuller account of his post-war career can be found in Neville's updated reprint of his very successful book *Test Pilot*, which was first published in 1953. The reprint, by Grub Street Publishers, came out in 1992, in time for the 40th anniversary of his record-breaking flight in WB188, the preserved red Hunter being on display at the Tangmere Aviation Museum, with which Neville has close ties.

Meanwhile, Neville flies whenever he can, and is still the highly respected and highly experienced test pilot he has been for almost 50 years, which has to be some kind of record. Certainly there can be very few men still flying solo who first flew in the early days of WW2.

This too has been quite a journey. Flying has given him a full life and he has given much in return, to his country, the Royal Air Force and the British aircraft industry.

APPENDIX I

Record of Service

RAF Uxbridge	30 Apr 1940—1 May 1940	
RAF Padgate	19 Jun 1940—22 Jun 1940	
4 ITW, Bexhill	22 Jun 1940—27 Jun 1940	
4 ITW, Paignton	27 Jun 1940—20 Aug 1940	
13 EFTS, White Waltham	20 Aug 1940—20 Sep 1940	
1 EFTS, Hatfield	20 Sep 1940—27 Sep 1940	
5 FTS, Sealand	27 Sep 1940—17 Dec 1940	
5 FTS, Ternhill	17 Dec 1940—15 Feb 1941	'Wings' 17 Feb 1941
58 OTU, Grangemouth	17 Feb 1941—31 Mar 1941	
92 Sqn, Biggin Hill	2 Apr 1941—25 Sep 1941	COs S/L J Rankin DSO DFC
„ Gravesend	25 Sep 1941—20 Oct 1941	
„ Digby	20 Oct 1941—2 Nov 1941	S/L R N Milne DFC
HQME, Cairo, Egypt	7 Nov 1941—11 Nov 1941	
112 Sqn, Sidi Hannish	12 Nov 1941—15 Nov 1941	CO S/L F V Morello
„ LG110	15 Nov 1941—19 Nov 1941	
„ Ft. Maddelena	19 Nov 1941—6 Dec 1941	
„ El Adem, Libya	13 Dec 1941—19 Dec 1941	
„ Gazala	19 Dec 1941—20 Dec 1941	
„ El Mechili	20 Dec 1941—27 Dec 1941	
„ Msus	27 Dec 1941—13 Jan 1942	CO S/L C R Caldwell DSO DFC
„ Antelat	13 Jan 1942—21 Jan 1942	
„ Msus	21 Jan 1942—24 Jan 1942	
„ El Mechili	24 Jan 1942—28 Jan 1942	
„ Gazala	28 Jan 1942—7 Feb 1942	
„ Gambut	7 Feb 1942—15 Feb 1942	
„ El Adem	15 Feb 1942—16 Feb 1942	
„ Gambut	16 Feb 1942—22 Feb 1942	
„ „ satellite	22 Feb 1942—9 Mar 1942	
„ Gambut	9 Mar 1942—15 Mar 1942	DFC 11 March 1942
„ Sidi Hannish	15 Mar 1942—15 Apr 1942	
„ Gambut satellite	15 Apr 1942—20 Apr 1942	
1 MEFS, Ballah, Egypt	23 Apr 1942—4 Jul 1942	CO F/L R E Bary DFC
1 MEFS, Muqubelia, Pal.	4 Jul 1942—31 Jul 1942	
1 MEFS, Ballah, Egypt	31 Jul 1942—16 Nov 1942	
92 Sqn, Gambut, Libya	16 Nov 1942—24 Nov 1942	CO S/L J H Wedgewood DFC
„ Msus	25 Nov 1942—3 Dec 1942	
„ Hassirat	3 Dec 1942—9 Dec 1942	
„ Nogra	9 Dec 1942—21 Dec 1942	CO S/L J M Morgan DFC
„ El Merduma	21 Dec 1942—31 Dec 1942	
„ El Chel	31 Dec 1942—9 Jan 1943	
„ Tamet	9 Jan 1943—19 Jan 1943	CO S/L W J Harper

„	Waddi Sarri	19 Jan 1943—15 Feb 1943	
„	Castel Benito	15 Feb 1943—26 Feb 1943	Bar DFC 13 Feb 1943
„	Medenine	26 Feb 1943—1 Mar 1943	
„	Ben Gardan	2 Mar 1943—10 Mar 1943	
„	Grara	10 Mar 1943—11 Apr 1943	DSO 27 March 1943
„	Fauconnerie	11 Apr 1943—15 Apr 1943	
„	Goubrine	15 Apr 1943—6 May 1943	
„	Hergla	6 May 1943—20 May 1943	CO S/L P H Humphreys DFC
„	Ben Gardan	20 May 1943—1 Jun 1943	
73 OTU, Abu Sueir		11 Jun 1943—27 Feb 1944	COs G/C W J Satchell DSO
			G/C J Grandy DSO
145 Sqn, Marcianise, It.		3 Mar 1944—23 Apr 1944	OC 244 Wing:
„	Venafro	23 Apr 1944—21 May 1944	G/C C B F Kingcome DSO DFC
„	Lago	21 May 1944—3 Jun 1944	
„	Venafro	3 Jun 1944—12 Jun 1944	2nd Bar DFC 3 Jun 44
„	Littorio	12 Jun 1944—17 Jun 1944	
„	Fabrica	17 Jun 1944—3 Jul 1944	Wing Leaders:
„	Perugia	3 Jul 1944—14 Aug 1944	W/C P S Turner DSO DFC
„	Rosignano	14 Aug 1944—16 Aug 1944	
„	Perugia	16 Aug 1944—25 Aug 1944	
„	Loreto	25 Aug 1944—4 Sep 1944	W/C H S L Dundas DSO DFC
„	Fano	4 Sep 1944—13 Oct 1944	
3 BPD Naples		13 Oct 1944—31 Oct 1944	
13 Gp Comm Flt, Inverness		4 Dec 1944—19 Dec 1944	
Hawkers Ltd, Langley		1 Jan 1945—31 Dec 1945	
ETPS, Cranfield		2 Jan 1946—30 Jun 1946	
High Speed Flt, Tangmere		1 Jul 1946—30 Sep 1946	
ETPS, Cranfield		30 Sep 1946—6 Jan 1947	
RAE, Farnborough		6 Jan 1947—6 Feb 1947	
ETPS, Cranfield		6 Feb 1947—12 Mar 1947	
A&AEE, Boscombe Down		28 Mar 1947—25 Jun 1948	Awarded AFC 10 Jun 48
Left RAF		25 Jun 1948	
Hawkers Ltd		19 Jul 1948—31 Oct 1956	OBE 1 January 1953
615 Sqn, Biggin Hill		Aug 1950—Aug 1951	

APPENDIX II

Awards and Citations

The *London Gazette*, Friday 17 March 1942:

Distinguished Flying Cross
Pilot Officer Neville Frederick Duke (61054) RAFVR, No.112 Squadron

One day in February 1942, Pilot Officer Duke was the leader of a section of a wing when he sighted 35 enemy aircraft. He informed the wing leader and led his section to attack. In the ensuing combat 11 enemy fighters were destroyed by the squadron, 2 being destroyed by Pilot Officer Duke. This officer's leadership contributed materially to the success achieved. He has destroyed 8 enemy aircraft and probably destroyed and damaged a further 6.

The *London Gazette*, Friday 19 February 1943:

Bar to Distinguished Flying Cross
Flying Officer N F Duke DFC (61054) RAFVR, No.92 Squadron

One day in January 1943, this officer led his flight in an engagement against a large force of enemy fighters over Beurat. During the combat, Flying Officer Duke fought with great resolution, destroying 2 enemy aircraft before all his ammunition was expended. Since being awarded the Distinguished Flying Cross he has destroyed 3 hostile aircraft, bringing his victories to 11. Flying Officer Duke has led his section and the flight with distinction.

The *London Gazette*, Friday 9 April 1943:

Distinguished Service Order
Flight Lieutenant N F Duke DFC (61054) RAFVR, No.92 Squadron

In recent intensive air fighting this officer has led his flight and often the squadron on most of the sorties which have been undertaken. He has displayed exceptional skill and dash, achieving great success. During the first week in March, 1943, he destroyed 7 enemy aircraft, bringing his total victories to 19. His courageous leadership and fine fighting qualities are worthy of the highest praise.

The *London Gazette*, Tuesday 20 June 1944:

Second Bar to Distinguished Flying Cross
Acting Squadron Leader N F Duke DSO DFC
(61054) RAFVR, No.145 Squadron

This officer has displayed the highest standard of skill, gallantry and determination, qualities which have been well reflected in his squadron which has destroyed 23 hostile aircraft within a period of several weeks. Recently, over Anzio, he led the squadron in a sortie during which 8 enemy aircraft were shot down. Four of them were destroyed by Squadron Leader Duke himself. He has destroyed 26 and damaged several other enemy aircraft.

The *London Gazette*, 10 June 1948:

Air Force Cross
Acting Squadron Leader N F Duke DSO DFC (61054) RAFVR

Czech War Cross — 1946.

Made an Officer of the Order of the British Empire—1 January 1953.

Queen's Commendation for Valuable Service in the Air—1955.

APPENDIX III

Victories

Date	Destroyed	Probable	Damaged	a/c flown	Remarks
1941					
92 Sqn					
			Spitfire V		
26 Apr	—	—	Me109F	R6904 'Y'	Channel Patrol
23 Jun	—	—	Me109F	R6904 'Y'?	Circus No.21—Le Touquet
25 Jun	Me109F	—	—	R6904 'Y'	Circus No.23—St Omer
9 Aug	Me109F	—		W3319 'X'	Sweep—St Omer
31 Aug	—	—	Me109F	AB125 'Y'	Circus No.90—St Omer
112 Sqn			**Tomahawk IIB**		
21 Nov	CR42	—	—	AK402	'F' Tobruk area, ⅓ share with PO Jeffries & Sgt Carson
22 Nov	Me109F	—	—	AK402	'F' Tobruk—El Adem area; Ofhr Waskott of I/JG27 baled out, PoW
30 Nov	Fiat G50	—	Me109F	AK402	'F' 20 Gruppo; El Gobi area—then shot down by Ofw Otto Schulz of II/JG27
4 Dec	MC 200	Ju87	—	AN337	'F' El Adem—Tobruk area
22 Dec	Me109F	Ju87	—	AK354	'L' over Megrun airfield;
„	—	Ju52	—	„	S. of Benghazi, shared with Sgt Carson. 109 pilot was probably Fw. Erich Wassermann of 7/JG27
1942			**Kittyhawk I**		
14 Feb	MC200	—	—	AK578	'V' SW of Acrona
„	MC200	—	—	„	Shared with Sgt Reid 3 RAAF Sqn
1943					
92 Sqn			**Spitfire Vb**		
8 Jan	MC202	—	—	ER220	'R' Zidan area
11 Jan	MC202	—	—	EP338	'S' NW of Tamit; S.Ten. Tellerchi 18 Gruppo, baled out, PoW
„	MC202	—	—	„	Magg. Gustavo Garretto of 18 Gruppo, baled out, PoW
21 Jan	Ju87	—	—	ER220	'R' S of Castel Benito: III/StG.3: pilot baled out
1 Mar	MC202	—	—	ER821	'R' NW Medenin—both baled out;
„	MC202	—	—	„	One was S.Ten. Antonio Roglai of 3 Stormo—PoW
3 Mar	Me109F/G	—	—	ER821	'R' N Gabes, either Uffz Werner or Fw Herbert Schwarz, III/JG77; or Uffz Willi Streba 9/JG77
4 Mar	Me109F	—	—	ER821	'R' Nr Medenin Uffz Herbert Muller, I/SG2;
„	Me109F	—	—	„	Pilot baled out—PoW
7 Mar	Me109F	—	—	ER821	'R' Nr Berka; Ltn. Heinz Schiedat of I/SG2—PoW (am)
„	Me109F	—	—	BR519 'T'[1]	Noffatia airfield, pilot baled out (pm)
25 Mar	—	—	Ju88	ER689	'J' 15 miles W of Gabes
29 Mar	Me109G	—	—	ES121	'R' 25 miles N of Gabes

			Spitfire IX		
16 Apr			SM82	EN333	Cap Bon area
„	SM82	—	—	„	Cap Bon area

1944					
145 Sqn			**Spitfire VIII**		
13 May	Me109G	—	Me109G	JG241	'J' Arezzo, Perugia area
14 May	Me109G	—	—	JG241	'J' Cassino
21 May	FW190	—	—	JG241	'J' NE of Velletri; I & II/SG4
„	FW190D	—	—	JG241	'J' NE of Velletri; I & II/SG4
3 Sep	Me109G	—	—	MT775	'J' Nr Rimini, pilot baled out
„	Me109G	—	—	MT775	'J' Nr Rimini, pilot baled out

Total: 26 and 3 shared destroyed, 3 probables, 6 damaged

Enemy Types:	**Destroyed**	**Probable**	**Damaged**
	14 Me109F/G	2 Ju87	5 Me109F/G
	5 MC202	1 Ju52	1 Ju88
	3 MC200		
	2 SM82		
	2 FW190		
	1 CR42		
	1 G50		
	1 Ju87		

---

[1] Log book records ER821 QJ–R; combat report quotes BR519 QJ–T

APPENDIX IV

Squadron Combat Reports

No.145 Squadron Combat Reports for 13 May 1944:

Flight Lieutenant W A R MacDonald:

> I was flying No.5 in a formation of 6 a/c flying S near AREZZO at 17,000' when 6 ME109s passed below us. I turned into them with the rest of the formation but unfortunately all E/A appeared to be engaged by the rest of the formation. I dived down with our own a/c to 4,000' but then gave it up so pulled up gaining altitude rapidly. Of a sudden I saw 2 of the ME109s diving towards me. I fired a short burst at one but did not see any results. I then turned about and dived after the E/A and fired a fairly long burst from 200 yards and saw strikes on the fuselage and engine cowling, then a large part of his tail plane flashed passed my a/c and I saw that the port tailplane had disappeared altogether. E/A engine had stopped and went down in a steep side slip in area (W) Q.73.

Claim: 1 ME109 Destroyed. Fired 240 × .303, 60 × 20mm.

Flight Lieutenant C R Parbury:

I was flying No.3 in a formation of 6 Spitfire VIIIs when we sighted 6 ME109s in the AREZZO area. Closing astern of them they turned to port. I engaged the No.2 on the starboard side of their formation and when I was about to open fire from 300 yards, he started taking evasive action so that I could not get a steady shot so I did not fire. This evasive action went on for about 3 minutes and consisted of steep turns, half rolls and vertical climbs. After about three minutes I got in a short burst from 100 yds in a climbing attitude. I saw about ten strikes on the fuselage behind the cockpit and three or four fairly large pieces flew off. At that moment my engine temporarily cut and I lost E/A.

Claim: 1 Me109 Damaged. Fired 200 × .303, 80 × 20mm.

Lieutenant S M Greene SAAF:

I was flying No.2 to F/Lt Parbury. I saw 6 ME109s do a 90° turn to port as we closed in on them. I picked out one ME109 which did a violent turn to port as I closed in and fired from 400 yards quarter astern. With my first burst I saw strikes (m/g) on the port wing root. E/A again made a violent turn to port and I tried to follow but being in a clipped wing Spitfire I spun about 2,000 ft and lost E/A. Unfortunately my port cannon jammed after firing one or two rounds.

Claim: 1 ME109 Damaged. Fired 1,000 × .303, 160 × 20mm.

Flight Sergeant D H Lorimer:

I was flying No.2 to F/Lt W A R MacDonald when 6 a/c were reported below our formation flying in the opposite direction. After turning about and giving chase, our leader reported them as ME109s. I lost my No.1 in the dive and pulled up to cover another Spitfire which was shooting at a ME109 and saw another ME109 on this Spitfire's tail. I therefore climbed up into it and it broke away in a very steep dive. I followed and opened fire at about 300 yards range but saw no strikes. As I closed to 50-100 yards, E/A began to turn slowly to port. I fired again and saw blue smoke coming from his wing tips. My next burst brought smoke and flashes from his engine. The E/A then flew straight and level and from about 50 yards I fired a long burst which brought more smoke from his engine and his hood and part of his cowling flew off. The E/A was now pouring clouds of smoke and what I took to be the pilot passed me to port. Flak was now bursting very close and I broke away. Lt F M DuToit, who had been following me, saw the E/A crash into the ground area (W) R.15.

Claim: 1 FW190 Destroyed. Fired 1,020 × .303, 240 × 20 mm.

Combat Reports for 14 May 1944

Second Lieutenant D J Beisiegel SAAF:

After we had turned about and intercepted 8 ME109s, my No.1 went down after an E/A which was diving away. I followed and another Spitfire joined in the chase behind my No.1. I observed a 109 following to the left and I turned into him. This was at approx 10,000'. He engaged me and we had a dog-fight down to 6,000' during which E/A made 2 head-on attacks. At 6,000' he levelled out and flew N and I closed astern to 100 yards and opened fire with my cannons observing strikes on the engine cowling. The pilot immediately baled out and I saw his parachute open. The E/A crashed in flames into a wood (area G.83) and I heard someone (presume a ground station) report it.

Claim: 1 ME109 Destroyed. Fired 360 × .303, 180 × 20mm.

Flight Sergeant D H Lorimer:

On sighting 8 ME109s flying head-on at us and slightly above near AQUINO, my No.1 climbed and then dived on E/A. I was about to follow him when I saw 2 more 109s above and to port. I climbed behind the No.2 who was doing a shallow turn to port and I fired from 200 yards. The E/A flicked on his back and went into a dive. I fired again from about 150 yards and saw strikes under the cockpit. The E/A then passed under my nose and on rolling over to contact it again, I was unable to see him.

Claim: 1 ME109 Damaged. Fired 160 × .303, 40 × 20mm.

Flight Sergeant R W McKernan:

I picked out one of the eight ME109s which jettisoned their bombs immediately we attacked. Following it down to ground level I closed to 300 yards astern and fired, seeing no strikes. E/A took evasive action by turning steeply to port. Closing on him again I fired 4 short bursts seeing strikes on the fuselage forward of the tailplane. I then broke away as I was myself attacked and turning steeply to port and climbing, I fired at my attacker, a ME109, but saw no strikes and returned to base as my fuel was getting short.

Claim: 1 ME109 Damaged. Fired 468 × .303, 142 × 20mm.

Lieutenant S M Greene SAAF:

I saw the ME109s approaching head-on at 15,000'. I rolled over on one of them and the pilot immediately jettisoned his bomb or LR tank, rolled over on his back and dived. I followed him in the dive, gaining on him slowly, but when he levelled out at mountain top height I closed rapidly. I fired first from 500 yards but my port cannon jammed. I closed to 50 yards and fired with m/g, seeing strikes on the fuselage and around the cockpit, pieces flying off. Short of fuel I broke off, my ammunition finished and last saw E/A going N at 1,000' very slowly.

Claim: 1 ME109 Damaged. Fired 1,120 × .303, 125 × 20mm.

Flight Sergeant A G Newman:

On sighting 8 ME109s in the AQUINO area I singled out one of them and chased it NW up Highway 6 but before I was in range I lost it in haze. Returning to base at 8,000' I saw 2 a/c just SE of FROSINONE flying NE at 7,000' at high speed. Turning in behind them I selected the one on the left, identifying it as a FW190. At the same time I noticed two Spitfire IXs on their tails. Closing in to fire, the FW190 crossed over to the righthand side of the other E/A. I therefore crossed over the Spits and fired a quick burst hitting the FW on the side of the fuselage. I fired again from 200 yards astern, seeing strikes on the wing roots and tail unit and a flame from the underside of the fuselage. Then there was a sheet of flame and the E/A went down in a spiral. This is the last I saw of the E/A but 111 Sqn saw it crash in area G.4848.

Claim: 1 FW190 Destroyed. Fired 320 × .303, 120 × 20mm.

Combat Reports for 21 May 1944

145 Squadron engaging aircraft of I and II Gruppen of Schlachtgeschwader 4

Flight Lieutenant J Wooler:

When E/A had split up and made for home, I chased 3 FW190s, one of which left the other two and dived down to the ground. Following it I fired from 150 yards dead astern, seeing strikes all over E/A which blew up (area F.79). I did not see E/A jettison its bomb and from the size of the explosion, it was probably still on E/A.

Claim: 1 FW190 Destroyed. Fired 600 × .303, 160 × 20mm.

Lieutenant J M G Anderson SAAF:

I followed 1 FW190 in a shallow dive N and closed to 250 yards and opened fire from dead astern, seeing strikes on the tail unit. I fired again from 150-200 yards and saw a large white flash on port side of the engine. I then pulled up over E/A, turned and saw it crash into the hillside (area F.9999) and blow up. Before I fired, E/A had jettisoned its bomb.

Claim: 1 FW190 Destroyed. Fired 400 × .303, 180 × 20mm.

Flying Officer J S Ekbury:

When our leader went into attack, I attacked a section of six E/A above him. Chasing them in a dive, I fired short bursts at one of them from 200 yards astern, seeing strikes on the fuselage and port wing, and E/A began to pour blue-black smoke. It then dropped out of the formation and went down like a falling leaf, apparently out of control, from 3,000' (area G.0647). I then chased the next E/A firing short bursts from 200 yards dead astern, seeing strikes on wings and fuselage. E/A jettisoned hood and pilot baled out (area G.0162). I continued to chase the rest of the E/A when one of them turned to port. I closed on it quickly and fired 2 bursts from port quarter astern, seeing strikes on fuselage and port wing root. E/A started to smoke and then went straight into the ground from 500' and burst into flames. All these E/A were FW190s and had Dark Green and Brown camouflage.

Claim: 2 FW190s Destroyed, & 1 Probably Destroyed. Fired 600 × .303, 100 × 20mm.

Lieutenant G E Milborrow:

I saw a FW90 pulling away from the main formation and I chased it N in a dive. After some time I got to 200 yards astern, seeing strikes on fuselage around the cockpit. I was then attacked myself and was forced to take evasive action and lost E/A. Flying S towards our own lines, I saw 2 FW190s flying N below me at 400'. I went down on them and attacked one of them from 50 yards astern. I observed strikes all over E/A and the pilot baled out from 400' (area G.8595) and I saw his 'chute open.

Claim: 1 FW190 Destroyed. Fired 1,000 × .303, 40 × 20mm.

Flight Sergeant J C Stirling:

I attacked one section of FW190s, 2 of them breaking away from the other 4. Of these four I fired at 2 or 3 without observing results. I finally singled out one of them and closed 100-75 yards dead astern at ground level and fired, seeing strikes all along the fuselage and pieces flew off. I then saw flames in the cockpit and the E/A pulled up to 150-200 ft, flicked over and went in to the ground (area F7596). Pilot not seen to bale out. I saw the E/A burning on the ground and I also saw another similar fire NE of it. I believe this to be the FW190 claimed by F/Lt J Wooler.

Claim: 1 FW190 Destroyed. Fired 1,100 × .303, 210 × 20 mm.

SG4 lost the following pilots in this action:

I Gruppe — Oberleutnant Robert Reiprich
          — Hauptmann Rolf Strossner   both to the east of Rome
II Gruppe — Leutnant Herbert Bertram   near Cassino
          — Oberfeldwebel Hans Schmitt
          — Unteroffizier Rolf Manske   both at Fabrica di Roma
          — Unteroffizier Gerhard Assmann
          — Leutnant Horst Kulpa   both at Viterbo

APPENDIX V

Aircraft Serial Numbers

For those readers interested in aircraft serial numbers, here are the numbers of those aircraft flown by Neville Duke during his operational service.

Spitfire Mark V—No.92 Squadron, RAF Biggin Hill 1941

Number	Letters	First flown	Remarks
R6770	QJ–W	May 1941	
R6882	QJ–N	May 1941	
R6904	QJ–Y	April 1941	Usual machine
R6923	QJ–S	May 1941	
W3319	QJ–X	July 1941	
W3381	QJ–P	July 1941	
AB125	QJ–Y	August 1941	

P40 Tomahawk IIB—No.112 Squadron, Western Desert 1941–42

Number	Letters	First flown	Remarks
AK354	GA–L	December 1941	
AK402	GA–F	November 1941	Shot down 30 November
AK413	GA–K	November 1941	
AM390	GA–W	November 1941	Crashed first flight
AN337	GA–F	December 1941	
AN340	GA–B	December 1941	

P40 Kittyhawk I—No.112 Squadron, Western Desert 1942

Number	Letters	First flown	Remarks
AK578	GA–V	January 1942	Usual machine Jan–Feb
AK595	GA–Y	January 1942	
AK602		January 1942	
AK652	GA–D	January 1942	
AK653	GA–G	January 1942	
AK673	GA–F	January 1942	
AK682	GA–U	January 1942	
AK707	GA–Y	February 1942	
AK900	GA–A	March 1942	
AK957	GA–D	March 1942	

Spitfire Vb/c—No.92 Squadron, Libya/Tunisia 1942—43

BR519	QJ—T	March 1943	
EP338	QJ—S	January 1943	
ER821	QJ—R	February 1943	Usual machine Feb—Mar
ER220	QJ—R	November 1942	Usual machine Nov—Feb
ER393	QJ—B	November 1942	
ER405	QJ—V	November 1942	
ER689	QJ—J	April 1943	
ES121	QJ—R	March 1943	Usual machine Mar—May

Spitfire IX—No.92 Squadron, Tunisia 1943

EN143	April 1943	
EN147	April 1943	
EN152	May 1943	
EN308	March 1943	
EN333	April 1943	Usual machine Apr—May
EN444	April 1943	
EN446	March 1943	

Spitfire VIII—No.145 Squadron, Italy 1944

JF873		May 1944	
JG110	ZX—D	May 1944	
JG121		June 1944	
JG186		June 1944	
JG241	ZX—J	March 1944	Usual machine Mar—Jun
JG246	ZX—A	April 1944	
JG250		August 1944	
JG337		June 1944	
JG838		April 1944	
JG953	ZX—J	March 1944	Usual machine Jun—Jul
JG959		March 1944	
LV729		July 1944	
MT775	ZX—J	July 1944	Usual machine Jul—Sep
MT777		September 1944	

PERSONNEL INDEX